W9-ABG-356

Jonathan Haynes's *The Social Relations of Jonson's Theater* is about the Elizabethan playwright Ben Jonson as a realist, and as an astute observer of the transition from feudalism to capitalism. Many of the forms and purposes of his realism spring from the social dynamics of the theaters in which he worked. Jonson's art arose in circumstances fraught with social pressures, and although his plays cannot be reduced to these pressures neither can his art be understood apart from them. This is a study of the social relations represented *in* Jonson's plays, but it is also about the social relations *of* the plays themselves, of what happened between Jonson and his audience in the theater.

Haynes makes a detailed literary historical argument about the sources and consequences of Jonson's realism. The book polemicizes against the moral and formal preoccupations of the last two generations of Jonson criticism; it is informed by the new social history and by the sociology of Pierre Bordieu and Norbert Elias.

The Social Relations of Jonson's Theater

The Social Relations of Jonson's Theater

JONATHAN HAYNES
Bennington College

CAMBRIDGE
UNIVERSITY PRESS

Published by the Press Syndicate of the University of Cambridge
The Pitt Building, Trumpington Street, Cambridge, CB2 1RP
40 West 20th Street, New York, NY 10011-4211, USA
10 Stamford Road, Oakleigh, Victoria 3166, Australia

First published 1992

Printed in the United States of America

Library of Congress Cataloging-in-Publication Data
Haynes, Jonathan.
The social relations of Jonson's theater / Jonathan Haynes.
   p. cm.
Includes bibliographical references.
ISBN 0-521-41918-2
1. Jonson, Ben, 1573?–1637 – Political and social views.
2. Theater – Social aspects – England – History – 17th century.
3. Literature and society – England – History – 17th century.
4. Social problems in literature. I. Title.
PR2642.S58H39 1992
822'.3 – dc20   91-38728

A catalog record for this book is available from the British Library.

ISBN 0–521–41918–2 hardback

for Ann
and
for David Konstan

Contents

Acknowledgments

Chapter 4 first appeared in *Studies in Philology* 86 (1989), and Chapter 5 in *ELH* 51 (1984); some bits of Chapter 3 are cannibalized from "The Elizabethan Audience on Stage," in *Themes in Drama 9,* edited by James Redmond (Cambridge University Press, 1987). I thank the editors for permission to reprint this material. I also want to thank the American Council of Learned Societies, Albion College, and Bennington College for grants that helped support the writing of this book. Bennington also gave me a much-needed leave.

I'm grateful to the friends and colleagues who read some or all of this work and had useful things to say: Mike Bristol (with whom I first read Jonson as an undergraduate at McGill University), Dick Burt, Charles Crupi, Reed Dasenbrock, Paddy Fumerton, Thomas Greene, Richard Halpern, Thomas Haynes, Didi Heller, Larry Manley, John Mepham, John Smyth, Julie Solomon, and Richard Tristman. I owe heartfelt thanks to the four true and loyal friends who stayed with me on the whole long march from beginning to end, and hauled me out of the Slough of Despond as often as I fell in – my fit audience, though few: Linda Bamber, the civilizing angel of my prose; Chris Kendrick, formidable dialectician; Joe Loewenstein, formidable scholar and Jonsonian; and David Konstan, who showed me how to read plays, and also showed me how much intellectual generosity could fit into a single human being. This book began in conversations with him one Cairene spring.

MITIS:	I trauell with another objection, signoir, which I fear will bee enforc'd against the author, ere I can be deliuer'd of it.
CORDATUS:	What's that, sir?
MITIS:	That the argument of his *Comoedie* might haue beene of some other nature, as of a duke to be in loue with a countesse, and that countesse to bee in loue with the dukes sonne, and the sonne to loue the ladies waiting maid: some such crosse wooing, with a clowne to their seruingman, better then to be thus neere, and familiarly allied to the time.

Every Man out of his Humour, III.6.191–201

I can assure those unprejudiced readers who are solicitous to become acquainted with the domestic manners and pursuits of our forefathers, that they will find more to gratify their rational curiosity in the dramas of this great poet, than in all the writers of his age.

Gifford, *Jonson's Works*

Le fait théâtral déborde constamment l'écriture dramatique, puisque la representation des rôles sociaux, réels ou imaginaires, provoque une contestation, une adhésion, une participation qu'aucun autre art ne peut provoquer.

Jean Duvignaud, *Sociologie du Théatre*

1
Introduction: Jonson's Realism

"A MEERE EMPYRICK"

In *The Second Part of the Return from Parnassus,* performed at Cambridge University about 1601, Ingenioso and Indicio find time to pass judgment on the current literary scene; eventually they get to "Beniamin Iohnson":

> *Indicio.* The wittiest fellow of a Bricklayer in England.
> *Ingenioso.* A meere Empyrick, one that getts what he hath by obseruation, and makes onely nature priuy to what he endites; so slow an Inuentor, that he were better betake himselfe to his old trade of Bricklaying; a bould whorson, as confident now in making of a booke, as he was in times past in laying of a brick. (I.2.295 ff.)[1]

"A meere Empyrick" is one who has not had theoretical training in his art, a strange charge to our ears, since Jonson has usually been thought of as the great pedant of Elizabethan drama, or as combining seamlessly and in ideal proportions classical art and English matter. What also strikes us immediately about this speech is its intolerable class condescension:[2] arrogant and stupid, yet clearly representing powerful prejudices, it seems motive enough for Jonson's prickly and defiant project of public self-definition as artist and playwright. But what I want to pursue at the moment is the claim that Jonson "getts what he hath by obseruation." The charge of "Empiricism" is not only a matter of class hatred obscuring Jonson's learning and art, but a backhanded tribute to his realism, which, even if mistaken for artlessness, is taken to be his defining artistic characteristic.

It is not presented as an artistic characteristic, but as stealing. This was a familiar accusation, and probably a reverberation from the War of the Theaters: In the Induction to Jonson's *Cynthia's Revels* (1600–01) a representative of the

---

[1] J. B. Leishman, ed., *The Three Parnassus Plays* (London: Ivor Nicholson & Watson, 1949), I.2.292 ff.

[2] Leishman thinks this passage is probably ironic (p. 60), but even if this is true the attitudes it expresses were real, and Jonson would not have been consoled by the sort of irony Cambridge students could afford as they reproduced the prejudices of their class.

audience admonishes playwrights not to glean wit from "obseruation of the companie they conuerse with; as if their inuention liu'd wholy vpon another mans trencher" (183–4),[3] and it must have been in response to an already public slander, or to advance knowledge of Dekker's *Satiromastix* (1601), that in *Poetaster* (also 1601) Jonson has Demetrius/Dekker say of Jonson's own persona Horace, "hee is a meere spunge; nothing but humours, and obseruation; he goes vp and downe sucking from euery societie, and when hee comes home, squeazes himselfe drie againe" (IV.3.104–07). Indeed during the final chastening of Horace in *Satiromastix* he is made to "sweare not to bumbast out a new Play, with the olde lynings of Jests, stolne from the Temples Revels" (V.2.29).[4] In the Prologue to *Volpone* Jonson defends himself again: "Nor made he' his play, for iests, stolne from each table,/ But makes iests, to fit his fable" (27–8).

It was not only Ben Jonson who was accused of trafficking in stolen jests – the notion that some playwrights, not always of the best social class, were making a living by aping the manners and conversation of their betters was fairly widespread. The humorous Cripple of Heywood's *The Fayre Mayde of the Exchange* (c.1602–07) could (if he were not a paragon of virtue) make enquiry

> Where the best-witted gallants use to dine,
> Follow them to the taverne, and there sit
> In the next roome with a calves head and brimstone,
> And over-heare their talke, observe their humours,
> Collect their jeasts, put them into plays
> And tire them too with payment to behold
> What I have filcht from them.[5]

The traffic went both ways: That foolish gallants cribbed matter for social display from literary and especially dramatic professionals was a current commonplace (amply dramatized in the scenes of *The First Part of The Return from Parnassus* in which the fop Gullio employs Ingenioso, and in many other places; in Webster's Induction to *The Malcontent* [1600–01?] a gallant comes to the theater equipped with a notebook, as does, in *Poetaster*, the citizen Albius who wants to learn how to talk to courtiers).

A few preliminary observations are in order. One, that the premise of all this is that life and art had gotten mixed up with one another with peculiar intimacy. It does not need saying that life and art are always intimately mixed up, but the modalities change, and this degree of proximity and lively reciprocity were unprecedented and therefore scandalous and exciting. One could not have

---

[3] All references to Jonson are from C. H. Herford and Percy Simpson, eds., *Ben Jonson,* 11 volumes, (Oxford: Clarendon Press, 1925–52). Dates in parentheses are of the first performance, not publication.

[4] Thomas Dekker, *Satiromastix,* in *The Dramatic Works of Thomas Dekker,* vol. 1, ed., Fredson Bowers (Cambridge: Cambridge Univ. Press, 1953), V.2.295–6.

[5] Thomas Heywood, *Dramatic Works* (1874; rpt. New York: Russel and Russel, 1964), pp. 46–7.

dined out on the lines stolen from *Gorboduc,* nor garnered ideas for *Tamburlaine* from table talk.

Second, the whole business of life and art imitating one another is situated quite exactly in the social world of the London theaters, whose composition and dynamic are the formative influences. The charge of imitation is bound up with negative scrutiny of the artist's (or socialite's) social affiliations and motives. Jonson is an impudent bricklayer; playwrights eavesdrop on their betters; social climbers think they can dine out on play scraps.

Third, this new artistic mode was not yet very well understood, either by its critics or by all its practitioners, though Ben Jonson had a pretty clear idea of what he was about. The satirists constantly needed to defend and explain what sort of art they were practicing.[6] This defense took a standard form: The satirist had high moral purposes and classical antecedents, and intended no topical allusions. Brave words and partially true, and amply glossed by a critical tradition concerned to rescue Jonson from the charge of mere empiricism; but both defense and gloss tend to make us forget what the above examples will remind us of, that this art arose in circumstances fraught with social pressures. Jonson's art cannot be reduced to these pressures, but neither can it be understood apart from them. Our criticism needs to recover a sense of this art *in society* as a weapon, or tool, or organ. This study is about the social relations *of* as well as *in* Jonson's plays.

There is a tradition of casually dismissing or condescending to the realist function of drama with phrases like "mere realism," seeing it as subartistic and so beneath notice. Perhaps one reason for this is that we take realism for granted, and can hardly imagine a literary tradition without an urban comedy of manners. Another reason is that the importance and interest of this art are as much social as they are literary, and drama and society in the age of Jonson are still usually thought about separately, as separate things, though this is changing rapidly in the wake of the New Historicism. It is no surprise that Jonson criticism, and the books on city comedy (the genre roughly corresponding to the development I am interested in), are with a few exceptions entirely shaped by the great themes of bourgeois criticism, formal and moral analysis. This criticism has accomplished a great deal, reaching a level of interpretation and a degree of consensus about Jonson's art and moral imagination that are unusual; and the categories of the moral and the formal certainly loom very large in Jonson's own thought – I will be arguing in a later chapter that he played a

---

[6] Maria Gottwald points out that "the abundance of various satirical writings in that period appears to be a natural product of contemporary life; they developed spontaneously, almost without any theoretical foundations," and that English poetics showed little interest in satire. *Satirical Elements in Ben Jonson's Comedy* (Wroclaw: Travaux de la Societié des Sciences et des Lettres de Wroclaw, Series A, no. 137, 1969), p. 163. But see the summary of ideas about satire in England in Alvin Kernan, *The Cankered Muse: Satire of the English Renaissance,* Yale Studies in English, vol. 142 (New Haven: Yale Univ. Press, 1959), chap. 2.

decisive role in reformulating what they meant for his theater, a reformulation with which New Criticism is historically continuous. But the interesting questions, now, are against what did Jonson have to struggle to reformulate them, and why did he want to?

It seems to me that the emphasis on the moral and the formal in Jonson has been extreme and is now – may I say? – worn out, if only because of its own successes. Discussions of Jonson's historical situation are governed so entirely by these terms that the situation becomes inert and undialectical, mere material toward which Jonson could take moral and formal positions.[7] Historical relationships get turned into a morality play about the Artist and the World. Symptomatically, two recent books on Jonson[8] and on city comedy[9] share essentially the same argument, that Jonson's theater endlessly reflected on social and generic stereotypes, and always to the same end: to transcend them. One needs to be steeped in refined moral and formal analysis to be able to make such an argument; one also must have lost all sense of the theater as a place where real social conflicts were going on. Roughly the first half of this book tries to recapture that sense of conflict and ritualized combat as pervading the theater, and of Jonson's drama as rooted in it.

I should make it very clear, before going any further, that I am interested in Jonson's realism not for empiricist purposes, but for dialectical ones: The

---

[7] Both L. C. Knights' *Drama and Society in the Age of Jonson* (London: Chatto and Windus, 1937) and Brian Gibbons' *Jacobean City Comedy*, 2d ed. (London: Methuen, 1980) segregate the historical material in separate chapters, as background. Knights' book retains its power as historical analysis, and is a provocation to debate with a materialist historical criticism ("The exasperating haziness of all those who have attempted to make some correlation between economic activities and culture is not due merely to the lack of a satisfactory definition of the latter term. Perhaps it is due . . . to the fact that 'the materialist interpretation of history' has not yet been pushed far enough," p. 4.) In Gibbons it is pretty clear that the historical chapters are a dutiful gesture, and he never really returns to them. On another level, Kernan has written the most eloquent description we have of Jonson's materialism, of how crowded with things his world is, and of how incessant is change within it – but this is presented undialectically as a universal and unsited cyclical change that never changes the world, and leaves the moral observer looking for a place outside it from which to look down on the spectacle (*The Cankered Muse*, pp. 168 ff.). The cyclical character of Jonson's thought, which is certainly real enough, is discussed in the context of his idea of history by Achsah Guibbory, *The Map of Time: 17th Century English Literature and Ideas of Pattern in History* (Urbana: Univ. of Illinois Press, 1986), chap. 4, and specifically in the context of social conflict by Gail Kern Paster, who says that the predation of city comedy is cyclical and so by its nature cannot change anything (*The Idea of the City in the Age of Shakespeare* (Athens: Univ. of Georgia Press, 1985), pp. 158–9.

[8] Robert N. Watson, *Jonson's Parodic Strategy: Literary Imperialism in the Comedies* (Cambridge, Mass.: Harvard Univ. Press, 1987).

[9] Theodore Leinwand, *The City Staged: Jacobean Comedy, 1603–13* (Madison: Univ. of Wisconsin Press, 1986).

object is not to show that Jonson's realism reflected social reality in an unprob-
lematic way (though I do believe we can learn about Elizabethan life by observing Jonson, a position perhaps less unfashionable today than it was recently,
now that we have a history of everyday life to make our curiosity respectable),
but to show that it was part of a historical process of social representation.[10]

The object of my study is Jonson-in-the-theater. I hope a clear sense of
Jonson's personal contribution will emerge. His personality and personal status
became public issues to a highly unusual degree which makes them an
inevitable topic, but my emphasis is on what happened *between* Jonson and his
audience. I intend a more detailed analysis of the sort found in some radical
pages of Muriel Bradbrook's *The Rise of the Common Player,* where the development of the most fundamental features of Elizabethan drama is seen as depend-
ing on the establishment of new dramatic conditions with the founding of the
commercial theaters:

> [R]egular performances created a regular audience; this produces a quite dif-
> ferent kind of attention and response with more trained and expert attention
> to the actors. . . . To transform their social "commoning" or intercourse to
> attentive watchfulness at the theater meant a shift of social habit in the audi-
> ence: to transform their art from the narrative to the dramatic form was a more
> exacting test for the poets. . . . Alongside the transformation of the Minstrel
> into the Comedian, a transformation in the social presentation of literature
> replaced narrative by drama. Elizabethan drama was created on the common
> stages, by fusing the art of orator or presenter with that of the mime, so
> turning a recital accompanied by gesture and costume display into a complete
> action. . . .
> It was a search for literary form, which should capture and display the social
> relations between player and audience as they shared together the imaginative
> acts which the poet had conceived for them.[11]

The attention of the audience is the *materia prima* of the theater and it has a great
deal to do with such things as whether the audience is sitting down or not: The
entirely seated audience at the Blackfriars was different from the partially
standing audience at the Globe, and the innyard Red Bull theater was different
again, where "opportunities for coming and going into the private rooms

[10] For a sophisticated brief discussion of this point see Kate McLuskie, " 'Tis but a
Woman's Jar: Family and Kinship in Elizabethan Domestic Drama," *Literature and
History* 9:2 (Autumn 1983), 228–39. See also Michael D. Bristol, *Carnival and Theater:
Plebeian Culture and the Structure of Authority in Renaissance England* (New York and
London: Methuen, 1985): "The critical intensification of collective life represented
and experienced in the theater, and the possibility it creates for action and initiative,
is the subject of this book" (p. 3).

[11] M. C. Bradbrook, *The Rise of the Common Player: A Study of Actor and Society in
Shakespeare's England* (London: Chatto and Windus, 1962), pp. 98, 118–19. A similarly radical sense for the primacy of the audience informs Jean Duvignaud, *Sociologie
du Théâtre: Essai sur les ombres collectives* (Paris: Presses Universitaires de France, 1965).

opening on the galleries, the full provisions for eating and drinking . . . must have given the audience a life of its own, distinct from that of the play."[12] My study is not of the variety of theaters Jonson worked in, but of his exploitation, exhortation, denunciation, and seduction of the modes of attention his audience brought with it – social modes being mixed up with aesthetic ones. This is the matrix of Jonson's realism.

JONSON'S REALISM

Since the term "realism" means nothing until it is defined, I had better say now what I mean by Jonson's realism. The most serious discussions of Elizabethan realism, like Bradbrook's, center on realism of character and the integration of word and action into a fully dramatic whole. Robert Weimann explicitly denies that it is a realism of subject matter.

> Rather, it is a new sense of the interdependence of character and society, and a fully responsive interplay between dramatic speech and dramatic action in the process of reproducing the cause and effect of human behavior that defines "realism" in the Renaissance theater.[13]

This is true of the realism of *Tamburlaine,* but the satiric realism of the turn of the century *was* a realism of subject matter, a social realism whose direction was guided by the social dynamic in the theater no less than by the moral reaction L. C. Knights found to be the ideology of drama in the age of Jonson. If *Tamburlaine* is a product of a theater that expressed the conditions of the Elizabethan settlement, the satirical realism of city comedy was a major instrument of social thought in a period of intensified social competition. It was a sharper realism, the cutting edge of artistic intervention in the social imagination.

It seems to me that the five interrelated elements Raymond Williams says form the basis for bourgeois realist drama, and which he finds for the first time in Restoration comedy and mid-eighteenth century tragedy, are all essentially present much earlier, in Jonsonian comedy: (1) contemporary and (2) indigenous subjects, (3) the generalization of quasi-colloquial speech, (4) a new social extension and inclusiveness, and (5) a secularism that does not necessarily deny supernatural agency but conspires to get along without it.[14] It will be convenient to discuss these five elements in some detail.

First, contemporary and indigenous subjects pertaining directly to the world the audience would walk out into – meaning, more or less, London – appeared precisely in the first years of Jonson's career as a playwright. In *Every Man out of his Humour* (1599) Jonson registers the novelty of this new dramatic project through the critics he has positioned on stage. Mitis wonders whether some

[12] M. C. Bradbrook, "Shakespeare and the Multiple Theatres of Jacobean London," in *The Elizabethan Theatre VI,* ed., G. R. Hibbard (Toronto: Macmillan, 1978), p. 90.

[13] Robert Weimann, *Shakespeare and the Popular Tradition in the Theater* (Baltimore: Johns Hopkins Univ. Press, 1978), p. 197.

[14] Raymond Williams, *The Sociology of Culture* (New York: Schocken, 1982), p. 166.

will not think comedy should concern itself with a (Shakespearean) romantic confusion among the aristocracy:

> some such crosse wooing, with a clowne to their seruingman, better than to be thus neere, and familiarly allied to the time.
>
> *Cordatus.* You say well, but I would faine heare one of these *autumne* judgements define once, *Quid sit Comoedia?* if he cannot, let him content himselfe with Ciceros definition (till hee haue strength to propose to himselfe a better) who would haue a *Comoedie* to be *Imitatio vitae, Speculum consuetudinis, Imago veritatis.*
>
> (III.6.199–207)

A stronger defense than this seems called for, however; *Speculum consuetudinis* tends to be overshadowed by its neighboring terms, reduced to dressing up the eternal in contemporary fashions. The connotation of traditional manners that hangs over *consuetudinis* obscures the novelty of the fashions paraded over the Elizabethan stage. The reflection of the times in constantly changing dress is not a constant in comedy. The Italian *comedia erudita* sometimes ignored it, and in the Roman *comedia palliata* the dress never changed. In the history of the drama its subjects are quite commonly not contemporary and indigenous.[15] The hunger for contemporary realism and novelty on the Elizabethan stage needs a specific historical explanation.

The event must have appeared as something radically and spectacularly new to playgoers, though theater historians have given it little attention. Even ten years later the contemporary London setting was so standard it must have been hard to remember a time before it was invented. Plays had been set in all manner of exotic locales, from Scythia to Italy to pastoral Arcadias; comedies were set in the English countryside; chronicle histories presented a realistic England, and sometimes London, but a London of the historical past.

The excitement of discovering the contemporary London scene swept through all the theaters at once starting about 1598 (William Haughton's *Englishmen for my Money* of late 1597 or early 1598 is thought to be the first London comedy). The fairly compact fraternity of playwrights worked in close collaboration and competition, exploring together this new source of dramatic power and interest. A new power was on the loose in London, setting off explosions of satiric realism in one neighborhood or social milieu after another, exciting the audience, worrying the authorities, and getting its handlers in trouble.

It was all good business: The dynamics of the literary historical event are obviously bound to the exploitation and marketing of a fashion, a fad. The thinly disguised *ad hominem* attacks of the War of the Theaters spiced with topicality a more fundamental fascination with contemporary social life, also (still) thinly disguised as Gargaphie or Rome or the London of King William Rufus. The theater had entered into a qualitatively new relationship with society: When it began representing contemporary manners it began participating

---

[15] Williams makes this point in *The Sociology of Culture,* pp. 161, 166.

more directly and powerfully than ever before in the creation of manners and fashions of all kinds – a participation noticed equally by those who denounced and those who defended the theater.

One might object that given their weakly developed sense of anachronism, English playwrights in fact had difficulty imagining any time and place besides their own. The contemporaneity of the scene had a new character, however, which should be distinguished from the anachronistic insertion of contemporary local matter into a scene ostensibly set elsewhere. This last had been going on since English shepherds found their way into the Palestine of the *Second Shepherd's Play;* it was particularly liable to happen in the subplot with its lower-class characters. When London figured in history plays or in celebrations of London heroes like Simon Eyre or Dick Whittington, there was little effort to distinguish London's past from its present; and Julius Caesar was dressed up like an Elizabethan.

One might object further that the morality play tradition intended to represent the world its audience lived in, and if this was by definition not thought of in secular terms, the allegorical tradition fostered, as the complement to its abstraction, an often extreme topicality that sponsored a kind of realist tradition employing advanced techniques of mimicry. Nashe reports that a Cambridge play in Latin carried an impersonation of Gabriel Harvey as far as stealing his gown to play in.[16] Such topicality in the Tudor interludes was intended to rile and challenge the audience. As Craik says, the Tudor interlude was on closer terms with its audience, physically and one might say sociably, than either the medieval theater or the Elizabethan; it could literally talk to the audience more easily.[17]

Jonson's drama grows straight out of this tradition. I will have more to say about that historical connection in the next chapter; I will say here only that the principle that makes Jonson's drama different and new is its secularism (which brings us to the fifth of Williams' elements of realism). The method of the

---

[16] In *Have with you to Saffron-Walden,* quoted in Leishman, p. 37. Such topicality, Bradbrook suggests, is inherent in the genre: "The difficulty of a moral play is that there is no necessary particular action for such an abstraction as Love, Conscience, or Lucre, except the reflection of some highly topical and local event." *Rise of the Common Player,* p. 269. There was also a genre of plays on current events, a sort of dramatic journalism that was topical in the extreme. Chambers quotes a letter from R. Whyte to Sir R. Sidney on 26 October, 1599: "Two daies agoe, the ouerthrow of Turnholt, was acted vpon a Stage, and all your Names vsed that were at yt; especially Sir Fra. Veres, and he that plaid that Part gott a Beard resembling his, and Watchet Satin Doublett, with Hose trimd with Siluer Lace. You was also introduced, Killing, Slaying, and Ouerthrowing the Spaniards; and honorable Mention made of your Service, in seconding Sir Francis Vere, being engaged" (*Sidney Papers,* ii.136; quoted in E. K. Chambers, *The Elizabethan Stage, Vol. I* (Oxford: Clarendon Press, 1923), p. 322.

[17] T. W. Craik, *The Tudor Interlude* (Leicester: Leicester Univ. Press, 1958), p. 24.

morality play was deductive, working out from given principles; this certainly allowed it to touch secular reality, but piecemeal and with its arbitrary mechanisms showing. Secular extension comes with a formal commitment to the surfaces of social life, an inductive method, the "obseruation" of an "Empyrick." Deductive and inductive modes are not absolutes, only a question of weight or emphasis on a continuum – but there are breaks, moments when the weight shifts. Such a break comes with Jonson's early plays; and when there is a resurgence of the old allegorical style in his last plays, we can see that however clearly Lady Pecunia is descended from *Everyman*'s Goods, for instance, there is nevertheless a decisive difference: The playwright who took such care to set *The Alchemist* in the very year and month and neighborhood of its performance[18] is still giving each play a different and definite, localized and specific setting, and infusing each play with a new set of observations and a fresh idea about what area of social life could be a fit subject for satire. These plays, individually and collectively, are set in an extended, secular, social dimension; the predominance of setting over the moral and spiritual structures of the morality is ironically demonstrated in *The Devil is an Ass* (1616), where an old-fashioned devil can't make his way in modern London. The moral and imaginative inheritance of the moralities is still very much alive in Jonson, but they have been reformulated in the new secular environment.[19]

Within this newly extensive secular space the familiar gallants and usurers from the moralities were handled with similar satiric methods: a scandalized pointing at horrible new abuses through techniques of exaggeration. Even citizen heroes who are not being handled satirically tend to hold their manners aloft for observation. This is a *demonstrative* realism, always displaying and pointing to its objects. Its language is a generalization of quasi-colloquial speech, Raymond Williams' third requirement, and thus much closer to conversation than that of Elizabethan tragedy or romantic comedy,[20] but it is regularly intensified to display social characteristics or individual humors, making it different from later, quieter realisms or naturalism. This demonstrative realism can contain elements of the fantastic and of parody, whether of behavior or – as in *Eastward Ho* (1605) – of its own genre.

The analysis of social behavior is carried through the amplifications of its representation, not through the "discovery" of a slice of life, presented naturalistically in the box behind a proscenium arch. G. K. Hunter has made very clear

[18] R. L. Smallwood, "Here, in the Friars: Immediacy and Theatrically in *The Alchemist*," *Review of English Studies* n.s. 32, no. 126 (1980), 146–7.
[19] Compare Middleton's *Michaelmas Term* (1607), where a very sharp analysis of the contemporary economy is conveyed using a variety of old techniques, like the allegorical dumb show.
[20] Polyvocality, capturing the diversity and richness of urban speech, is one of the marks of city comedy generally, and in playwrights other than Jonson it is not unusual to find a romantic plot amidst the city comedy material, conducted in a very unrealistic romantic poetry. *The Shoemaker's Holiday* (1600) is a good example.

the distinction between the modern stage, with its assumption that environment creates a character and its technique of finding its characters amidst a
painted representation of an environment then used to interpret the character,
and the technique of the Elizabethan theater where the landscape is "a landscape
of persons" on a bare stage, and "the character, his entry and his movement
create, in so far as we are required to assume one, the environment that is
appropriate to his deeds."[21] It is probably because Elizabethan realism has
nothing to do with the development of set design, and inherits its techniques
rather from the morality play, that Williams and others start the history of
stage realism with the Restoration.

Hunter goes on to point out that the assumption governing Elizabethan stage
practice was that character was formed not by environment but by social
status, which was clearly visible from the character's entrance, because of his
costume.[22] Social status is the *problematic* of city comedy, where appearances
are often deceptive and the world is full of social climbers; all the features of the
social world need to be talked over as well as shown. These plays typically
slacken their plots so the action unfolds at a leisurely rate leaving plenty of time
for characters to stand around on stage and *talk,* venting a constant stream of
social observations. Hustlers hang around in the middle aisle of St. Paul's and
discuss business. Bawds compare Court ladies and City dames, and whores
discuss their clients. Reflections are offered on the follies of young heirs.
Everyone talks about usurers. Innumerable foolish gallants have their humors
analyzed and then appear on stage to confirm the diagnosis. Images of the city
pour in through similes: "men and women are borne, and come running into
the world faster than Coaches do into Cheap-side vppon *Symon* and *Iudes* day:
and are eaten vp by Death faster, then Mutton and porridge in a term time."
(Thomas Dekker and John Webster, *Westward Ho* [1605]).[23] The audience
evidently had an insatiable appetite for these observations, stereotypes, propo-
sitions about social behavior and relations, and images of their own lives.

Any art this thick with social references and so clearly social in its intentions
deserves the name of social realism – which is not to say we should expect
Balzac or Zola.[24] Nineteenth-century realism had a body of sophisticated economic and social theory to direct its investigations and form its purposes,
which did not exist at the turn of the seventeenth century. Economics was in
its infancy as a science and could not explain the changes that were occurring;
the official social ideology of the period also lagged seriously behind developments. By retreating from transcendent principles and mythic origins, and

---

[21] G. K. Hunter, "Flatcaps and Bluecoats: Visual Signals on the Elizabethan Stage,"
    Essays and Studies 1980 (n.s.33), pp. 21–5.
[22] Hunter, pp. 25 ff.
[23] *The Dramatic Works of Thomas Dekker,* ed., Fredson Bowers (Cambridge: Cambridge
    Univ. Press, 1955), vol. 2, II.1.171–4.
[24] Gibbons also distinguishes Jonsonian from nineteenth century realism, p. 3.

focusing instead on concrete interactions and proximate causes, city comedy
managed intelligently to represent new aspects of social life. That city comedy
was so far ahead of social and economic theory is one of its glories but also a
very real limitation; it leaves us with questions about its motivations and social
functions. What guided and informed and empowered it? Why was there a turn
toward the sociological at this moment?

L. C. Knights' answer was reaction: the ideology of the drama was the
conservative economic and social morality formed under medieval conditions,
and its attitude toward the historical changes it observed was oppositional,
satiric, moral. This is still a powerful argument, though Harbage noticed long
ago that Knights' "crypto-feudal" sympathies led him to underestimate the role
played in the drama by the new pride and assertiveness of the middle class.[25]
Knights is notoriously bad at making sense of plays that do not embody this
position, such as Middleton's, or *Bartholomew Fair*. There is now something
like a consensus that the theater was implicated in social change as well as
opposed to it, if only by virtue of the anomalous status of players and playwrights under the old order.[26] Louis Adrian Montrose points out that the
political position of the theaters was to represent the interests of the theater
people.[27] Jonson's own position often lay athwart that of the theaters, but he
was also a "new man."[28]

I share Knights' belief that Jonson was an acute and intelligent observer of
society, and of nascent capitalism in particular – a claim being taken up again
after half a century, but from the left rather than the right. (I am thinking
particularly of recent books by Peter Womack and Walter Cohen.)[29] First and
last I am concerned with Jonson's perception of the social volatility that accompanied the transition from feudalism to capitalism. Later chapters explore the
extent to which Jonson could connect the phenomena of social volatility to
historical change; much of the earlier part of the book is about how Jonson's
realism is constituted by the volatile social situation in the theaters. An analysis

[25] Alfred Harbage, *Shakespeare and the Rival Traditions* (1952; Bloomington: Indiana
Univ. Press, 1970), p. 267.

[26] See Don E. Wayne, "*Drama and Society in the Age of Jonson: An Alternative View,*"
Renaissance Drama, n.s.13 (1982), 103–29; Nicholas Grene, "L. C. Knights' *Drama and
Society in the Age of Jonson: A Retrospective Review*," in *Themes in Drama I*, ed.,
James Redmond (Cambridge: Cambridge Univ. Press, 1979); Margot Heinemann,
Puritanism and Theatre: Thomas Middleton and Opposition Drama Under the Early Stuarts
(Cambridge: Cambridge Univ. Press, 1980).

[27] Louis Adrian Montrose, "The Purpose of Playing: Reflections on a Shakespearean
Anthropology," *Helios* n.s.7, (1979–80), 51–74.

[28] This is a major theme of the new biography by David Riggs, *Ben Jonson: A Life*
(Cambridge: Harvard Univ. Press, 1989).

[29] Peter Womack, *Ben Jonson* (Oxford: Basil Blackwell, 1986); Walter Cohen, *Drama of
a Nation: Public Theater in Renaissance England and Spain* (Ithaca: Cornell Univ. Press,
1985), especially pp. 299–300.

of the form and social conditions of Jonson's art is as indispensable as ideology-critique of its content in ascertaining its social meaning. Social competition and conflict are the origin and subject of comical satire and city comedy, but while their social realism is shaped by social and political struggle – it can*not* be taken as the disinterested product of moral reflection – it is not itself the creation of any one social class, though some figure more largely than others, nor is it reducible to a narrow ideological position. The celebrated diversity of the Elizabethan theater is responsible for its usefulness as an arena of conflict; hence both public and private theaters and men as different as Marston, Middleton, and Dekker could be involved in the development of social realism out of the several realisms of Elizabethan drama.

I begin in the next chapter with a survey of the origins of Jonson's realism, above all in the morality play tradition. The crucial elements are a dramatic tradition of social criticism, a set of stage techniques for analyzing social behavior, the topic of fashion associated with the issue of social mobility, and the gradual appearance of London as a dramatic scene – a concrete and extended secular space where social conflict and competition were most highly concentrated. Jonson inherits all these elements quite directly, but they are fused together into a new and more powerful whole in the pressurized situation of the London theaters. Chapter 3 focuses on some of the specific mediations through which the social pressures in the audience burst onto the stage: the sway of the gallants in the theatrical milieu; a mapping of the social space of the theater, and beyond it, of London; a fashion competition in the audience that the stage satirizes but also plays to, participating in a new urbane sense for manners and in the establishment of a fashionable *monde*. Jonson's theater expresses, albeit ambivalently, that new urban formation and its sensibility, and therefore expresses values no longer merely conservative. *Epicoene* is generically halfway between satire and the comedy of manners; culturally it represents a new organ of social perception. Such organs are a part of a society's ideological apparatus, of the means by which it understands and reproduces itself symbolically. Raymond Williams notes that some artistic forms, like the portrait or Greek drama, are created in and determined by specific historical circumstances, but become the general property of subsequent traditions.[30] Something like this is true of Jonson's social realism. It is the response, ultimately, to deep structural pressures having to do with demography and the shift from postfeudal to capitalist relations. Once achieved, Jonson's kind of representation of contemporary manners was a permanent acquisition of the English stage. In Jonson himself the constitution of this realism is always unstable and combative, bound up as it was with his own stormy social relations.

[30] Williams, pp. 137, 150.

2

The Origins of
Jonson's Realism

THE MORALITY PLAY

One might say that the kernel from which Jonson's realism grew, or the node around which its elements began to crystallize, is the alehouse or tavern scene, whose roots go back to the late medieval morality play. This is not to identify realism with everything that is crude, obscene, or lower class, as has been done often enough in talking about the medieval fabliau. The very ubiquity of the tavern scene in the moral interlude tradition suggests it is stereotyped, as if it were impossible to encounter sin without being led by bad companions to an alehouse, to dissipate oneself in wine, women, and song, gambling and thievery. To be sure the alehouse was a central institution in early modern society, for the lower classes particularly, providing a valuable source of protein in its ale, and a warm, lighted, and convivial alternative to dismal lodgings. As a cultural institution it was central also, harboring all sorts of popular traditions and values, many of them opposed to the official order of church and state.[1] It is therefore not surprising that this familiar scene should turn up on stage, nor that its functions should be stigmatized – it probably *is* true that the alehouse is where medieval or early modern man or woman would go if looking for trouble, but the association of alehouse with iniquity is partial enough that one would hesitate to call its representation "realistic."

The argument about realism thus begins with the striking fact that the alehouse or tavern is very often the only social setting defined with any specificity at all in the morality play. In *Mankind* (1465–70), for instance, the alehouse is one of only two locations, the other being the very vaguely imagined field in which the universal Christian peasant Mankind delves. When the Vice Titivillus seduces Mankind he immediately heads from the field to the place where one goes bad:

[1] Peter Clark, *The English Alehouse: A Social History 1200–1830* (London and New York: Longman, 1983), especially chap. 7.

13

A-dew, fayer mastere! I wyll hast me to the ale-house,
And speke with Newgyse, Now-a-days & Nought.
Ande geett me a lemman with a smattrynge face.[2]

The alehouse is not sketched in with a lot of realistic detail, beyond a free and natural handling of the sort of behavior that went on there, which includes serving as the base of operations for the criminal gang Titivillus has organized with Newgyse, Now-a-days and Nought. From Nought's early speech alluding to gambling and the "comyn tapster of Bury" (line 267), these three bring this culture with them whenever they tumble onto the stage, singing or dancing wildly to the minstrels' music. The *topos* of alehouse culture matters more than direct representation of the alehouse as a place, both in the moral scheme of the play and in medieval stagecraft, which, like the Elizabethan, creates the requisite sense of place through the behavior of actors on a bare stage; it is a matter of relative indifference whether scenes are actually set in the tavern, or the tavern is merely talked about by its habitués. The realistic achievement is to convey a definite sense of a particular culture, a style of social interaction on a concrete basis. The ebullience of the writing at these points stems at least as much from this as from the supposed fact that evil is more interesting than good. The good people wander about in a void that soaks up spontaneous liveliness, with no basis of interaction except a pale mutual respect, while the bad can immediately begin roistering together, improvising exuberantly on a stock of familiar situations. The scene is developed in the direction of clowning rather than social analysis, but it still serves to give the impression of a full, dense, random life.

In the Digby *Mary Magdalene* (1480–90) – significantly a generic hybrid of mystery, miracle, and morality – the seduction is set in a tavern, not an alehouse. The two institutions were distinct: Taverns served wine, not ale or beer, and hence were more expensive and catered to a wealthier clientele than the much more numerous alehouses.[3] Thematically the drama treated alehouse and tavern interchangeably for the most part, transposing the same seduction up or down the social scale, but the social difference encouraged, as here, the association of the tavern not with criminality but with elegant if still sinful consumption. Our heroine, traveling to Jerusalem in the company of the seducer Lady Lechery, stops at a tavern. The taverner praises his fancy wines, and then Curiosity, "a Galaunt," enters, looking for a pretty barmaid to talk to. He is a dandy, a lover, and a sharp dresser, the ancestor of all the fops and men about town who will occupy the English stage for centuries to come. At Lechery's bidding Mary Magdalene calls him over, and eventually leaves with him. Satan rejoices over her fall.[4] Decorum is kept by making the upper class

[2] *Mankind*, in *Specimens of the Pre-shakespearean Drama*, ed. John Matthews Manly, vol. I (Boston: Athenaeum, 1897), lines 602–04.
[3] Clark, chap. 1.
[4] *The Digby Mysteries*, ed., F. J. Furnivall (New Shakespeare Society Series 8) (London: N. Trubner, 1882), lines 470–546. Robert H. Bowers points out that the tavern

characters speak in aureate language, setting this scene apart from the colloquial energies of most other tavern scenes.[5]

In the Tudor interlude *Youth* (performed 1513–14) Youth has just inherited his father's lands. Ian Lancashire argues plausibly that the play was produced in the household of Henry Algernon Percy, fifth earl of Northumberland, who thought his son was ungovernable.[6] However this may be, the tavern is here associated with the theme of prodigality, which is taking on a specific class setting and meaning, having to do with estate management. (Mary Magdalene's father had just died, too, but since she is a woman her sexual morality is emphasized.) We never actually see the tavern, but most of the play is a movement toward it, as Riot offers to take Youth there and pay for his wine and wench, accompanied by Pride, who urges Youth to exalt his mind, put down the poor, and arrogantly assert class status: "Be in company with gentlemen. / Jet up and down in the way, / And your clothes – look they be gay" (346–8). Later we see them returning from the tavern, Youth very drunk; there is a debate over whose counsel to follow, Charity and Humility's or Riot and Pride's, in which Riot offers to teach Youth card games and dicing, further education in the tavern culture clearly intended to dissipate his fortune.

The setting is also more specific in that London names begin to appear. As Riot enters he tells (like *Mankind*'s New Guise) the story of his escape from hanging: "I come lately from Newgate . . . The Mayor of London sent for me / Forth of Newgate for to come / For to preach at Tyburn" (234, 253–5). These London references are rather surprising, given the northern provenance of the play. Newgate and Tyburn function as symbolic locations, proverbial landmarks of a moral landscape, as one would speak of Hades or Jerusalem. In *Hick Scorner* (1514), however, a play produced in the London area, the tavern world has expanded to include constant talk about Tyburn and Newgate, and about

seduction is a unique addition to the accounts of Mary Magdalene's life: "Although the tavern episode is striking, and is probably the earliest tavern seduction scene in English literature, it has received no careful consideration by historians of the English drama." "The Tavern Scene in Mary Magdalene," in *All These To Teach: Essays in Honor of C. A. Robertson,* ed., Robert Bryan et al. (Gainesville: Univ. of Florida Press, 1965), p. 26. *Mankind* would seem to be earlier (Bowers dates it from the reign of Edward IV, making it after 1471), but it, too, is set in an alehouse.

[5] Bowers emphasizes this point: "This is not a scene of low realism, nor is the tavern like that operated by Skelton's Eleanor Rumming of Leatherhead or Shakespeare's Mistress Quickly of Eastcheap. The main characters all talk in aureate language, far from the colloquialism or immediacy of even upper-class speech" (p. 28). Bowers adds that the author confuses didactic with mimetic modes, which also militates against colloquial freedom of speech. The notion of decorum prevalent in most Elizabethan drama would continue to keep the speech of upper-class characters from being rendered naturalistically; on this point see Madeleine Doran, *Endeavors of Art* (Madison: Univ. of Wisconsin Press, 1954), pp. 78–9.

[6] Ian Lancashire, ed., *Two Tudor Interludes: The Interlude of Youth, Hick Scorner* (The Revels Plays), (Baltimore: Johns Hopkins Univ. Press, 1980), pp. 27 ff.

other features of the criminal underworld: the Surrey gibbet site at Saint Thomas of Watring, the sanctuary and the law courts in Westminster, the famous highwaymen's ambush at Shotter's Hill, the Bell and Hart's Horn whorehouses, and so on. Cony-catching anecdotes are plotted through the streets of London. As in *Youth* we hear about these places but never see them; the conversations in which they occur are held in unlocalized allegorical space. Pity and the other virtuous characters still wander about in a void, because they are allegorical and because the criminal geography of London is – strikingly – the only aspect of the city mentioned at all.

As Alan C. Dessen has pointed out in his study of Jonson and the morality tradition, far from expiring as the sixteenth century wore on, there was an efflorescence of the genre during the Elizabethan era: "On the basis of the total number of both extant and lost plays, for example, one *could* argue that the period between 1558 and 1590 represents the golden age of the morality play," he says, citing the fifty or so plays listed in Harbage's *Annals* for these thirty years.[7] Moreover, as he goes on to say, following the lead of Louis B. Wright, the bulk of these plays concern current social and economic problems.[8] The generic basis for this access of social analysis is the confluence of the morality play and the medieval complaint tradition, which had expressed itself in various forms – sermon, verse, and mysteries like the *Second Shepherd's Play*. In *Mankind* the names Newgyse and Now-a-days suggest the complaint theme of the badness of modern times, but it is very hard to find any historical content in the play's handling of it. There is no comment on changing fashions, even as Mankind's side coat is cut down into a fashionably short jacket, with the cony catchers keeping the profit from the extra cloth: The joke is an eternal one. Even the rudiments of a specifically sociohistorical analysis do not emerge.

There is more room for such analysis in the later morality play, which, as Dessen has shown, shifts its emphasis from a psychomachia in a single central figure representing Humanum Genus to a survey of the social evils besetting Respublica, run by a public Vice. A typical structure is represented by Thomas Lupton's *All for Money* (1577):

> In accordance with his promise on the title page of "plainly representing the manners of men and fashion of the world noweadayes", Lupton has offered his audience a specific demonstration of how the venality in various parts of society contributes to the corruption of justice. Through a combination of allegorical personae, who embody the thesis (All for Money, Sin), and social types or "estates", who provide the demonstration, the moral dramatist has made his point about the materialism of society.[9]

[7] Alan C. Dessen, *Jonson's Moral Comedy* (Chicago: Northwestern Univ. Press, 1971), p. 10; S. Shoenbaum's revision of *Annals* (London, 1964).

[8] Dessen, p. 12; Louis B. Wright, "Social Aspects of Some Belated Moralities," *Anglia*, 54 (1930), 107–48.

[9] Dessen, p. 22

The estates satire element provided a great impetus to the development of an array of representative social types, which later provided a ready-made stock of characters for city comedy.

The Jonsonian theme of fashion, latent in the gallantry associated with tavern seductions, becomes prominent in these plays as a symptom of social malaise. To take a garden variety example, the topic of fashion is all over Ulpian Fulwell's *Like Will to Like, quoth the Devil to the Collier* (1568), which features a Vice called Nichol Newfangle, who was apprenticed to Lucifer as a tailor. Lucifer fell from heaven because of his pride, he reminds us, and he instructs Newfangle "Such pride through new fashions in men's hearts to show / That those, who use it, may have the like overthrow." Newfangle assures him that knaves already seek to go gayer and more brave than lords, and Tom Collier utters the commonplace about the badness of the times: "It is a common trade nowadays, this is plain, / To cut one another's throat for lucre and gain."[10] The title expresses the often repeated Calvinist premise of the play, that Like Will to Like, naturally illustrated with a class metaphor: "For the virtuous will always virtue's company seek out: / A gentleman never seeketh the company of a lout" (15). Wielding this mighty premise, Fulwell cuts through social problems before they can truly appear. The action of the play is a sorting operation, a flushing of the social order; fashion never disguises social differences, and people are what they seem, their names disclosing their natures. In spite of its prominence, the fashion theme thus stays pretty inert; it is hard to believe that such a simple formula spoke to its audience with much force or immediacy. The writing is bad and the stagecraft is worse – getting characters on stage and introduced is painfully laborious, the allegorical procedures obscuring how people really interact and reveal themselves. When this sort of thing is done badly it produces the dullest, most poverty-stricken plays in our language.

The continuing vitality of the tradition might be illustrated by the anonymous *The Contention between Liberality and Prodigality*, probably a play of 1567–8 dusted off for performance before the Queen by the Children of the Chapel Royal in 1601, and published in 1602,[11] making the play not only a representative precursor of Jonson's drama, but contemporary competition as well. Some of what seems Jonsonian about it has nothing to do with realism, like the strong dramatic imagination which creates the rapid metamorphoses of Money, ruffled and torn by Prodigality, then kissed, bound with ropes and carried off by Tenacity the country miser. The old dramaturgy was far from worn out, as Jonson believed, returning to it in his last plays. At other times Liberality and Prodigality touches on the sorts of subsidiary social topics that

---

[10] *The Dramatic Writings of Ulpian Fulwell*, ed., John S. Farmer (London: Early English Drama Society, 1906), pp. 7, 9.

[11] *The Contention between Liberality and Prodigality*, ed., W. W. Gregg (Malone Society Reprints) (Oxford: Oxford Univ. Press, 1913).

interested Jonson: The courtier Vanity sells access to his mistress Fortune, as in *The Staple of News,* while the good courtier Liberality assures the poor but virtuous Captain Well-done that his virtue has already been recognized by his Prince without the need of some base mechanism of patronage – the sort of mystification to which *Cynthia's Revels* and *Poetaster* are dedicated.

This play's realism has nothing to do with the ambition of its social analysis. The cheerfully modest Prologue, which should be taken at face value, disclaims all ambition beyond entertainment. This is entertainment of a virtuous sort, to be sure, but the author is not setting himself up as a teacher of virtue, social or otherwise, who has seized on the theater as an instrument of instruction. Its realism arises rather from its easy and pleasant dramatic instincts – the action gets going with a swirl of life around the inn which descends from the old tavern scenes and looks forward to the bustle around Ursula's booth in *Bartholomew Fair* – and, above all, its feeling for character, which slips out incidentally. The Hostess of the inn comes and goes quickly, but she has a name, Dandaline, and we catch a strong whiff of the kitchen from her speech. The Sheriff enters saying "I supplying, though vnworthy, for this yere, / The place of an Officer, and Sherife of the Shiere" (V.4.1164). Being a sheriff is not a metaphysical essence, but a role a real man plays for a while. The abstraction of the morality play is humanized from within by the assumption that characters are people who have complex motives and responses; this accounts for the fine gay cynicism of the play as well as for its colloquialism.

This is an example of the general Elizabethan realism that culminates in Shakespeare, growing within the morality tradition. Jonson is also heir to this, but developments specific to the morality plays feel more characteristically Jonsonian. W. Wager's *The Longer Thou Livest* (1559)[12] anticipates Jonson, particularly the Jonson of the comical satires, to a degree that is startling. Discipline, hailed by Piety as one whose nature it is "both comely manners to teach / And also to minister correction" (190–1), is a direct ancestor of the more socialized and psychologized Asper of *Every Man out of his Humour* and Crites of *Cynthia's Revels.* Discipline speaks with Asper's causticity and with his images as he brandishes a whip over the central character, Moros the fool:

> You begin to be scabby and worm-eaten;
> It is time salt upon you to strow.
> Sirah, do you see what I have here?
> The wise man willeth an ass to have a scourge;
> You have learned folly many a year,
> From the same now I must you purge.
>   (329–34)

On the other side Idleness and Ignorance set up for Moros a course of study with inverted values, in dicing, whoring, quarreling, and the handsome wearing

---

[12] *The Longer Thou Livest and Enough Is as Good as a Feast,* ed., R. Mark Benbow (Regents Renaissance Drama Series) (Lincoln: Univ. of Nebraska Press, 1967).

of a sword, as Jonson's Asotus and Mathew and Sogliardo have their swagger-
ing trainers who will also quail at the sight of the figures representing Discipline. Jonson took over this method for setting up a character for observation
by surrounding him with advisors and commentators; the method obviously
descends from the whole psychomachia tradition in a general way, but in this
particular form it becomes a vehicle for concentration on and discussion of
stylish gestures and postures. The handling of the foolish character is also very
much the same: The newly tricked-out Moros reenters, priding himself on his
appearance, like Pennyboy Junior (1293), and is so infatuated by his feather that
he stumbles and falls while looking up at it (1535). He has a kind of beguiling
foolishness of gesture, like Dapper and Cokes and Littlewit and the rest,
allowing a pleasure in the expression of idiocy, its yearnings and self-satisfac-
tions. The playwright really does want to beat the fool, but without real
hatred, and there is a certain gaiety as he is carried off to hell, as he must be,
since the Calvinist assumption is that his folly is irremediable: "the longer thou
livest, the more fool thou art."

What then are the differences between Jonson and Wager? One might speak
of two, both turning on a more or less developed sense of social context. In
Wager there is little dramatic sense of an ambient society of which the fool is
an enlivening or tedious part, but in any case part of a colorful social scene.
There are occasional topical references to London, and later in the play Moros
inhabits an estate with a gang of retainers, but on the whole the location and
definition of the scene still do not matter much.

On the ideological level the social thinking of Wager's morality is more
directly and topically political than that of Jonson's comedy. There are many
references to the Marian persecution (the sort of tyranny that can be expected
from Moros in power), and the play takes a very strong conservative line on
social order, including propaganda in favor of the Statute of Artificers which
would be issued in 1563 (1032–3 and note). Wager's later *Enough is as Good as
a Feast* (1570?) is even more forthright in its condemnation of ambition and its
advocacy of political passivity on the part of subaltern classes, who should
learn to be happy in their places. In *The Longer Thou Livest* social climbing is
a problem, handled without ambiguity or much sophistication of tactics, but it
is not really the root problem. The root problem seems – according to Piety –
to be lack of piety.

> But now, alas, what manners, what heavy time,
> Piety is utterly extinguished.
> What contempt is there, what crimes,
> More mischief than can be published;
> And as God's majesty is despised,
> So the love among men doth abate.
> Never was there greater hatred devised
> Than is among men of every estate;
> What falsehood, what deceit, and guile?

What subtilties are of men invented?
Who doth not his body with sin defile?
Who is with his own state contented?
I have read of many worlds and seasons;
Of so sinful a world did I never read.
(1177–90)

Falling away from God causes the social disintegration: There is no room for secular causation here, as the evils are each related directly to the principal cause, not tied to one another. The hyperbolic denunciation of the badness of these times and these manners is utterly conventional, which does not mean it did not express real feelings or a real situation. What makes it so unsatisfactory, even as moralizing, is that the temptation to rest here in this position – a quite natural temptation, as the formula has been fulfilled – prevents any further reformulation of the social problem, or the development of new tactics to deal with it. This is the ideological impasse of the postfeudal complaint tradition; as I shall be arguing later, Jonson managed in some ways to move beyond this impasse, though the elements of this conservative ideology are certainly still present in him (see below, Chapter 4).

Thus as the morality tradition wore on through the Elizabethan period it both sponsored and inhibited the development of a dramatic realism that could serve as the vehicle for social thought. In the 1580s and 1590s it produced some complex and ambitious plays, which filled out the possibilities of the genre and suggested the direction of its transformation.

R[obert] W[ilson]'s *The Three Ladies of London* (1581)[13] pushes the allegorical tradition a long way toward the representation of social life, and therefore out of the dramatic and ideological impasse. It is a fully elaborated example of the estates morality, adding to the roster of allegorical figures like Love, Lucre, Conscience, and Simplicity, figures representing social types like Tom Beggar, Gerontus the Jewish usurer, and Mercatore the Italian merchant. This produces a very large cast of characters milling about the stage doing a great deal of talking about one thing and another. Clumps of actors shift and re-form, brushing past each other. Finally a social network binds all the characters together, with no two characters more than one acquaintanceship apart. Social relationships – of service, calculated marriage, debt, friendship, antagonism, conspiracy, cheating and its exposure, the services of bawdry – are what are talked about and negotiated, providing what action there is.

All this bears the strongest resemblance to Jonson's comical satires. *The Three Ladies* is also vast, shapeless, interminable, and weakly plotted, if punctuated by local liveliness and strong symbolic actions; it too is concerned to illustrate an idea, not an action, a *logos* not a *mythos,* in Aristotelian terms.

[13] In W. Carew Hazlitt, ed., *A Select Collection of Old English Plays, originally published by Robert Dodsley in the year 1744,* 4th ed. (London: Reeves and Turner, 1874), vol. 6.

Wilson's later play, *The Cobbler's Prophesy* (1589–93), is more self-consciously literary, supplementing the allegorical figures with an array of pagan deities, handled with a sophisticated Lylian wit reminiscent of *Cynthia's Revels*. At one point the estates figures – Emnius the bad courtier, a rack-renting Country Gentleman, a Scholar with Machiavellian inclinations, and the good blunt Soldier who is the repository of the play's values – talk about going off to an ordinary, the upscale Elizabethan version of the old tavern.

Courtier:	Marry we will all to the eighteene pence Ordinary, how say ye Gentlemen?
Country Gentleman:	No sir, not I, tis too deere by my faith.
Scholar:	Why you shall be my guest for this once. How saye you master souldier?
Souldier:	No sir I must turne one of your meales into three. And euerie one a sufficient banquet for me.
Courtier:	Faith and you had kept your newes vntill now, yee should haue bin my guest, for your talke would haue serud well for the table.[14]

But the Soldier won't trade on his conversation that way, as Jonson similarly objected to soldiers and travelers dining off gossip of foreign news (for example, in *Epigrams* 107 "To Captain Hungry"). The relative subtlety of this social and moral judgment puts us a long way from the plain casting of oneself into perdition of the old tavern scenes; in every way this scene descends from that tradition, but it deals in more sophisticated distinctions. The expense of the tavern signifies prodigality, but in the precise form of an expensive fashion-ableness around which the characters sort themselves out. Again the issue is whether or not one affiliates with bad companions, but now their company is the structure of power in a semicorrupt state. In *Henry IV* Shakespeare famously made the tavern world a mirror of the world of politics; in *The Cobbler's Prophesy* the tavern world has begun to swallow up society, and in the process has lost its otherness. More and more social behavior is interpreted in its light as falsely sociable, unredeemed, and pernicious. Jonson will press this idea further.

As they are going off Contempt, the play's Vice, who is disguised as Content, calls to them:

Contempt:	Why Gentlemen, no farewell to your little God.
All three:	Suffice it without vaine Ceremonies we shew our selues dutifull.

(416–18)

This is typical of Wilson's witty and ironic handling of the problem of having characters from different ontological levels on stage together; the ease of writing

[14] Robert Wilson, *The Coblers Prophesie,* ed., A. C. Wood and W. W. Gregg (Malone Society Reprints) (Oxford: Oxford Univ. Press, 1914), lines 401–10.

social dialogue and their eagerness to network with one another nearly got the estates figures off stage before the allegory was sufficiently attended to. All the attention it needs is an airy wave, signifying a gentlemanly unceremonious-ness. The Vice is becoming superfluous; soon the devil will be an ass.

There is a great deal of such sprung, complex layering in this play, some of it rather sublime; the presence of a cobbler called Rafe is not the only reason to see this play as an important precursor of Beaumont's heavily metatheatrical *Knight of the Burning Pestle* (1607–10). Both have the problem of not adding up to what is conventionally thought of as a play; this one takes flight into a dense allegorical landscape, and finally succumbs to its variousness, its stylistic ener-gies squandered on displays of midlevel virtuosity in a dozen kinds rather than the consolidation of a coherent dramatic world.

Something rather similar might be said of *Histriomastix*,[15] a play of about 1589 which John Marston revised in 1599 (thereby inadvertently beginning the War of the Theaters), though in this case the squandered resources are more theatrical than rhetorical. The scene is crowded, broad, and kaleidoscopic; there are more than eighty speaking parts, plus various "harvest folkes," "contrimen," "morrice-dancers," "other Nobles and Gentles," "a sort of Rus-setings and Mechanichalls," and so on. The dramatic technique is a hyper-trophic development of that of the moralities, with its characteristic doubling of parts;[16] it permits a continual wash of new scenes played by small groups of actors, representing what seems like a potentially infinite variety of social types and milieus with brief, sinewy characterization. Clearly Marston was not making do with four men and a boy; the spectacular capacity of his theater can bring a whole market scene before us for just a minute before it is whisked away, and it runs to effects reminiscent of the masque. (Act III begins with the entrance of Pride, with her attendants, who "casts a mist, wherein Mavortius and his company vanish off the Stage," and the play ends with a stage full of mythological personages singing paeans to Astrea/Elizabeth.)

The play's technical capacity is matched by the ambition of its social thought. It is acute and full of meaty issues: the social ambitions of "Mechani-calls" who would be actors, the conflict between a high, witty, Italianate manner and blunter English hospitality, feudal retainers being dismissed by the fashionable Mavortius, who needs only a page, the bad emotions of an aristoc-racy which resents its dependence on merchants and lawyers, and of merchants and lawyers who resent the condescension and contempt of aristocrats whom they can buy and sell, the place of the artist in such a society and the envy that will gnaw at him, and so on. This is a compendium of the themes of the traditional economic morality described nostalgically by L. C. Knights, for-

---

[15] In *The Plays of John Marston*, vol. 3, ed., H. Harvey Wood (London: Oliver and Boyd, 1939).

[16] David Bevington, *From "Mankind" to Marlowe: Growth of Structure in the Popular Drama of Tudor England* (Cambridge, Mass.: Harvard Univ. Press, 1962).

mulated specifically and pointedly, but so global in its scope that the subset of issues that will dominate the War of the Theaters and city comedy do not emerge as definitive, although they are fully present.

Histriomastix's allegorical skeleton sticks out painfully through the flesh; the problem is clearest on the level of overall structure. Each of the play's six acts is presided over by an allegorical figure (Peace, Plenty, Envy, Pryde, War, and Poverty) who governs an epoch in what is understood as a recurrent historical cycle. It is a very abstract scheme, and, one may feel, an extraordinarily barren one for purposes of historical understanding. Its principal contribution would seem to be encouragement of the belief that periodic wars are a necessary and good thing. This apparatus lies heavily over the play. Meanwhile in the plot the paths of the various groups of characters begin to cross – Mavortius casts off the (Jonsonian) scholar Chrisogonus, hires the actors and entertains the lawyers and merchants – in conjunction with the intensifying theme of social mobility, competition, and resentment. Sometimes the times' transsshifting helps the development of this theme, as when both aristocratic and citizen factions expect to profit from the coming war, but in general the rapid lockstep march through the historical cycle keeps any theme or any scene from developing much beyond a quick sketch. On the level of the setting, the crossing of paths suggests a location, a determinate place where these social events can occur; there are clear signs that we are in the environs of London, but in the scheme of the play the locale cannot be very concrete. A concrete setting would invite speculation about concrete application of the historical model, which is pretty clearly not intended. (*The Three Ladies of London* is similar: In spite of its title it is not set in London, and although the social concerns of the play are numerous and explicit, and its purview is vast, the ground of all the issues is not concretized.)

The theme of social competition and fashion develops through two quite different dramatic modes. One is the overtly symbolic, organizing mode of the discussion of social issues – which must have looked old fashioned in 1599 – in which an enthroned Pryde declaims "If you will sit in throne of state with Pride, / The newest fashion (still) must be your guide" and then urges Lawyers and Merchants to break the sumptuary laws (pp. 268–9), and in which a merchant's wife expresses her social ambition in a rhetoric of pride patented by Christopher Marlowe, reminiscent of the flyting of Zenocrate and Zabina, a rhetoric whose symbolic topography is defined by just such things as the throne of Pryde:

> Shall I still stand an abject in the eye,
> Of faire respect, not mounted to the height
> To the top gallant of o're-peering state,
> That with Elated lookes of Majestie,
> I may out face the proud pild Eminence,
> Of this same gilded Madam *Bellula* . . . ?
>
> (p. 280)

Growing out of this is a more conversational mode from which we can learn a good deal about how social competition was felt – the symbolic importance of bodily gestures of kneeling or giving the wall, the envy of the citizen wife "pent / In nice respect of civill modesty" (p. 279) for the curled tresses and glittering ornaments of the lady. Mavortius' entertainment, which bridges Acts III and IV, is city comedy in embryonic form.

Like Jonson's work this is more subtle and exact because more empirical. Again one feels the distinction between a technique that elaborates deductively from allegorical principles, which is what is still going on in *The Three Ladies of London,* and one based more directly on observation of real social interactions. Jonson's generalizations are a step closer to his materials, and so include the finer mechanisms of social functioning in addition to basic moral principles. The new object emerging in *Histriomastix* is, in part, *style* – Marston and Jonson can catch its evolving nuances, even begin to theorize its motives and mechanisms, where Wilson can only trot out the conventional if colorful figures of Fraud as a blustering braggart soldier, Usury as a Vice, the stage Jew, and so on.

Jonson's great legacy from the morality is thus a structure of examination and judgment of social behaviors, a sense that it was the proper business of drama to analyze such things, and a set of techniques for posing them, including literally posing them, in the form of the posturing gallant and foolish heir. Jonson's greater commitment to secular extension, and so his ability to jettison much of the now inhibiting apparatus of the morality, comes with his adaptation of the new comic tradition, whose conventional scene is an ontologically coherent "world."

COMEDY

Comedy is the form associated with "private life" and, in its classic (new comic) form, with urban life. Less analytic in its view of society, it was closer to its surfaces, less problematically realistic – a mirror, as everyone said. The emphasis is on personality rather than spiritual state; the action is based on how people behave in society, and the plots often revolve around issues of social status. The conventions of new comedy included an array of social types, and a stage set which was normally a city street. When new comedy was revived in Renaissance Italy the stock set was immediately customized to look like the city in which the play was performed.[17] It took a long time for London to appear, as I have pointed out, but adapting new comic form to English content seems not to have taken any practice, or at least there were some immediate precocious successes – Gasgoigne's *Supposes* (1566) and William Stevenson(?)'s *Gammer Gurton's Needle* (printed 1575, but written as early as the early 1550s).

[17] Harry Levin, "Notes Towards a Definition of City Comedy," in Barbara Kiefer Lewalski, ed., *Renaissance Genres: Essays on Theory, History and Interpretation,* Harvard English Studies 14 (Cambridge, Mass.: Harvard Univ. Press, 1986), pp. 132 ff.

The first intersection of new comedy and a London setting is apparently the anonymous *Jacke Jugeler* (1562?), though both elements are present only fragmentally. This play is really in the old interlude tradition, though in the secular wing of it, the only classical elements being that it is based on the Sosia subplot of Plautus's *Amphytruo,* and the pedantry of its prologue with its nervous defense of comedy as harmless entertainment. We get glimpses of the fashionable urban lifestyle of the Boungraces, masters of the feckless page Jenkin Careaway, who accompanies his master to the tennis court, then gambles at the gate of the house where his master dines, and, when he neglects his errand to invite his mistress to join Master Boungrace for supper, tries to convince her she wouldn't like that occasion anyway:

> And besyds that there was such other compainye
> As I know your maistriship settith nothyng by:
> Gorges dames of the corte and galaunts also,
> With doctours, and other rufflers mo.[18]

He goes on to suggest that she lives, or wants to live, in a world where secret admirers provide banquets for her. Master Boungrace's bearing, when we see him, confirms the impression of urbanity. None of this is represented directly, and it is quite irrelevant to the main business of the play, which is set in the pages' youth culture and is occupied with beatings, scheming amongst the servants, and talk of fist sandwiches at the gate, but the fashionable lifestyle would have been a draw for a sophisticated audience.

The 1580s and 1590s saw the spectacular growth of the realism defined by Weimann as not of subject matter but of the relation of subject to environment. One does not want to exaggerate the separation of this development, associated with comedy and tragedy, from the tradition of the moralities: Marlowe and Shakespeare were the heirs of the morality tradition also, and their accomplishment would feed back into satiric comedy, which could take for granted a more supple technique and characters of greater psychological depth and social nuance. Basic matters like managing entrances and exits were now routinely handled with a newly realistic eye to how people actually enter a room. All this would permit the issues of the social realistic drama to be taken up on another level, in a medium of a different texture.

Shakespeare also had an interest in manners, and fills his comedies with social occasions and fashionable conversation, increasingly so in the period leading up to the comical satires (*The Merchant of Venice* 1596–7, *Much Ado About Nothing* 1598–1600, *Twelfth Night* 1599–1600). *Love's Labour's Lost* (1588–94) is his *Every Man Out,* an early examination of this material so exaggerated in technique that the preoccupation is unmistakable. But the difference in Shakespeare's approach to the topic must be noted.

---

[18] *Jacke Jugeler,* in *Four Tudor Comedies,* ed., William Tydeman (Harmondsworth: Penguin, 1984), lines 266–9.

The heir of Lyly and an admirer of the aristocracy, Shakespeare loved fine manners, but for him fashionableness does not imply a competition in fashion, as it always does for Jonson. To be sure he has his fops and dandies – Oswald and Osric, the popinjay who enrages the battle-heated Hotspur, even Richard II and his silken caterpillars – and some of them, like Sir Andrew Aguecheek, have clearly wandered out of the city comedy matrix; Aguecheek is more truly stranded on the Illyrian coast than Viola is. Normally there is only one such figure in each play, and so they are fish out of water. No one is playing the game of emulation with them. This has everything to do with the fact that none of Shakespeare's plays is set in contemporary London, where the issue of fashionableness would become acute and combative. The elegant worlds of Verona, Illyria, or Navarre are not foreign, because their high style is international, but they are timeless and remote from the jostling of the city.

This sort of concern for good manners is characteristic of the popular dramatic tradition, close as Shakespeare's connections with the aristocracy were. In *The Book of Sir Thomas More* (c.1592–1601, by a raft of playwrights perhaps including Shakespeare)[19] More is the exemplar of good manners, always lecturing his wife on how to behave, not to leave her guests alone, to seat them quickly and make merry with them (scene ix); he even forces a young man with a bad attitude to cut his hair and straighten up (viii.b). His precepts of courtesy consist essentially of graciousness and merriness, a manner that has nothing in it to date, to go out of fashion, and with no element of competition. It is a fantasy of a stable middle class (which values manners as a mark of distinction but is not in fashion and does not want to be) of how its social and cultural superiors might act, a fantasy containing nothing to offend it or put it down, nothing it can't aim at. In Dekker's *Satiromastix,* the last shot in the War of the Theaters but nonetheless not satirical at heart, so much pleasure is taken in wedding customs – the strewing of flowers, the distribution of gloves and rosemary, the marshaling of the guests – that from this source alone it would be possible to write a pretty full ethnographic account of a late sixteenth-century wedding. There is no analysis of innovation here, only affirmation of the way things are done.

1597

In the year before Jonson's *Every Man in His Humour* (September 1598) two plays emerged out of the mainstream comic tradition which initiated developments Jonson was to carry forward: George Chapman's *An Humorous Day's Mirth,* which began the line of "humor" plays, and William Haughton's

[19] *The Book of Sir Thomas More,* ed., W. W. Gregg (Malone Society Reprints) (Oxford: Oxford Univ. Press, 1911). The manuscript of this play was so heavily censored by the Master of the Revels that it was never performed.

Englishmen for My Money, the first regular comedy deliberately to exploit the London setting.[20]

An Humorous Day's Mirth promptly runs the word "humor" into the ground, and endlessly employs techniques whereby the behavior of some character is set up for observation – this is a social game everyone is playing. In scene vii everyone gathers to watch, from hiding, the humor of Lord Dowsecer, a melancholic. Various objects have been left about for him to moralize on – a picture, hose, a codpiece, a sword – and he discourses on the standard topics of worldliness. He turns out to be a moralist of the classical variety, and the crowd is smitten by his virtue. Usually, however, the point is a comedy of mechanical social behavior. In scene viii Lemot, the King's minion and chief organizer of the fun, says: "Thou seest here's a fine plump of gallants, such as think their wits singular, and themselves rarely accomplished; yet to show thee how brittle their wits be, I will speak to them severally, and I will tell thee before what they shall answer me" (viii.209–13). And so the game is played out. It is scarcely an exaggeration to say that the whole play is composed of such exposures, especially if one includes catching out people – notably the King – in erotically embarrassing situations.

These scenes work somewhat better than one would expect them to, given the awkward straightforwardness of their technique. The technique of observation is quite like what we saw in *The Longer Thou Livest,*[21] but the object of attention has shifted, from vices to follies, as one might put it conventionally; from the spiritual to the psychological, conceived as improbably mechanical. This is a more secular domain: The lines Lemot knows the gallants will speak are a socially produced text, and their "stale proverbs" represent a social failure rather than a moral one.

But the behavior being observed is vaguely formulated, and the observation weakly directed, which is why the play does not have the bite of Jonson or later city comedy. The forms of comical satire are here, profusely, but the content is entirely absent. Few real personalities emerge out of the crowd, in spite of the

[20] Chapman, *An Humorous Day's Mirth,* in *The Plays of George Chapman: The Comedies,* vol. 1, ed., Thomas Marc Parrott (New York: Russell & Russell, 1961); William Haughton, *Englishmen for My Money, or A Woman Will Have Her Will,* ed., Albert Croll Baugh (Philadelphia: Univ. of Penn. Press, 1917); Baugh says it is, "so far as we can tell, the first regular comedy of realistic London life in the English drama," p. 40. Entries in Henslowe's diary date the play to the first few months of 1598 or the end of 1597.

[21] Baskerville commented on the derivation of "humorous" characters from medieval didactic, allegorical ones; tendencies in classical literature were assimilated to this native tradition. Charles Read Baskerville, *English Elements in Jonson's Early Comedy* (Austin: Univ. of Texas Press, 1911), pp. 26–8. See also Brian Gibbons, who points to the revival of elements from the Tudor Interlude and Estates Morality in *An Humorous Day's Mirth. Jacobean City Comedy,* 2d ed. (London: Methuen, 1980), p. 48.

"humors" business. The play succeeds at making art out of inconsequential matters, simply celebrating everyday life and observing social behavior, like snapshots at a picnic. It succeeds not through a journalistic sense of observation, much less a satiric combativeness, but through jests, humor, merriment: the sense of comedy, in a very pure form.

As the title indicates, the play is about a day's spontaneous social amusements in the leisure class, with only the mildest kind of plot tension, and no underlying social tensions. There is almost no social differentiation, or characterization, by class or manners or occupation. Everyone is made out of the same *materia prima,* which is generically aristocratic. Lemot represents the spirit of comedy, not a particular socially and culturally locatable class fraction, like the gallants Jonson introduced in the next year, who sport with folly in similar fashion. The King does not play any ideological role, because there are no problems above the level of the personal for him to resolve. The Puritanism of the pretty hypocrite Florilla, the nearest the play comes to topicality, is not meant to be taken seriously. The setting is French, but without proper names and so undefined that it is not easy to tell if we are in the city or the country.

The best defined location is – this should not surprise us – an ordinary, where the play's climax takes place. Many features suggest that the scene is built on the old tradition. The first guest to arrive, an impecunious heir with fancy clothes who has never been to an ordinary before, is enticed into learning to gamble at cards; another guest arrives fresh from prison, like New Guise or Riot, having been arrested in a whorehouse. But someone else arrives from the tennis court, and new associations mix with the old. This is the place for the elegant new custom of taking tobacco, and the ordinary's fine rooms are praised with apparent sincerity. Chapman goes to considerable lengths to portray the life of the establishment, with genial satire on the management's sharp practices, and plays on its social customs, for instance, the mild scandalousness of the presence of ladies at a private dinner there. (This dinner and its disruption may have given Jonson the hint for Ovid's banquet of the gods in *Poetaster.*) Chapman was clearly interested in the social life of ordinaries, which figures in his *All Fools* (1599–1604) and *May Day* (1601–09) as well, but it is an insider's amused interest and certainly not dominated by heavy moral condemnation. This is the point at which he comes closest to representing his own culture, and that of the relatively sophisticated audience for which this play seems intended.

Haughton's *Englishmen for My Money* finally supplies the London setting, and it is clear that the author did not merely stumble into it accidentally. He knew he had something to exploit, and he exploited it, most strikingly by setting a scene in a central London institution, the Exchange. The scene is long and full, and mimics the rhythm of a business session. It gathers momentum as business picks up and more and more transactions are juggled at once; we are shown the ripple of excitement as a post arrives with news.

Centering on the Portuguese usurer Pisaro, who seems to have lost a ship in the Mediterranean to Spanish galleys, this scene displays the global scope of the business conducted on the Exchange, and the consequent cosmopolitan knowledge of geography and geopolitics. It also explores the emotions of the Exchange: the toughness, the agitated excitement, the speed, the devastating loss amidst indifference, the rudeness in the press of business which must be smoothed over before "The Exchange bell rings" (s.d. line 658) and everyone goes off in various directions to dinner. As Pisaro gets off the day's emotional roller coaster he does a little conventional moralizing – "What is this world? or what this state of man, / How in a moment curst, in a trice blest?" (648–9) – which only illustrates the worthlessness of such talk compared to the theater's power to convey what it means to do business and the energy of mercantilism pulsating at the center of the city's life.

The attitude the play takes toward this spectacle is curiously neutral. It is not in the satirical mode of the scenes set in Paul's walk in Jonson's *Every Man Out* and Middleton's *Michaelmas Term* (Haughton has a brief scene in Paul's walk, too, though unlike the Exchange scene there is little attempt at recreation, and the interest is merely touristic), but neither is it celebratory in the mode of popular plays like *The Life and Death of Sir Thomas Gresham, with the Building of the Royal Exchange,* named with approval by the Citizen of *The Knight of the Burning Pestle* (he is probably referring to Part II of Heywood's *If You Know Not Me You Know Nobody* [1605]).

We get to the Exchange, as it were, with the three young English gentlemen who are pursuing the three daughters of the usurer Pisaro, to whom they are in danger of losing their estates. The Englishmen are sent there by the girls to borrow more money from him, with the promise that they will never have to repay it – "for vs you spend . . . Weele pay the intrest, and the principall" (374, 378). This is a fantasy economy, where prodigality pays, and borrowing is an investment, and foreigners can be milked as a source of credit but without the danger of real wealth passing out of English hands – "Englishmen for My Money." The Exchange is Pisaro's element, but the foreign usurer does not own it. In fact there are strong social sanctions operating against him. A friend asks why he couldn't be found there an hour earlier, and he replies

> Fayth sir I was here but was driuen home,
> Heres such a common hant of Crack-rope boyes,
> That what for feare to haue m'apparell spoyld,
> Or my Ruffles dirted, or Eyes strucke out:
> I dare not walke where people doe expect mee.
>
> (550–4)

The indifference of other businessmen to the loss of his ship is extreme, and he complains about it in lines that recall Shylock's. (There is other evidence that this play is a response to *The Merchant of Venice* [1596–97] – as in the Jessica plot the usurer's daughters return his wealth to the community, and here, too, there are three foreign suitors.) This scene makes Shylock's treatment look civil and benevolent, though Pisaro the bottlenosed usurer is not a Jew and so does not come in for such vicious ethnic stigmatizing even in this racist play.

The arrogance of the young men as they ask for money is extreme:

> Gentlemen, you know, must want no Coyne,
> Nor are they slaues vnto it, when they haue:
> You may perceiue our minds: What say you to't?
> (447–9)

and they complain throughout the scene that Pisaro's distraction over the loss of his ship is keeping them waiting ("What an old Asse is this to keepe vs here: / Maister Pisaro, pray dispatch vs hence." 594–5). This is class aggression, and they turn it idly on the Post while they wait, tormenting him until he flares up.

> Walgrave: What will you swagger sirra, will yee swagger?
> Browne: I beseech you Sir, hold your hand; Gette home yee patch, cannot
>   you suffer Gentlemen Iest with you?
> Post: Ide teach him a Gentle trick and I had him of the burse.
> (580–4)

Walgrave, in particular, is a hothead whose hyperphallic aggression culminates at the end of the play as he tells Pisaro off, having stolen his daughter:

> Here is my wife, Sbloud touch her, if thou darst,
> Hearst thou, Ile lie with her before thy face,
> Against the Crosse in Cheape, here, any where.
> (1894–6)

Repellent though he may be, all the signs are that he is the hero of the play. He is "fun," and the audience can rally behind him because they can identify with his aggression – as everyone's wish fulfillment, perhaps, and because his aggression against the foreigners unites even those in the audience who will have to swallow his class arrogance in the bargain. The 'prentices in the audience liked to riot against foreigners, too. Pisaro is pushing as rivals to the English gentlemen three foreign merchants (one French, one Italian, and one Dutch) whose class status, possibly a point of contention in another city comedy, is completely overshadowed by their national identity. It occasions endless jokes on the level of the comment that Frenchmen say "awee, awee" like pigs. It seems possible that the impulse to represent English life is (among other things) a reflex of the hatred of foreigners which crops up frequently in Elizabethan drama. In any case the uneasy truce in the class war permits a view of the Exchange as a center of national wealth.

The multifarious and smoothly run intrigue plot eventually crowds out the London setting as the main interest, but not before Haughton has given it a couple of other dimensions. One is a thoroughgoing circumstantiality: As Pisaro shows his neighbor Moore out, he says "Take heed how you goe downe, the staires are bad, / Bring here a light" (1334–5). As the stairs are concretely imagined, so is the neighborhood. Moore's daughter Susan is given permission to sleep at Pisaro's since Mrs. Moore has given birth and the house is noisy and full. When Pisaro's servant Frisco meets the Bellman late at night their conversation makes it clear that they are old though somewhat estranged friends. Social relationships are concrete, with a history and more detail than the plot requires.

Pisaro's treacherous stairs also indicate how carefully space is handled. It is usually made clear where in Pisaro's house we are, and there is a lot of playing around the front door, in the new comic tradition. But unlike the new comic convention we are not simply to imagine the forum off stage in one direction and the harbor in the other. The implied space opens out, using the map in the audience's mind, to include a great deal of London. This map is most elaborately played on in Act III when at night the Englishmen stand in front of Pisaro's house in Croched-friers and misdirect their foreign rivals through the dark streets of London, telling one he is in Fanchurch Street, another Leadenhall, another Towerstreet. There is much play with finding landmarks in the dark: Is it the four spouts in Leadenhall Alvaro hit his head against? Frisco, leading the regrouped strangers and hoping they will knock their horns into the pissing Conduit, claims to smell London-stone on Canning Street, feels the Maypole on Ivie-bridge going to Westminster, and so forth. The confusions in the night are specific, the jokes based on the integrity of the space of the city.[22]

Haughton and Chapman's innovations seem complementary, from the vantage of the Jonsonian synthesis. Haughton provided a deeply realized sense of the London setting, concrete and full of social tensions, the groundwork of the city comedy to follow. His representation of London is motivated by the politics of the Elizabethan settlement, submerging (without obscuring) class differences in the interests of a bully nationalism. The ideological power of the play is carried mainly by the comic plot form (the thwarting of a miser and rival suitors by young love), with the attendant identification with the English gentlemen heroes. This identification is powerful and crude: The gentlemen and their culture are not critically investigated. They are not gallants, either in the old tradition of the moralities or in the sense in which Jonson would create them in *Every Man In* (see below). Chapman with his "humors" had introduced a new wrinkle into the satirical display of the cultural fabric of the ruling class, and of gallantry in particular – a modernized version of the morality techniques turned to secular topics, but depoliticized and without analytic force. Jonson restored the social purposes of this sort of observation by grounding it in a (proto-) Jacobean cultural politics in which social tensions and class styles were the central preoccupation.

[22] Gibbons points out that jest books and cony-catching pamphlets also set episodes in specific London locations "to give sensational interest to otherwise very commonplace material," p. 107. A sense for the contribution of jest books and *lazzi* to city comedy runs throughout his study.

Both *Englishmen for My Money* and *An Humorous Day's Mirth* were written for Phillip Henslow and produced by the Admiral's Men, for whom Jonson began to write in the same year. One imagines Jonson watched the work of these two playwrights with special attention – Chapman had the kind of learning and the social connections Jonson aspired to, and Haughton, making a big hit at the age of twenty-three or twenty-four, perhaps a bit younger than Jonson, may well have seemed like a rival. Jonson started working for Henslow immediately following his imprisonment for his coauthorship (with Thomas Nashe) of the (now lost) play *The Isle of Dogs,* apparently a satire on the Queen's courtiers. This play so enraged the authorities that the Privy Council issued an order banning all stage plays, accompanied with instructions that the theaters be "plucked down." In the event the direst sanctions were not enforced, but the theaters were closed for some months and Pembroke's Men, the offending company, dissolved and was forbidden to perform in London ever again.[23] The *enfant terrible* Ben Jonson thus began his career as a playwright by pushing things too far, threatening with destruction the very institution in which he was still finding his forms and purposes.

His plays regularly got him into trouble (in 1601 the "Apologetical Dialogue" appended to *Poetaster* was prohibited on stage, and Jonson was threatened with prosecution before the Chief Justice; in 1603 he was called before the Privy Council because of suspected poperie and treason in *Sejanus;* in 1604 he was imprisoned for the satire on the Scots in *Eastward Ho,* and threatened with having his nose and ears cut off; in 1609 Lady Arabella Stuart took offence at *Epicoene,* which, according to one account, was "suppressed" as a result; and in 1616 he was "accused" for *The Devil is an Ass,* and "The King desired him to conceal it," as he told Drummond of Hawthornden (presumably referring to the satire on the Duke of Drowned Land, *Conversations,* 409–15). He continued to skirt the edges of the permissible, for instance, by provocatively inventing comical satire just at the moment satire in verse was banned. In any case, the profession of playwright left one open to false accusations by "politic picklocks." His armed prologues show how aware he was of the danger. It has been plausibly suggested that he turned to nonaristocratic subjects to protect himself from charges of libel, and introduced local color to ward off the suspicion of dangerous allegory.[24] His adoption of the conventions of comedy in *Every Man in his Humour* might be seen as a strategic retreat from a more overtly political and topical kind of play descending from the moralities.

In spite of – or rather through – the crisis of the *Isle of Dogs,* 1597 is considered the year in which the relationship of the theaters with the government was stabilized, as they came more directly under the control of the Court. This control also served as protection from the City administration which had

[23] David Riggs, *Ben Jonson: A Life,* (Cambridge: Harvard Univ. Press, 1989), pp. 32–4.
[24] Fran C. Chalfant, *Ben Jonson's London: A Jacobean Placename Dictionary* (Athens: Univ. of Georgia Press, 1978), p. 9.

long wanted to close the theaters down.[25] Royal control was soon intensified when the Stuart monarchy took over direct patronage of the companies. Compensating for the considerable (if far from total) curtailment of political freedom this involved was the theaters' new autonomy and confidence with respect to the rest of society, including their audience. Jonson sensed and exploited this social possibility. In comedy he could hope to be provocative without getting into trouble with the law or the government, instead organizing contention in civil society and helping to reform and redefine it.

[25] E. K. Chambers, *The Elizabethan Stage,* vol. 1 (Oxford: Clarendon Press, 1923), p. 309.

3

"Thus neere, and familiarly allied to the time"

EVERY MAN IN HIS HUMOUR

As is well known, Jonson buried all his early dramatic work, beginning his official career, as monumentalized in the 1616 folio *Works,* with *Every Man in his Humour*. It is equally well known that the 1616 version is a revision of the original, which was performed in 1598 and published in a quarto in 1601, the major change being the shift of setting from Florence to London. The date of the revision is disputed,[1] but whatever the date Jonson carefully inserted topical allusions not to the year of revision but to 1598,[2] as if to admit, in a further redefinition of the beginning of his career, that the original version *should* have had a London setting all along. I agree: It should have. Literary history, particularly the one I am constructing here, would be neater and altogether more satisfying if it had. Editors of the play, who like to compare the two versions, all find the revision to be an improvement, introducing a new coherence, energy, and allusiveness: "With the action transferred to London, the play becomes crowded wih off-stage life and activity. . . . The English setting, moreover, suggests a more vivid, concrete use of language and figures of speech."[3]

[1] Herford and Simpson say about 1612; J. W. Lever agrees with E. K. Chambers on about 1605, in preparation for a Court performance on February 2, 1605. This fits in with the use of an English setting in *Eastward Ho* (1605), on which Jonson collaborated with Chapman and Marston [E. K. Chambers, *The Elizabethan Stage* (Oxford: Clarendon Press, 1923); J. W. Lever, ed., *Every Man in his Humour,* Regents parallel text edition (Lincoln: Univ. of Nebraska Press, 1971)]. Gabriele Bernhard Jackson in her edition discusses the issue at length and concludes 1607–08 or 1612–13 are probable (New Haven: Yale Univ. Press, 1969), pp. 221–39.

[2] Jackson, p. 225.

[3] Lever, xxi. A. Richard Dutton quotes Swinburne and Herford and Simpson on the Folio's greater realism, but accuses them of naiveté, discounting the historical setting ("the setting is essentially passive and incidental to the story") in order to take up the position this study seeks to revise: "The realism that matters to Jonson is neither verisimilar nor, ultimately, psychological – though these are pieces of the pattern, means to an end – but moral." "The Significance of Jonson's Revision of *Every Man in His Humour,*" *Modern Language Review* 69, no. 2 (April 1974), 241–9.

Even in the Italian version, the sense of place is very strong, though not of a particular place. The references to Italy are pretty general and coexist with allusions to Jonson's favorite London taverns (the Mitre, the Mermaid) in the old manner which we might call anatopic as well as anachronistic. This is something Jonson would not do by the time he returned to an Italian setting in *Volpone* (1606), where he maintains decorum by introducing English material only through traveling English characters. In *Every Man in his Humour* it is the urban landscape as such that emerges very palpably. Anne Barton has excellently described the detailed evocation of

> the life of a great, mercantile Renaissance city as it moves through a typical day: from the early morning distribution of fresh water from the conduits, sordid awakenings in small lodging houses, breakfast and social calls, the routine work of warehouses and offices, desultory talk in taverns and ordinaries, to supper and bed. The city is the true centre of the comedy and, to a large extent, its main character. As hour succeeds hour, a series of petty quarrels, misunderstandings, sexual jealousies and minor infringements of the law ("the malady of the quotidian", in Wallace Stevens' phrase) grow in certain areas to the point where they require some rough and ready resolution by a justice of the peace. They subside, at least temporarily, in sleep.[4]

It is hard to resist comparison with the Dublin of *Ulysses* as the paths of Jonson's wandering characters crisscross, building up a mass of cross-references and weaving a texture of relationships that implies the whole city.

The scene is precisely that of city comedy, most of whose elements Haughton had brought together, but Jonson develops them fully: the roving gallants, with their entourage of gulls and hustlers, the citizen household with its jealous head and women ripe for seduction by aristocratic manners, the genre scenes of London lowlife, and the social occasions that throw all these characters together.

Above all, Jonson achieved, even in the early version, unprecedented concentration on the theme of social competition. At first glance this most classical of Elizabethan comedies may appear simply to be holding up a mirror to the life of the middling sort, as new comic principles would have it (in contrast to Jonson's later comical satires, where the focus is more exclusively on the world of fashion), but already Jonson has his play straddle the major status division in Elizabethan society, between those who were gentlemen and those who were not. Most city comedies will be similarly poised, and the division is a tense and conflicted one, not the traditional sorting out of the dramatis personae into an aristocratic main plot and a lower class subplot.

The dramatis personae are still grouped by family relationships, but the important defining characteristics, and the real business of the play, are matters of social status and public space. As David Konstan has shown, new comic plots are typically structured around the violation of status barriers by erotic

---

[4] Anne Barton, *Ben Jonson, Dramatist* (Cambridge: Cambridge Univ. Press, 1984), p. 46.

impulses; the status barriers in ancient Athens and Rome were absolute, so the conventional conclusion with a marriage required a conventional quick reversal, usually through the convenient revelation that the girl was after all of the correct status.[5] In English society the status barriers were much more permeable, and in *Every Man In* everything is more diffuse: The urbane young gentleman Wellbred/Prospero[6] has two demisiblings, a half brother who is a downright country gentleman, culturally and emotionally at odds with him, and a brother-in-law who is a citizen. This family spread across three distinct cultural formations generates a lot of talk and argument about what manners should be. The marriage plot arises from the citizen's sister recognizing and being captivated by the true manners of Wellbred's friend, and thus marrying into the gentry. Readers will be forgiven if they forget there is a marriage plot – these relationships are not given much real importance, being only a framework on which the subject of social roles and social climbing can be hung. J. W. Lever has made the point acutely:

> Plautus and Terence had focused almost exclusively on personal or domestic relationships: Jonson left the conventions of family life unquestioned, to concentrate on the absurdities of social climbing. Snobbery is the universal folly derided in *Every Man In,* whose real key word is not "humour" but "gentleman." Through all the class graduations of its characters, from squire's nephew to shopkeeper's son, from seedy gallant to small clerk and semiliterate water-bearer, the aspirations to gentry typify the fool. The fashionable cults of the day – hunting, duelling, tobacco-smoking, vociferous oaths – are ridiculed chiefly because they are practised as short cuts to the status of a gentleman. . . . Social ambition is the real impulse behind the cultivation of pseudo-humours. . . .
>
> Braggarts and gulls were the stock-in-trade of Elizabethan authors; Jonson's individual contribution was to trace in minute detail their unending quest for social status.

The English tradition of comedy of class affectation, Lever goes on to say, really begins with this play.[7]

The theme is started immediately: In the opening speech Lorenzo/Knowell Senior ruminates on his son's education and predilection for poetry but is quickly interrupted by the appearance of his nephew Stephano/Stephen, a status seeker in search of another sort of education, in the social arts. The two sorts of education will be contrasted throughout the opening scenes and indeed through the whole play. Stephano asks after

> a booke of the sciences of hawking and hunting. . . . and a man haue not skill in hawking and hunting now a daies, ile not giue a rush for him; hee is for no

[5] David Konstan, *Roman Comedy* (Ithaca: Cornell Univ. Press, 1983).
[6] I will quote as it pleases me from the 1598/1601 Italian Quarto and the 1616 English Folio versions, but will use the English names for convenience after the first reference.
[7] Lever, pp. xvi, xxiv.

gentlemans company, and (by Gods will) I scorne it I, so I doe, to bee a consort for euerie *hum-drum;* hang them *scroiles,* ther's nothing in them in the world, what doe you talke on it? a gentleman must shew himselfe like a gentleman.

(Q I.1.30–43)

In the Folio local references, simultaneously geographical and social, provide concrete indices against which the climbing can be measured: "Because I dwell at *Hogsden,* I shall keepe companie with none but the archers of *Finsburie?* or the citizens, that come a ducking to *Islington* ponds?" (F I.1.47–50).

Knowell Senior responds with a stern lecture, in the accents of humanist ethics, against prodigality and social climbing:

> Learne to be wise, and practise how to thriue. . . .
> I would not haue you to inuade each place,
> Nor thrust your selfe on all societies,
> Till mens affections, or your owne desert,
> Should worthily inuite you to your ranke.
> He, that is so respectlesse in his courses,
> Oft sells his reputation, at cheape market.
> Nor would I, you should melt away your selfe
> In flashing brauerie, least while you affect
> To make a blaze of gentrie to the world,
> A little puff of scorne extinguish it.

(F I.1.66, 70–9)

He concludes with a favorite humanist topic, that true gentility cannot be inherited.

Like Henry IV's speech to Prince Hal in *Henry IV Part I,* this is a lecture on managing one's social reputation, with the issues transposed down from the political to the social register. The plain good sense of this speech, amounting to the class wisdom of the gentry, rests not only on firm ethical principles but on an acute sense for what things are worth in the marketplace. The commercial imagery may suggest something unflattering about Knowell's character, but surely this is secondary to the frank grounding of individual reputation in a solid social economics. The commercial imagery indicates not a contamination of the aristocracy by bourgeois values but a common sense shared by the two branches of the ruling class, both too secure to make a fetish of exclusivity, as the climbing Stephen does. Social status maintains its value only if it is managed carefully, beyond the "flashing brauerie" of social ostentation and the answering "puff of scorne."

The point is promptly enacted and extended as a servant appears and Stephen shows himself incapable of dealing with him: Stephen is too familiar, bothers to impress where he shouldn't, then suspects the servant is flouting him and threatens to beat him. Knowell is appalled at the disorder thrust needlessly into class relations, while "the honest man demeanes himselfe / Modestly to'ards you" (F I.2.32–3). The dramatic emphasis is all on Stephen's folly, but this strategically placed episode establishes the class framework of the theme of social climbing: Knowell's solid ethics depend on and support a solid class hierarchy.

At the other pole of social status the citizen Thorello/Kitely is, like Knowell, equally sure of and unostentatious about his own status (though he also feels acutely that it puts him at a disadvantage in dealing with his dissolute but gentle brother-in-law Wellbred), and therefore can speak an ethical language much like Knowell's. The disruptive play of social status takes place between these two stable poles and threatens them: Knowell comes into the city, where he loses his bearings; Kitely complains that Wellbred "makes my house here common, as a *Mart,* / A *Theater,* a publike receptacle / For giddie humour, and diseased riot; / . . . a tauerne, or a stewes" (F II.1.61–4). If Knowell and even Kitely are normative figures, they are also (a common enough paradox) block-ing figures in Northrop Frye's comic paradigm,[8] in ways not related to their classic miserly psychological symptoms. They try to block not so much a romance as Edward Knowell and Wellbred's immersion in the milieu of social climbers, a social dissolution that substitutes for the confusing erotic energy of the standard comic plot. This again suggests that the dissolute social realm is where the real interest of the play lies.

This element of the plot is also introduced in Act I as Knowell Senior intercepts a letter the abused servant is carrying to his son from Wellbred. Knowell's sense of status has none of the exaggeration of Stephen's, but it is actually nicer: He is curious about Wellbred ("A yong gentleman? is he not?" F I.2.54–55), hoping he is a companion of the proper sort of distinction for the young gentleman his son. He expects the letter, addressed "*To his most selected friend, master EDWARD KNO'WELL,*" to be "greatly varied from the vulgar forme" (Q I.1.139). But the letter is a nasty surprise, the very salutation of the Quarto version, "Sirha *Lorenzo,*" being a calculated affront to class decorum.

This letter is one of the most heavily revised – effectively rewritten – parts of the play. The Quarto version continues in the praise/abuse style of the exchanges between Falstaff and Hal – "Sirha, sweete villayne, come and see me" (Q I.1.151–2). Its theme is the conflict between devotion to the Muses and Apollo and the recreations of social life. This is the sort of topic on which Milton would be assigned to write academic prolusions, jazzed up with witty, low-style handling of the literary apparatus. Most of this is thrown out in the revision, which is shorter and more sophisticated, hitting the note of urbanity for which Jonson was fumbling in 1598. Instead of a moral argument and scattered insults we get a finely tuned social invitation of studied, even outra-geous, informality.[9]

---

[8] Northrop Frye, *The Anatomy of Criticism* (Princeton: Princeton Univ. Press, 1957), "The Mythos of Spring: Comedy," pp. 163–86.

[9] Knowell's reaction is also modulated a bit: In 1598 his horror leads him to call the letter "a blacke and criminall *inscription*" (Q I.1.188); in the Folio his judgment is more focused on Wellbred's "manners" (F I.2.97). A very similar transformation is visited on Lorenzo Senior's long discourse on will and governing reason (Q II.2.1–35), which

Why, NED, *I beseech thee; hast thou for-sworne all thy friends i' the old* Iewrie? *or dost thou think vs all* Iewes *that inhabit there, yet? If thou dost, come ouer, and but see our fripperie: change an olde shirt, for a whole smocke, with vs. Doe not conceiue that antipathy betweene vs, and* Hogs–den ; *as was betweene* Iewes , *and hogs-flesh. Leaue thy vigilant father, alone, to number ouer his greene apricots, euening, and morning, o' the north-west wall. . . . But, pr'y thee, come ouer to me, quickly, this morning: I haue such a present for thee (our* Turkie *companie neuer sent the like to the* Grand-SIGNIOR.) *One is a Rimer sir, o' your owne batch, your own leuin; but doth think himselfe* Poet-maior, *o' the towne: willing to be showne, and worthy to be seene. The other – I will not venter his description with you, till you come, because I would ha' you make hether with an appetite. If the worst of 'hem be not worth your iorney, draw your bill of charges, as vnconscionable, as any Guild-hall verdict will giue it you, and you shall be allow'd your* viaticum.

From the wind-mill.   (F I.2.70–91)

Peter Womack has written brilliantly on the revised version of the letter, unpacking its dense and miscellaneous allusions to London and its stylistic pastiche, from fairground barker through the commercial and legal. It is, using Bakhtin's terminology, multivocal.[10] Knowell, reading Wellbred's letter, enacts the conflict Bakhtin finds in Renaissance culture between the centralization of the verbal–ideological world attendant on the formation of nation states, and the heterogeneous speeches of the city street.

> The "heteroglossia of the clown" is a neat summary of what Wellbred's letter, albeit in somewhat gentrified form, introduces into the play. What the scene enables us to add to Bakhtin's account is the significance, as a term in his dialectic, of the city. The size and heterogeneity of Jonson's London . . . makes the centreless interchange of diverse language types a matter of individual verbal experience. . . . speech types jostle, relativize and, as both Bakhtin and Jonson emphasize, make fun of one another. *Every Man In* as a whole is, among other things, a stylization of such a babel.[11]

The generational conflict, with its linguistic dimension of classically based unitary and "true" speech in opposition to the casual juxtapositions of the urban *flaneur*, cannot be resolved clearly. Knowell will be mildly humiliated in the course of the play, but his wisdom is still wisdom.

> The paternal-ethical discourse can characterize the follies of the heteroglot city, trenchantly and eloquently, but from a distance: the very universality of its moral categories disables its intervention in the urban speech world itself.

becomes Knowell Senior's tirade on the corruption of manners through bad example (F II.5.1–65). Again concrete social examples replace abstract argument as Jonson finds the social ground of his theme. G. B. Jackson has shown that the revised version is a tissue of adaptations from Juvenal, Quintillian, and Horace, but this only demonstrates once more that imitation of classical literature could bring an author closer to Elizabethan reality.

[10] Womack, *Ben Jonson*, pp. 76–9.
[11] Ibid., p. 80.

> If, on the other hand, that eloquence were to be overwhelmed by the verbal play of the wits and gamesters, then the rhetorical centre of values would be dispersed, and the comedy would become morally incomprehensible.[12]

Womack is right to point to an unresolved tension, but it is also important to see that Jonson has attempted a compromise through the figures of Wellbred and Edward Knowell, who stands symbolically between his father and his cousin Stephen – he shuttles between the security of landed wealth and the social dissolution of the city. This is not a novel critical point, but it is rarely historicized.[13] P. K. Ayers has noted the emergence in Jonson (especially in *Epicoene*) of

> the "man-about-town" as a recognizable figure in the brave new world of fashionable London. The gallant is by birth and education a member of the gentry, but in certain respects a displaced one; he is a member of the traditional ruling class who has for practical purposes abandoned both his traditional power base and his traditional residence, his place in the country, together with its demands and responsibilities, in favor of the more exciting world of town life.

Wellbred and Edward Knowell are "the first true gallants on the English stage."

> They live in a self-contained and relatively coherent culture of their own; their manners and morals are in a sense self-created, and owe little to traditional social patterns or sources of value. They are defined by their polished good-breeding and easy good manners, and represent qualities quite different from those displayed by the usual swaggerers, wits, intriguers, and ruined prodigals who inhabit the London of Jacobean city comedy generally. Unlike their cousins, they live in the city not because they need to restore their fortunes or seek a place at court, but because it is the only place a man of fashion can live. Urbanity is their distinctive excellence.[14]

This is an extremely important development. The gallant, who had for centuries been a principal target of the morality plays as a figure for foppery, novelty, and urban degeneracy, is rehabilitated (or split, becoming Edward *and*

---

[12] Ibid., p. 81.

[13] See, for example, how Judd Arnold makes the point. I share his sense of the importance of the gallant in Jonson's drama, but disagree with his premises. He thinks Jonson's gallants "understand that they inhabit a fallen world, but not a world falling apart. Jonson may have thought the real world was. But his comic worlds are stable. His 'humours' comedy deals intentionally with fixed patterns of behavior. Within these unregenerate worlds of Bergsonian mechanical man, the gallants – a sort of aristocracy of wit – achieve a kind of happy security. They stand not only conservatively, but successfully, against all who would undermine established orders." *A Grace Peculiar: Ben Jonson's Cavalier Heroes* (University Park: Penn State Univ. Press, 1972), p. 16.

[14] P. K. Ayers, "Dreams of the City: The Urban and the Urbane in Jonson's *Epicoene*," *Philological Quarterly* 66 (Winter 1987), 74–5.

Stephen) as the model for a new balance, a new class style that can cope with and dominate the city. The need of the gentry to produce such a figure is obvious; an increasingly important sector of the theater audience could identify with such a figure directly and powerfully.

A new ethical posture could be founded on this figure, though that would take time, and some moral ambivalence tends to cling to him, along with residual ethical schemes associated with the generic origins of the play. In the last lines of F III.7, for example, Justice Clement, speaking out of the classical ethical tradition, counsels the elder Knowell to let his son run his course; in the opening lines of the next scene Downe-right's language puts his brother's friends in the context of the moralities: They "hant him, vp and downe, like a sort of vnluckie sprites, and tempt him to all manner of villanie. . . . a little thing would make me play the deuill with some of 'hem. . . . I'ld make the house too hot for the best of 'hem: they should say, and sweare, hell were broken loose" (F IV.1.7–13).

Both schemes are formative on a fundamental level, but neither really accounts for the characters of Wellbred and Edward, let alone for the world they inhabit. Wellbred in particular is prone to flying off the handle, and something causes him to abandon his studies and make improper suggestions to his sister, but whatever it is it is not the traditional form of sexual or financial excess associated with the prodigal in both classical and Christian traditions. The study of gulls is a different sort of hobby. As with Prince Hal's bad companions, it is not really true that they are corrupting him. The urbane gallant's first characteristic is mastery.

Jonson's attitude toward the gallant and the world he represents is nothing if not critical, but moral critics have often been too distracted by individual faults to see a generic social hero, or rather a triumphant cultural norm. Even Ayers is uneasy with the gallants' way of coming "to terms with the city by diverting the moral dimension of life into a variety of the aesthetic,"[15] and lapses into a typical discussion of their moral ambiguity. Faults may be emphasized not only to individualize, as here, but to make distinctions (for example, between gallant and fop) all the more important *within* the community of gallants.

I will return to the topic of the normative cultural function of the gallant later. Here I want to note that the coincidence of the newly invented gallant and the newly invented genre of "humor" plays is not accidental – playing on humors is the gallant's most characteristic action. The gallant may well be humorous himself, both in the sense (which Asper approves in *Every Man out of his Humour,* Prologue "After the Second Sounding," 102–09) of suffering from a psychological imbalance, and in the sense (which Asper rejects, but which is certainly also operative in Jonson and more relevant here) in which a humor is a social affectation, an assertion of individual style that usually takes

[15] Ayers, p. 79.

the form of an exaggerated display of a current fad like smoking tobacco, extravagant oaths, melancholy, and so on.

> But that a rooke, in wearing a pyed feather,
> The cable hat-band, or the three-pild ruffe,
> A yard of shooetye, or the *Switzers knot*
> On his *French* garters, should affect a Humour!
> (110–13)

Such affectations arise in a situation where individual style is highly prized, is in fact becoming necessary and a principal source of social value, but where the field is crowded and increasingly extreme measures have to be taken to define oneself in a saturated system of distinctions.

The other response to such a situation – that of the gallants like Wellbred and Edward Knowell who are in some way normative figures, if only because their response is so close to the play's own method and sensibility – is to develop a connoisseur's sense for the new varieties of urban style and play with them, which often means playing *on* them sadistically. Where Knowell Senior sees in Stephen a kinsman in need of reclamation, his son sees a monster to be shown, or an animal to be bet on in competition with Wellbred's town gulls: "we may hap haue a match with the citie, and play him for fortie pound" (F I.3.134–5). Whether or not this normative, nuanced, and ironic consciousness was represented by figures in a play, as it is in *Every Man In,* it was represented in the audience, and was increasingly the dominant sensibility, especially in the private theaters. In the humor plays it becomes the structuring force.

Peter Womack has written an analysis of the principles of Jonson's characterizations, including a rapid sketch of the history of the term "character," worthy of Raymond Williams, in which he reminds us that in Jonson's day it meant a description of a person, something apart from him, a sign, and only gradually came to be interchangeable with "person."[16] Humors are an exaggerated form of this structure. "Characters" get regularly bandied about in humors comedy before the person appears, but

> humor is not really a method of characterization [in our sense of the word]. For instead of approaching the union of sign and person . . . constitutive of realist character, the humours model drives them apart, usually presenting them as two separate figures on the stage, and even deriving the dramatic action from the conflict between the two. In other words, stage humours depend for their effect on a deeper structural principle, which is the writing down of a person by another – the *Jacobean* type of character.[17]

This is a power relation, and Womack links it both with a managerial discourse ["It's not a coincidence that charactery flourished during a period when the centralization of state power and the demilitarization of the aristocracy were

---

[16] Womack, pp. 34–5, but the whole of chap. 2, "Characters," is relevant.
[17] Womack, p. 53.

obliging the ruling class to acquire (in the first instance through a training in rhetoric) bureaucratic skills"] and with the apparent authorial sadism of the comical satires, which makes monsters of men by invading rather than constituting their interiority.[18]

Womack is right to link the mode of perception of humors comedy with the ruling class. When the water carrier Cob asks the merchant's apprentice Cash what a "humor" is, Cash tells him "It is a gentleman-like monster, bred, in the speciall gallantrie of our time, by affection; and fed by folly" (F III.4.20–22); and when the humble Cob objects to the humor of taking tobacco, which Bobadill affects, Bobadill beats him, and Justice Clement agrees that one of Cob's position shouldn't meddle with such fashions (F III.7.49–70). It was a gentlemanly audience that sponsored the craze for humors. In the Blackfriars play *The Case is Altered* (published 1609) Jonson has Antonio Balladino, a figure for the popular playwright Antony Munday, say

> mary you shall haue some now (as for example, in plaies) that will haue euery day new trickes, and write you nothing but humours: indeede this pleases the Gentlemen: but the common sort they care not for't, they know not what to make on't, they looke for good matter, they, and are not edified with such toyes.
>
> (I.2.60–5)

In the Induction to *The Magnetic Lady* (1632), as Jonson closes the circle of the humors comedies which began with *Every Man In*, he points to their topicality: They are based on "recent humours still, or manners of men, that went along with the times" (103–04), caught up in the flow of fashion. The Induction begins with the Boy hawking "characters" to the gentlemanly audience in the theater, which is described in a continued metaphor as a "Poetique Shop": "What doe you lack, Gentlemen? what is't you lack? any fine Phansies, Figures, Humors, Characters, Idaeas, Definitions of Lords, and Ladies? Waiting-women, Parasites, Knights, Captaines, Courtiers, Lawyers? what doe you lack?" (1–5). Formulations of social types were a principal commodity the theater had to offer, mass producing professionally a form of social apprehension gentlemen produced amateurishly, as a sign of their urbanity, in their conversation and in coterie forms such as verse satire.

COMICAL SATIRE

There are many continuities between *Every Man in his Humour* and *Every Man out of his Humour* (1599–1600). Both plays open with a country gull

---

[18] Womack, pp. 53–4, 55–9. The argument about bureaucracy is more suggestive than conclusive. He also probably goes too far in making of "humor" a principle so individual and antisocial that it cannot signify anything, including itself, and is therefore antithetical to, and dependent for articulation on, an opposing intelligence. Some such antithesis is working in Jonson, but I would emphasize the relation of "humor" to fashion, that is, social trends.

eager to appear as a gentleman and seeking instruction, but it is symptomatic that Stephen is cut off by his uncle the moralist, while *Every Man Out* stays with the long lecture Carlo Buffone gives Sogliardo on how to be fashionable; whereas Stephen is casually relegated by Doctor Clement's judgment at the catastrophe to eat with Cob and Tib in the buttery while the real gentry feasts above, Sogliardo does manage to buy his coat of arms, and Saviolina's (failed) judgment of his pretensions to gentility is perhaps the central episode in *Every Man Out,* insofar as it makes sense to talk in such terms about the exploded structure of this play.

The principles of construction in *Every Man Out* are very different, deserving the generic description, "comical satire" – " 'tis strange, and of a particular kind by it selfe, somewhat like *Vetus Comoedia,* " says the critic Cordatus (Prologue, 231–2). Intrigue, which in *Every Man In* was not weighty in its motivation but was handled with skill and elan, no longer pretends to serve as the organizing principle. *Every Man Out* relies on other principles of organization, deriving more directly from a satiric vision of society as *spectacle.* This was a spectacular culture, accustomed to displaying itself to itself in visually readable ways.[19] In Jonson the spectacle is delegitimized and problematic, a spectacle of ostentation and folly, a display of surfaces to be examined as surfaces, of objects constituted as objects by a satiric observer. In *Every Man In* this spectacular aspect is more or less confined to the running of the gulls, but in *Every Man Out* all the characters are defined by their relation to it: Macilente is the satiric spectator, Carlo Buffone the professional critic and jester, Sogliardo an actor manqué, Fastidius Briske the (false) image of success, Puntarvolo a real knight who makes a spectacle of himself purely out of humor.

This is not the sort of theatrical spectacle that employs a lot of props or battle scenes – it is a social spectacle, "deedes, and language, such as men doe vse" (EMI Prologue, 21), being translated into the theater with modest means, though not without a newly elaborated stagecraft, whose features and execution are pointed up by the extraordinary device of the commentators Cordatus and Mitis, positioned on the stage.

[19] See Michel Foucault, *Discipline and Punish,* trans. Alan Sheridan (New York: Vintage, 1979), and Steven Mullaney, *The Place of the Stage: License, Play, and Power in Renaissance England* (Chicago: Univ. of Chicago Press, 1988). In a sense closer to the issue of the theatrical display of identity, G. K. Hunter points to how easy it is to read the social hierarchy of the court of Denmark at the opening of *Hamlet.* This legibility is immediately disrupted by Hamlet's anomalous position and appearance, but the disruption is internal, a subversion from within a closed ordering of social appearances. "Flatcaps and Bluecoats: Visual Signals on the Elizabethan Stage," *Essays and Studies 1980* (n.s.33), on *Hamlet,* pp. 26–7, 33–5, but the theme runs throughout the article, which contains a splendid analysis of the social meaning of clothing in *Eastward Ho,* pp. 29–31. Jonson deals in another kind of problematizing of social appearances.

One feature is the realistic representation of London institutions: As Haughton had done the Exchange, Jonson does Paul's as his bravura piece, though the play also has scenes at Court, the Mitre tavern, and the Counter prison. Most of Act III takes place in the middle aisle of Paul's, London's central meeting place for all kinds of social and business transactions.[20] Cordatus is there to set the scene, which he does carefully, exploiting the audience's knowledge: "we must desire you to presuppose the stage, the middle isle in *Paules;* and that, the west end of it" (II.6.183–4). Jonson fills the stage with his dramatis personae, and the careful stage directions move shifting groups about in the pattern in which one would walk in Paul's. Never is it clearer that getting large numbers of actors on stage is the way to visually imitate the city in a theater without scene painting. The citizen-fops Clove and Orange appear and Mitis asks

> What be these two, signior?
> *Cor.* Mary, a couple sir, that are meere strangers to the whole scope of our play; only come to walke a turne or two, i' this *Scene* of *Paules,* by chance.
>
> (III.1.16–9)

This is arch: Clove and Orange fit in in several ways – they enlarge the social scope and the satirical themes, and carry a jab at John Marston – but Cordatus points exactly to the pseudoextraneousness of realism, the sense that they are simply "there" and so can shoulder their way into the work of art.

The sense of a London setting is not, however, all that strong or concrete, so much so that *Every Man Out* is often overlooked as a London play, the first of Jonson's plays to have a London setting. Indeed it is set part way on the road to Gargaphie, the Lylyan court of *Cynthia's Revels* which shadows that of Elizabeth but is not to be taken for it literally. We are told *Every Man Out* is set in *"Insula Fortunata,"* a not very dark conceit explained by Macilente when he says it is fortunate because Queen Elizabeth is on the throne (in the canceled ending performed before the Queen, 21). The Italian names and "signior"s are distracting, but the real problem is that urban space is not palpably felt the way it is in *Every Man In;* the object of vivid representation is not the life of the whole city but a certain way that people look at each other and interact. This is the medium of the play, its action, its style, its accent, its structure.

To create this focus Jonson resurrects all the techniques of the morality play for posing and analyzing characters (in particular gallants) discussed in the last chapter: the weakened plotting, the extensive social groupings, the posturings of the fool, the surrounding advisors and commentators, and so on. The morality techniques are stiffened now by the overlapping influences of "humors," the Theophrastan character (which was also enjoying a vogue,

---

[20] Paul's became a favorite object of description by contemporaries. See Dekker, *The Gull's Horn-Book,* and so forth.

Theophrastus having been newly translated),[21] and the formal verse satire of the 1590s by Hall, Marston, and Donne. These influences are most directly evident in the prose "characters" of the dramatis personae Jonson printed with the play.

As for acting style, it is in the nature of the case hard to say anything with assurance. Andrew Gurr tells us a new term for acting appeared at exactly this moment, 1599–1600, to replace "acting," which originally referred to the gestures accompanying the declamation of an orator, and "playing," which was what the common players did. The new term was "personation," and it denoted a new, naturalistic style of acting Gurr believes was now the standard style, although it must have coexisted with other more stylized forms.[22] This might well be the style in which Wellbred or Knowell would be played, a subtle presentation allowing for the suggestion of psychological depth and polished, uncaricatured manners. The mode in which humors were presented, however, the conception of character Womack traces, has different purposes and works against the fusion of the presenter and the mime, to use Bradbrook's terms. The technique of the morality play, with its tradition of exact but demonstrative mimicry, would serve better.

One would expect that technique to have been extended as the styles of social behavior became central subjects of representation. The Chamberlain's Men would themselves be familiar with the middle aisle of Paul's, as would the audience; to deliver this new dramatic object in a way that both produced a shock of recognition by its realism and interpreted the gestures performed there, doubtless through exaggeration, would test the skill and initiative of the company. From later and better documented periods we can get a sense of what effects were possible: Cibber played Vanbrugh's Lord Foppington over the years, and "as the fashions of the times altered, he adjusted his action and behaviour to them, and introduced every species of growing foppery"; a contemporary wrote of Garrick in his *Miss in her Teens,* "It is said he mimics *eleven men of fashion.*"[23]

Jonson's plays are full of studies of social gestures, the small arts of everyday life, from Bobadill's urging Mathew to twine his body into a more gentleman-like guard in *Every Man In,* through Fastidius Briske's courting of his mistress with tobacco and viol and his advice to Macilente on how to brush up his hair just before he enters the presence at Court, to its most spectacular development in the Master of Courtship competition in *Cynthia's Revels,* in which the stage is turned into a model's runway where the gestures and postures of courtship – the bare Accost, the better Reguard, the solemne Addresse, the perfect Close

[21] Benjamin Boyce, *The Theophrastan Character in England to 1642* (Cambridge: Harvard Univ. Press, 1947).
[22] Andrew Gurr, *The Shakespearean Stage 1574–1642,* 2nd ed. (Cambridge: Cambridge Univ. Press, 1980), pp. 97–8.
[23] Quoted in Susan Staves, "A Few Kind Words for the Fop," *SEL 22* (1982), 417–18.

– are performed, subjected to minute inspection, and graded by a panel of experts.[24] Such studies of gesture are called for so often by the text that one must conclude that the performance was a more or less continuous play on social gestures. Surely Anne Barton is wrong when she complains that the delivery of a "character" by one actor leaves the one whose part is being described with nothing to do on stage.[25] One suspects it left room for virtuoso displays of closely observed behaviors, a whole gestural language shared with the audience but lost to us. Stephen and his like are always preening and interrupting to ask inanely if a stocking does not look well. The actor would presumably be able to keep up the visual patter without verbal prompting.

On another level of dramatic organization, Jonson's hypertrophied examinations of fashionable gestures and social interactions in extended secular space permit one to talk about a new object of dramatic realism: the party. The comical satires, which display Jonson's most original and characteristic idea about how plays might be constructed, are almost entirely staged parties, with large groups of people on stage at almost all times; the smaller scenes often show preparations for the larger ones.[26] Again, the technical innovation is re-marked on by the critics of *Every Man Out:* After most of the cast has wandered on through a long continued scene and been absorbed into an expanding social group, Cordatus asks, in answer to Mitis's objection to the scene construction,

> and is it not an obiect of more state, to behold the *Scene* full, and reliev'd with varietie of speakers to the end, then to see a vast emptie stage, and the actors come in (one by one) as if they were dropt downe with a feather, into the eye of the spectators?
>
> (II.3.297–301)

It took Jonson's very special gifts for and ideas about plot construction to make this focus on parties work at all. When he returns to this strategy in *Epicoene, Bartholomew Fair, The Staple of News,* and *The Magnetic Lady,* the plotting is better integrated, but the formal principle is still much the same. The innovation in stagecraft brings a new object onto the stage: In contrast to verse satire, which dropped individual portraits into the eye of the reader, attention shifts from single humors to social interactions; in contrast to the stage tradition,

---

[24] These scenes from Act V are not in the original 1601 Quarto. Herford and Simpson follow Fleay's suggestion that the Quarto gives the text of a performance at Court on January 6, 1601, for which Jonson suppressed some of the satire on the Court. Presumably the suppressed material would have been included in other perfor-mances, and was restored in the 1616 Folio.

[25] Barton, pp. 69–70.

[26] Compare G. K. Hunter: "The economy of the Elizabethan theatre does not seem to allow the stage to be crowded for more than brief and special occasions. The average stage scene (measured across the fifty or so plays I have analysed) has three or four speakers present at one time, though the impression of a crowded public life is often sedulously promoted." "Flatcaps and Bluecoats," p. 23n.

these plays are designed not so much to follow plots as to examine the dynamics of a social field.[27] The party is no longer incidental to the plot, as parties
generally are in Shakespeare, whether they are the festive occasions that
provide the background for the meeting of Romeo and Juliet or of Benedict and
Beatrice, or the roistering scenes of *Henry IV* or *Twelfth Night* which grow out
of the prodigal plays, or the closing celebration inherited from ancient comedy.
The party is now the center of attention.

 This formal displacement of the party from its place in the ritual structure of
festive comedy is most significant. In Jonson's unfestive comical satire the
party no longer represents the solution to social problems, but illustrates the
problem, is a symptom rather than a cure. We are almost always being offered
a study in social pathology; most of the bondings we observe are false, or
degrading, or both. This satirical emptying out or displacement of the festive
content of parties is a necessary precondition for the comedy of manners,
which starts here.

 The formal fact of Jonson's organization of his plays around satirically
observed parties, and the literary historical fact of the emergence of parties on
the stage at this moment, are clearly related to socioeconomic developments.
Such fashionable parties had a new character, were, within limits, a new
phenomenon. These are *private* parties, and so are structurally opposed to
festivity which, Bakhtin tells us, always tends to include everyone;[28] the basic
demarcation of these private parties is not of a festive time, but of a social space,
their play impossible without that constitutive limit. This privacy has to do
with the retreat from the hall to private rooms and the annual migration from
country seats to the new fashionable neighborhoods around the Strand, the
decay of "good lordship" so frequently noticed by contemporaries and
described by Stone and others.[29] The social life of the upper classes was no

---

[27] Compare Neil Rhodes: Jonson tries in *Every Man In*, and succeeds in *Bartholomew Fair*, in breaking up "the integrity of the plot in order to reveal the diffuseness and variety of actual social relationships. And it is in this sense that the plays attempt a form of realism with which Shakespeare was never concerned. (That is to say, they seek to embody in their dramatic structures the realities of human intercourse in a certain kind of society). . . . The serial quality of nondramatic satire . . . is reproduced in *Every Man Out* by the play's insistence on the fragmentary nature of urban social relations; the hiatuses between character descriptions in, say *Pierce Pennilesse* are turned by Jonson into the spaces between people which the city creates, and the impossibilities of relation in pamphlet satire become failures of social communication in 'comicall satyres.' " *Elizabethan Grotesque* (London: Routledge and Kegan Paul, 1980), pp. 132, 135.

[28] Mikhail Bakhtin, *Rabelais and his World*, trans. Helene Iswolsky (Cambridge, Mass.: M.I.T. Press, 1968).

[29] Lawrence Stone, *The Crisis of the Aristocracy*, abridged ed. (Oxford: Oxford Univ. Press, 1967), pp. 87–8. For a handy conservative summary of Stone-inspired social history as it applies to the drama see Ann Jennalie Cook, *The Privileged Playgoers of*

longer played out before a large unsophisticated audience of social inferiors, with a consequent largeness of gesture constantly demonstrating social status; the modes of social interaction become more nuanced and subtle, the participants more nearly equal in status.[30]

Unlike ceremonial occasions, where various ranks could sit together but hierarchically, at different ends of the table, so they never had to make conversation with each other at all, or at least not beyond the conventions of social relations between unequals, in these parties all are potentially social partners and must talk together as provisional equals, no matter what the difference in rank might be. The guests do not come to an entertainment to mark by their presence an occasion or the patronage of their host, but to *entertain one another*.

Conversation thus moves into center stage in these parties, replacing gluttony, ceremonial displays of one kind and another, the ostentatious serving of courses, paid jesters and musicians, and so on.[31] Not that these features disappeared, from the Court or from such celebrations of corporatism as the Lord Mayor's feasts or Simon Eyre's in *The Shoemaker's Holiday*, but a new beau monde with its own sense of style grew up beside these customs. Our ears tell us when we have come upon such scenes; the cadences of their conversation are unlike anything else. *Every Man Out*, the talkiest play ever written, leaves a ringing in the ears that is the sharp and cloying rendition of the observed speech of a certain set, variously inflected but held to a conversational pitch with few streaks of the poetic splendor which breaks out in most of Jonson's other plays.

The new importance of conversation requires that everyone present be able to participate, have a highly developed and refined talent for it. This is the real price of admission, though the scene is always littered with people comically

Shakespeare's London 1576–1642 (Princeton: Princeton Univ. Press, 1981); and as applied to Jonson, Ayers, p. 74. See also Frank Whigham, *Ambition and Privilege: The Social Tropes of Elizabethan Courtesy Theory* (Berkeley: Univ. of California Press, 1984), p. 65.

[30] The search for privacy and more intimate social interactions had been going on for a long time – see Georges Duby, ed., *A History of Private Life: II Revelations of the Medieval World*, trans. Arthur Goldhammer (Cambridge, Mass.: Harvard Univ. Press, 1988) – but Jonson's does seem to have been a watershed period. Patricia Fumerton is doing interesting work on Jonson from this angle, for example, "Tearing Down the Masque," presented at the Modern Language Association convention, 1987.

[31] "The best banquets were those, wher they mistered no Musitians to chase tym." *Conversations with Drummond of Hawthornden*, Herford and Simpson, 1, p. 145, lines 460–1. But paid musicians still followed the smell of the venison going through the streets (*Epicoene* III.3.85–90). They and the ostentatious serving of courses are part of the torture inflicted on Morose. Quentin Bell notices a parallel development in dress and ornamentation, *On Human Finery*, 2d ed. (New York: Schocken, 1976), pp. 30–1.

unable to meet the standard. They are the *alazons*[32] to be discredited, whose failure defines the boundaries of this society, which is structurally apt to continuous invasion by impostors because the criteria for inclusion are so subtle.

These fashionable parties are always marked by social tension. There is a certain self-conscious sense of mission about setting and maintaining the standard of fashion, a project inherently exclusive and (in Veblen's sense) invidious. Moreover the social composition of these parties is almost invariably mixed; whatever the range in individual plays, it almost always spans the status distinctions between aristocracy and citizens. In an age of rapid social mobility this mixture is inherently unstable. In *Every Man In* the party is at the citizen Kitely's house, but is attended by real and would-be gentlemen; Kitely himself has married a gentlewoman, which is why the gallants are there. In *Every Man Out* the party moves around town, from one haunt of gentlemen to another, but the presence in it of Sogliardo (with his disreputable if not entirely unfashionable adjunct Captain Shift) and his nephew Fungoso, who are at different stages of evolution out of yeomanry, and the outsiders Macilente (an impoverished gentleman) and Carlo Buffone (no gentleman at all – "I am not for court") keeps things lively. There is a citizen household here too, at which people collect, but its mistress's social pretensions seem not to take the form of fashionable entertaining. Virtually the whole cast is either rising or falling or maintaining a parasitical existence dependent on dissimulating true social status or financial means (like the seriously indebted courtier Fastidius Briske). Only Puntarvolo has untroubled claim to his status. *Cynthia's Revels* is set at Court, but during a festive open house when it is crashed by noncourtiers including the citizen son Asotus, and features the classless Jonson figure Crites. *Poetaster,* though set in Rome, clearly plays up and down the length of the Strand from the house of the citizen jeweler Albius, with his pretentious wife Chloe who eagerly entertains the small-time gallant Crispinus and a party of courtiers (whose status varies from the Emperor's daughter to Ovid, a younger son who has only "a bare exhibition"), to the Court where most of the same people gather again in fancy dress.[33]

---

[32] The term comes from Frye, *The Anatomy of Criticism,* p. 39.

[33] This analysis could be prolonged with more detail. A near constant is the group of gentlemen and their hangers-on at a party at the house of a citizen whose women are a sexual attraction. Haughton's *Englishmen for my Money* has such a scene, and it is very common in later city comedy. It is a sign of historical change that these parties have no ceremonial character, or ritual function – the sacrilegious feast of the gods in *Poetaster* proving the rule – but there is often a business motivation (in *Every Man Out* Briske is in debt to the citizen household, Puntarvolo is organizing a wager on his travels, and Buffone is a professional parasite; Albius hopes entertaining courtiers will help his jewelry business), and there is always some sexual intrigue or at least interest (Edward Knowell meets his bride at Kitely's; various people are interested in the pretty brainless Chloe, and at both the parties in *Poetaster* Ovid can meet his mistress and his fellow poets theirs).

These parties all have the same rhythm. There is always a moment when the initial excitement fades and spirits flag, to be revived by measures often leading to disorder (like Wellbred's suggestion that his married sister take a servant who will do "tricks" for her; everyone jumps on him, and soon swords are drawn).

Through these parties, then, we get studies of precisely those metropolitan milieus in which the classes mixed with one another, in which social mobility was at its height and the slippages between wealth, status, and power were most evident. Social status was so much an issue because it was no longer so clearly a fact. The standards of behavior in these milieus were complex, ambiguous, and worthy of exploration because their social bases were as well. This fashionable world served as a field of individual ambition and of collective status definition, since fashion provides a mechanism through which social competition can be managed.

FASHION

The fashion process was heating up. Fashion is by no means a universal phenomenon: It arises in societies undergoing adjustments between social classes, as the vehicle for competition and clarification of the social hierarchy.[34] Extraordinary attention was paid to clothing at the turn of the century – more perhaps than at any other period of English history – because clothing at that time both defined traditional social status through minutely graded conventions endowed (in theory anyway) with legal force[35] and a quasi-sacramental character as an expression of identity within a divinely sanctioned hierarchy,[36] and was simultaneously a means of displaying and achieving social mobility. The acceleration of fashion in late Tudor and Stuart society is thus functionally related to its social dynamics, as well as to the rapid increase in the quantities of cloth, furniture, and so on available as the material preconditions.[37] The

[34] On this well established theory of fashion see, inter alia, Georg Simmel, "Fashion," American Journal of Sociology 62 (1904), 541–58; Thorstein Veblen, The Theory of the Leisure Class (1899; New York: B.W. Huebsch, 1919), especially chap 7; Bell, op. cit.; Fernand Braudel, Civilization and Capitalism 15th-18th Century: Vol. I The Structures of Everyday Life, trans. Sian Reynolds (New York: Harper and Row, 1981), pp. 312 ff.

[35] See Frances Elizabeth Baldwin, Sumptuary Legislation and Personal Regulation in England (Baltimore: Johns Hopkins Univ. Press, 1926). For the history of English fashion in this period see F. W. Fairholt, Costume in England: A History of Dress to the End of the Eighteenth Century, rev. H. A. Dillon, 3d ed. (London: George Bell and Sons, 1885), vol. 1, and M. Channing Linthicum, Costume in the Drama of Shakespeare and his Contemporaries (Oxford: Clarendon Press, 1936).

[36] Staves, pp. 426–7.

[37] See Joan Thirsk, Economic Policy and Projects: The Development of a Consumer Society in Early Modern England (Oxford: Clarendon Press, 1978), and F. J. Fisher, "The Development of London as a Center of Conspicuous Consumption in the 16th and 17th Centuries," in E. M. Carus-Wilson, ed., Essays in Economic History, 2 (London, 1954), pp. 197–207.

population of London nearly quadrupled between 1500 and 1600, and nearly doubled again by 1660.[38] The increase was the result of immigration, and the immigrants moved into new social relations. This was as true of the poor being driven off the land by a protocapitalist agriculture as of the aristocracy which was making a habit of coming to London for the legal term, or to attend at Court, or to take advantage of the growing national markets in marriages, land, labor, and money.[39]

The demographic statistics are impressive enough, but the changes they indicate were further amplified and exaggerated in social consciousness because of the disproportionate increase in the numbers of the political class and its concentration in London.[40] There were an increasing number of people able and willing to pursue a fashionable lifestyle, and a specialized economy developed to meet their needs. A class fraction devoted to stylish consumption accelerated the process exponentially. A new world was created that had not existed before: "In the first half of the seventeenth century there emerged a world of fashion in London, persons whose life revolved around clothes, pictures, sculpture, newsletters, books, and plays."[41] The beginning of *The Devil is an Ass* measures how much things had changed in the last half century with a care and precision that go beyond the traditional lament over the degeneracy of the times. One detects a civic pride in the fashionableness of London as opposed both to the provinces and to days gone by. Satan tells the little devil Pug, who wants to try his hand on earth,

> The state of *Hell* must care
> Whom it imployes, in point of reputation,
> Heere about *London*. You would make, I thinke,
> An Agent, to be sent, for *Lancashire*.
>
> (I.1.29–32)

Satan is dismayed at Pug's choice of an old-fashioned Vice for a companion; the times have outrun the old tempters, who are now fit only for social backwaters:

> Art thou the spirit thou sem'st? so poore? to choose
> This, for a *Vice*, t'aduance the cause of *Hell*,
> Now? as Vice stands this present yeere? Remember,
> What number it is. *Six hundred* and *sixteene.*
> Had it but beene *fiue hundred,* though some *sixty*
> Aboue; that's *fifty* yeeres agone, and *six,*

---

[38] Lawrence Stone, "The Residential Development of the West End of London in the Seventeenth Century," in Barbara C. Malament, ed., *After the Reformation: Essays in Honor of J. H. Hexter* (Philadelphia: Univ. of Penn. Press, 1980), p. 168.

[39] On the growth of these markets, the reciprocal relations of London and the rest of England, and their ideological figuration, see Raymond Williams, *The Country and the City* (New York: Oxford Univ. Press, 1973), especially p. 51.

[40] Whigham, pp. 10–11.

[41] Stone, "West End," p. 183.

(When euery great man had his *Vice* stand by him,
In his long coat, shaking his wooden dagger)
I could consent, that, then this your graue choice
Might haue done that, with his Lord *Chief,* the which
Most of his chamber can doe now. But *Pug,*
As the times are, who is it, will reciue you?
What company will you goe to? or whom to mix with?
Where canst thou carry him? except to Tauernes?
To mount vp on a joynt-stoole, with a *Iewes*-trumpe,
To put downe *Cokeley,* and that must be to Citizens?
. . . .
Vnlesse it be a *Vice* of quality,
Or fashion, now, they take none from vs. Car-men
Are got into the yellow starch, and Chimney-sweepers
To their tabacco, and strong-waters.

(I.1.78–93, 111–14)

The speech points to a process with three axes, one temporal, another geographical (out from the metropolitan center, now the unquestioned arbiter of fashion), and the third down the class hierarchy. All of society, down to the menials, is caught up in a process once assumed to be restricted to the ruling class, and it expresses itself as a rippling series of displacements – what once was good for a great man now fits his chamber servants.

All this took place in the context of a great deal of stress and strain on the class system. There was a lot of rapid movement up and down between classes,[42] of which we see so much in city comedy, and there were new professions that were anomalous within the traditional status hierarchy – players and playwrights being the most relevant examples.[43] The code of manners not only allowed for such slippages but also controlled them. Gentlemen were supposed to be reasonably fashionable ["Is any man term'd a gentleman that is not alwayes i' the fashion?" (*Every Man Out,* IV.1.13–14) is wrong in theory, and in rural practice, but the force of the statement would be felt in the city], and by being fashionable one could hope to pass as a gentleman, or, like Sogliardo, secure a recently won status. Therein lay a danger to the whole system: It consisted of a set of outward signs that could be copied by those who had no right to them, thereby emptying them out. Fashion is the true sign of aristocracy as well as of vice and folly; in *The Devil is an Ass,* the fashion-seeking Fitzdottrel is an ass but his wife, who, we are repeatedly told, is a clotheshorse, is altogether admirable.[44]

---

[42] Stone, *Crisis,* passim.

[43] See M. C. Bradbrook, *The Rise of the Common Player: A Study of Actor and Society in Shakespeare's England* (London: Chatto and Windus, 1962), passim.

[44] In *Volpone* II.1.26 ff., Peregrine says Lady Would-Be has come to Venice to study fashion among the courtesans, and Sir Politic replies, "Yes, sir, the spider and the bee oft-times / Suck from one flower." These points are central to Whigham's powerful analysis of courtesy literature.

They haue their *Vices,* there, most like to *Vertues;*
You cannot know 'hem, apart, by any difference:
They weare the same clothes, eate o' the same meat,
Sleepe i' the self-made beds, ride i'those coaches,
Or very like, foure horses in a coach,
As the best men and women. Tissue gownes,
Garters and roses, fourescore pound a paire,
Embroydred stockings, cut-worke smocks, and shirts,
More certaine marks of lechery, now, and pride,
Then ere they were of true nobility!

(DA, I.1.121–30)

Therefore the signs, the marks of fashionableness, had to be constantly changed, so quickly that anyone not truly on the inside would be unable to catch up. So Fungoso, the son of a country miser, who has been sent to the Inns of Court to become a gentleman, is always copying the suits of the courtier Fastidius Briske, only to find that the courtier has a newer suit, which he cannot afford to reproduce (*Every Man Out*). Philautia in *Cynthia's Revels* bemoans the problem from the other point of view:

> And yet we cannot haue a new peculiar court-tire, but these *retain-ers* will haue it; these *Suburbe-sunday-waiters;* these courtiers for *high dayes;* I know not what I should call 'hem.
> *Phantaste.*   O, I, they doe most pittifully imitate.

(II.4.77–81)

The topic of fashion runs the length and breadth of Jonson's work, and it nearly always carries this charge. We almost never hear of anyone acquiring fashionable clothes or hiring a tutor merely to express a social status in which they are comfortably ensconced, though tutoring and attending dancing academies were a normal part of the education of the aristocracy. One of the frontiers we see being negotiated is between rustic country gentry and their fashionable urban cousins, not between social classes. The city was in the business of making the country fashionable. Kastril in *The Alchemist* is a country gentleman come to the city with his sister precisely for this purpose. Stephen and Sogliardo need to be citified but they also have a very insecure grip on the status of gentleman. In Jonson's drama, and city comedy generally, class emulation is clearly understood as the principal mechanism of fashion.

The psychosocial tension that could build up around clothing finds its strongest expression in the story of the missing dress in *The New Inn* (1629).[45] Lady Frampul has promised her chambermaid Prudence a new dress in which to preside as sovereign over the sports they have planned for their country vacation, but the tailor has failed to deliver it on time. The Lady decides to give Pru a dress of her own, which then will be sold to the Players:

[45] Jonson glances at the same story in *Underwoods* 42. "An Elegy," lines 39–42.

> Pru. That were illiberall, madam, and mere sordid
> In me, to let a sute of yours come there.
> Lad. Tut, all are *Players,* and but serue the *Scene.* (II.1.37–9)

The theme of theatricality and profanation comes back in extraordinary form when the tailor shows up at the inn, dressed as a footman, with his wife posing as a lady in the missing dress. They are exposed, and she spills the story: Whenever he makes anything fine that fits

> Then must I put it on, and be his *Countesse,*
> Befor he carry it home vnto the owners.
> A coach is hir'd, and foure horse, he runnes
> In his veluet Iackat thus, to *Rumford, Croyden,*
> *Hounslow,* or *Barnet,* the next bawdy road:
> And takes me out, carries me vp, and throw's me
> Vpon a bed.
> Lad. Peace thou immodest woman:
> She glories in the brauery o' the vice.
> Lat. 'Tis a queint one! (IV.3.68–76)

The tailor's transgressive fetishization of aristocratic fashions is matched by the ferocity of the aristocrats, who turn on him in a pack. They want to toss him in a blanket, and to rip the dress off his wife and burn it: "*Host:* And send her home, / Diuested to her flanell, in a cart. / *Lat.* And let her Footman beat the bason afore her" (IV.3.97–9). When the tailor and his wife beg for mercy, it is refused. Later the Lady assures Pru, amidst another hail of class insults, that "rich garments only fit / The partyes they are made for! They shame others," and that her putting on the clothes "hath purg'd, and hallow'd 'hem / From all pollution, meant by the *Mechanicks*" (V.2.3–4, 7–8).

Fashionable society always swings between hostility toward outsiders and solidarity with the fashionable; Jonson's plays are filled with nice observations of the process by which an outsider is accepted, like the ritual dueling between "The Spaniard" and Lady Tailbush in *The Devil is an Ass,* which ends in an adulatory embrace. Breaking through this moment of hostile testing is crucial for the impostor or climber, and a great deal of attention is lavished on it. In *Every Man out of his Humor* Carlo Buffone coaches Sogliardo on making his entrance into an ordinary:

> . . . the fashion is, when any stranger comes in among'st 'hem, they all stand vp and stare at him, as he were some vnknowne beast, brought out of *Affrick:* but that'll bee help't with a good aduenturous face. You must be impudent ynough, sit downe, and vse no respect. (III.6.174–81)

Jonson is working from a passage in Erasmus' Colloquy on *Diversoria* where a foreign guest in a German inn is met with a gaze of crude xenophobia;[46] in

---

[46] *The Colloquies of Erasmus,* trans. Craig R. Thompson (Chicago: Univ. of Chicago Press, 1965), "Inns (*Diversoria,* 1523)," pp. 149–50.

Every Man Out it is a gaze judging fashion that rakes over the newcomer. In a scene in *May Day* (1601–09), closely modeled on Jonson's, Chapman develops still further the pressure of the situation.

> *Quint.*   Marry Sir, when you come first in, you shall see a crew of Gallants of all sorts: . . . Now will all these I say at your first entrance wonder at you, as at some strange Owle: Examine your person, and obserue your bearing for a time. Doe you then ath' tother side seeme to neglect their obseruance as fast, let your countenance be proofe against all eyes, not yeelding or confessing in it any inward defect. In a word be impudent enough, for thats your chiefe vertue of society.[47]

The aggressive charge is very high in these encounters. The fashionable circles of Restoration and eighteenth century drama seem domesticated in comparison. The swagger is nearer violence than it will be later: The high temper of an aristocracy that can still remember its origins as a warrior class is channeled into fashion. A man's fashion is tested as his honor might be; Touchstone reminds us the cut of a man's beard could be the cause of a duel.[48] The hostility and impudence of these scenes are shot full of falsity and often enough are seen to mask cowardice and mere dandyism. But more than mere falsity is in play – we are also brought close to the modes of social pressure in the maintenance of class boundaries.

We are also brought close to a new sort of attention to manners and fashion, propelled ultimately by class emulation but involving a general rearticulation of social behavior. This is clearly of great intrinsic historical interest and has massive significance for literary history. If it is only beginning to get the attention it deserves this is because it can be captured only incompletely in the historical terms traditionally directed at this period, those of the politics of the Elizabethan settlement and the Civil War, or of a narrow economic interpretation. Hence the usefulness of Norbert Elias's *The Civilizing Process,*[49] first published in German in 1937. Recently translated into English, it seems very

[47] Quoted in Herford and Simpson, 9, p. 454.

[48] *As You Like It, The Riverside Shakespeare* (Boston: Houghton Mifflin, 1974), V.4.69 ff. Helen Ostovich has written an essay on Jonson's group psychology, " 'Jeered by Confederacy': Group Aggression in Jonson's Comedies," *Medieval & Renaissance Drama in England III,* ed., Leeds Barroll and Paul Werstine (New York: AMS Press, 1986), pp. 115–28. Ostovich says Jonson seems to see in his groups of jeerers "a desperate defense by the weak against the overcrowded, viciously acquisitive, status-seeking conditions of Jacobean London" (p. 115), but she does not otherwise examine the historical basis of this behavior, or the topic of fashion. Her essay is based on studies of aggression by modern social psychologists, with some interesting information on the life of rats.

[49] Norbert Elias, *The Civilizing Process, Vol. I: The History of Manners; Vol. II: Power and Civility,* trans. Edmund Jephcott (New York: Pantheon, 1978, 1982). For a review and evaluation of Elias and his reception see Helmut Kuzmics, "Elias' Theory of Civilization," *Telos* 61 (Fall 1984), 83–99.

contemporary: Its attention to the slow changes in the way Europeans ate and spat and blew their noses recalls the *Annales* school of historians of everyday life; its concerns for the sociohistorical determinations of psychic structures opens a problematic familiar to us now; the titles of the two volumes that comprise *The Civilizing Process, The History of Manners* and *Power and Civility,* have a Foucauldian ring. Elias helps us to see that Jonson was watching an important historical development, and was watching it in a new way. Though he says little about England, several parts of his theory are extremely well adapted to describing Jonson.

Very briefly, Elias's theory of the "sociogenesis of manners" runs as follows: As social and economic functions have become more and more differentiated under the pressure of competition, social behavior has had to become more refined, more precisely calculated, to transmit the right signals in an increasingly large and complex web of communication. This demands finer calibrations of codified behavior patterns, and a corresponding discipline and stability of the apparatus of mental self-restraint. The "civilizing process" has been continuous from the earliest history of the Occident to the present, but Elias focuses on a sea change between the Middle Ages and the eighteenth century. The relevance to Jonson's ethics is immediately obvious. Elias could be glossing Jonson's "An Ode: High-spirited friend" (*Underwoods* XXVI) when he writes

> The moderation of spontaneous emotions, the tempering of affects, the extension of mental space beyond the moment into the past and future, the habit of connecting events in terms of chains of cause and effect – all these are different aspects of the same transformation of conduct which necessarily takes place with the monopolization of physical violence, and the lengthening of the chains of social action and interdependence.[50]

Elias invites us to see Jonson's famous ego as not just big and strong but of world-historical significance, thereby inviting us to historicize our discussions of Jonson's morals, something those discussions badly need.

The sociogenesis of manners is effected through the diffusion of manners through the social structure, a process that takes different forms in each society – Elias's book opens with a comparative study of France and Germany. It is hard to overstate the extent to which Jonson's plays are devoted to observing this process of the diffusion of manners. He systematically covers a very wide field, often focusing precisely on the nodes of generation and distribution. *Cynthia's Revels* is set in "The Speciall Fountaine of Manners: The Court"; *Poetaster,* as has been said, runs the length of the Strand from the Court through the fashionable quarters of the gentry to the City; *Epicoene* is famous as the first English comedy to restrict itself to a fashionable West End milieu; *The Alchemist* watches cony-catchers encourage their bourgeois and gentle victims to climb on the lower and middling rungs of the social ladder, and *Bartholomew*

---

[50] Elias, *Power and Civility,* p. 236.

Fair watches the bourgeoisie slip; with *The Devil is an Ass* we are again on the fringes of the Court, in the subculture of those mixed up in fashions and "projects"; *The Staple of News* is set at the nerve centers of social gossip; in *The New Inn* the aristocracy withdraws to a country retreat where it can pursue the Court of Love fashion the monarchs were pushing. Nearly all Jonson's handling of his great theme, fraud, involves social pretense, the appropriation of manners from a superior class.

Nearly all his plays include characters who have set themselves up on a more or less professional basis to diffuse manners by teaching the social arts, and others who are looking for such instruction, like Bobadill and Mathew in *Every Man In*. At the beginning of *Every Man Out* Sogliardo tells Carlo Buffone "I will be a Gentleman, whatsoeuer it cost me. . . . if you please to instruct, I am not too good to learne" (I.2.3, 24–5), and Captain Shift, who is first seen posting ads for his services in Paul's, is hired as a sort of subcontractor to teach Sogliardo to take tobacco. *Cynthia's Revels* follows the transformation of the citizen son Asotus into a Master of Courtiership under the tutelage of Amorphus. In *Volpone* Sir Politic Would-Be offers to take Peregrine under his wing and instruct him in the arts of travel and politics (II.1.105 ff). In *The Alchemist* Face, for once telling the truth, tells Kastril, come for a quarreling lesson, that Subtle has made him the gallant he now is in two months (III.4.44–6). In *The Devil is an Ass* Fitzdottrel worries that his wife will not be able to play the part of a duchess:

> *Meercraft:*   Best haue her taught, Sir.
> *Fitz-dottrel:*   Where? Are there any Schooles for
>   *Ladies?* Is there
> An *Academy* for women? I doe know,
> For men, there was: I learn'd in it, my selfe,
> To make my legges, and doe my postures.

Yes there is, Meerecraft says, run by "The Spaniard," who "is such a Mistresse of behauiour; / She knowes, from the *Dukes* daughter, to the Doxey, / What is their due iust: and no more!" (II.8.18–22, 37–9). Fitzdottrel eventually hands his wife over to her:

> She is your owne. Do with her what you will!
> Melt, cast, and forme her as you shall thinke good!
> Set any stamp on! I'll receiue her from you
> As a new thing, by your owne standard!
>   (IV.4.253–6)

There are ironic overtones, since his wife's lover Wittipol is playing the part of "The Spaniard," but the more literal sense of the passages gives us the clearest possible expression of both the sense of social presence as something to be applied externally through a process one could buy, and the precision that characterized increasingly sophisticated manners, as set forth in Elias's model.

Such examples could be multiplied out of Jonson's plays, and multiplied more or less to infinity out of the plays of his contemporaries. London was full of tutors and academies of one sort or another, and many courtesy books were sold. All this indicates a general crisis in the social presentation of the self, a widespread sense that social behavior was changing, and was now an object not merely for a Chaucerian eye for variety, nor for satiric condemnation of novelty, though there was plenty of that, but for anxiety and study. Social behavior was increasingly governed by the idea of performance rather than ceremony. More and more people were being drawn into this problematic, and more and more of their behavior was being molded by it: "then for your observances, a man must not so much as spit but within line and fashion."[51] The Puritans had their own sense of the importance of the minutiae of behavior, and this immediately before the period in which the Country is formulated as a stylistic as well as ideological alternative to the leadership of the Court. In all cases the choices are made in the context of a heightened sense for style and manners.

For the most part manners are generated at Court and are diffused downward, but the old tradition of finding the courtier affected and ridiculous was intensified with a new resentment as the Court filled up with "new men" scrambling for advancement, driving out the natural leaders of the old aristocracy.[52] In *Cynthia's Revels* Jonson points to the muddying of the fountain of manners, though the mud is presented as welling up from below. We also see a sturdy bourgeois resistance to courtly fashions, from citizens like Touchstone in *Eastward Ho,* who hates his daughter's feverish infatuation with aristocratic styles, or from the City Dames in *Westward Ho* who are said (with some irony, probably) to know things they could teach Court Ladies.[53] Jonson does not defend the honor of the citizens of London, but neither does he endorse the view that citizen manners are inherently risible. He is interested in the play between class styles.

In *Poetaster* the jeweler Albius awaits the arrival of a group of courtiers, and tries to redecorate his house in a foreign style for their sake. He wants the cushions piled on top of one another rather than scattered about to give an effect that is not tavernlike; he pleads "hang no pictures in the hall, nor in the dyning-chamber, in any case, but in the gallerie onely, for 'tis not courtly else" (II.1.126–7). He sees that such things are subject to a *distinctive* reading, in the sense elaborated by Pierre Bourdieu – that all these details of decoration, dress,

[51] Thomas Middleton, *Michaelmas Term,* ed., Richard Levin (Lincoln: Univ. of Nebraska Press, 1966), II.1.92–3.

[52] Whigham, p. 10.

[53] "Taylor, you talk like an asse, I tel thee there is equality inough between a Lady and a Citty dame. . . . Your Citizen's wife learnes nothing but fopperies of your Lady, but your Lady or Justice-a-Peace Madam, carries high wit from the City" (I.1.23–4, 29–30). Joan Thirsk agrees that it was not always a matter of fashions and markets spreading down from above, p. 125.

speech, and behavior are encoded with class meanings.[54] He thinks he knows what the courtly style is, but must yield to the contemptuous authority of his wife Chloe – a gentlewoman born, she rushes to let everyone know – who is rehearsing her credentials with the gallant Crispinus, and getting his advice on how to entertain the ladies (he counsels hypocrisy). This is satire, but there is nothing inherently ridiculous about either arrangement of cushions or pictures. What is ridiculous is the anxious attempt to move from one to another, but even this satiric note is lost temporarily in the measurement and observation of class styles.

Through this process of the diffusion of manners a new way of seeing emerges, a new gaze fastened on manners and fashion. Elias answers the question of what separates Erasmus' *De civilitate morum puerilium* (1530) from the medieval courtesy books that preceded it by pointing not to a radically new content but to its new style, which is individual and perceptive, giving us scenes of social life rather than bare precepts. The change from medieval to Renaissance modes of behavior is not a rupture in manners themselves, but again a matter of a new way of looking, a more careful, thorough, and sensitive awareness of the people around one, involving more coercive expectations of "good behavior": "In this, too, a new relationship of man to man, a new form of integration is announced."[55]

The theater in England became a powerful instrument of this new way of seeing – one of the most powerful, though not the only one. Its importance came partly from its strategic relation to other institutions, notably "the special fovntaine of manners," the Court, the unrivaled source of fashion, where behavior was subjected to a scrutiny more stringent than anywhere else, and whose prestige rubbed off on the companies associated with it formally or informally; and the Inns of Court, an even more crucial influence on the theaters because they were a distinctively urban institution, culturally as well as geographically between Court and City, and having the recognized function of forming the manners of the gentry.[56]

We can trace in the culture of the Inns a change in the way manners were formed, or, better, the accumulation of successive modes of formation corresponding roughly to the heterogeneous dramatic languages of the theater, from the stiffly hieratic through the smooth charm of Shakespearean gallantry to Jonsonian satire. There still survived ceremonies like the Readers Feast, an installation rite involving "a stately dance accompanied by a number of ritualistic gestures in which the whole company, in order of precedence, followed the Reader in his 'measures'." This was out of favor by the Elizabethan period, and attendance had to be enforced. By the time of Sir John Fortescue's defense

[54] Pierre Bourdieu, *Distinction: A Social Critique of the Judgement of Taste* (Cambridge, Mass: Harvard Univ. Press, 1984).
[55] Elias, *History of Manners,* pp. 78–9.
[56] On the culture of the Inns see especially Philip Finkelpearl, *John Marston of the Middle Temple* (Cambridge: Harvard Univ. Press, 1969).

of the Inns, written about 1468 to 1471, they were already providing training in the social arts of music, dancing, literature, and the like, which were displayed in the Revels, performed, we hear from a seventeenth century source, "by the better sort of the young Gentlemen of the Society, with Galliards, Corrantoes, and other Dances; or else with Stage-plays." Not locked into the hieratic repetition of frozen gestures, the "better sort of the young Gentlemen" were allowed to cavort and perform mock ceremonials that trained them to perform real ones at Court or elsewhere.[57] Personal gracefulness and social bearing were part of the extracurricular cultural capital (to use Bourdieu's language) that residence at the Inns could bring.[58]

The Revels always contained the burlesque and satire typical of medieval school festivals, but in the Elizabethan period the satire took on a new immediacy and bite. Finkelpearl writes of

> the superimposition onto a set of traditional institutional complacencies of the attitudes and actions of a group of satirists, rhetoricians and disorderly wits. I do not refer only to the way their personal feuds imparted a special flavor to these revels. Within the old framework they managed to inject satire of the wealthy idlers, rakes, clotheshorses, and fools among whom they lived. . . . They inconspicuously shifted the emphasis in many parts of the revels so that the satire was often about the audience rather than the outside world.[59]

The Inns thus generated a complex and mobile discourse about manners that spilled over into the theaters.

Jonson had many connections with the Inns. He dedicated *Every Man Out* "TO THE NOBLEST NOVRCERIES OF HVMANITY, AND LIBERTY, IN THE KINGDOME: The Innes of Court," "*as being borne the Iudges of these studies,*" claiming friendships there, and associating his work with the Revels tradition by asking that his play not interrupt their serious studies, but be read "*when the gowne and cap is off, and the Lord of liberty raignes.*" His next play, *Poetaster,* was dedicated to Richard Martin, a prominent Innsman; in *Satiromastix* Jonson was accused of stealing jests from the Temple Revels. The highly visible literary connection is through the 1590s verse satire of Donne, Marston, and Hall, all Innsmen.

It is conventional to note that Jonson's comical satires follow directly on the banning of verse satire in 1599. Verse satire had also served effectively to respond to the new sense of observation and self display. The "fondling motley humourist" of Donne's "Satire I," who calculates like a broker the worth of

---

[57] Christopher Gordon Petter, ed., *A Critical Old Spelling Edition of The Works of Edward Sharpham,* The Renaissance Imagination, vol. 18 (NY: Garland Press, 1986), pp. 14–21.

[58] Orthodox humanist educational theory held that acquiring "good behauiour and audacitye . . . ease of bearing and self confidence" was one of the purposes of school dramatic performances. *Jacke Jugeler, Four Tudor Comedies,* ed., William Tydeman (Harmondsworth: Penguin, 1984), p. 17.

[59] Finkelpearl, p. 61, quoted in Petter, p. 30.

passers-by so he can raise his hat the right number of inches, foreshadows "The Spaniard"; Macrine, preening himself at the door before entering the royal presence in "Satire IV" (lines 197 ff.), anticipates Fastidius Briske's advice to Macilente on the same subject. I do not wish to overestimate the formal influence of formal verse satire on comical satire,[60] but to point to the diffusion of a cultural style from the Inns to the private theaters, where Innsmen were a decisive influence, and to the public theaters. After the controversy over Harbage's thesis about the rival coterie and popular traditions we have learned not to draw the boundaries between private and public theaters too sharply, but neither do we want to erase them. The point is transmission of manners, a process implying a permeable membrane but also differing pressures in different environments. As satire moved from the Inns to the stage, and from the private houses to the public ones, more and more people were drawn into a process operating in public space.

The most important transformation of verse satire is thus not visible to formal analysis: This is that it suddenly reached a much larger, even mass audience. "Rare poems ask rare friends," Jonson wrote to the Countess of Bedford, sending her a rare copy of Donne's unpublished satires; the pile of books burned when satires and epigrams were banned in 1599 cannot have been very large, but when the dramatists began to mock the fashion for extravagant feathers, the feather-sellers quailed.[61] As long as we are interested in the formative social role of art, this difference can hardly be overestimated.

With the translation of formal verse satire onto the stage and (therefore) into another more entirely urban social formation comes the replacement of the traditional rural values of the satirist (a constant in both Roman satire and English complaint) with new urban ones. As Kathleen McLuskie writes,

> Complaint . . . was subsumed into satiric comedy which increasingly embodied the values of a self-conscious urban community. The sharp critique of the pride and folly of urban life which had animated verse satire was blunted as the

[60] Printed and stage satire had always influenced each other and would continue to do so, from the Marprelate controversey to the cony-catching pamphlets (see, *inter alia*, Chambers, vol. 1, p. 294, and Lawrence Manley, "Cony-Catching: Anatomy of Anatomies," unpublished ms.). J. B. Leishman is right to argue that the distinctions between the classical and native English satirical traditions matter less than noticing that there was one satirical impulse that gathered unprecedented force in the 1590s, with a real burst in 1598 (pp. 42–5). There must have been strong social reasons for this boom, the consciousness of problems having reached a certain critical mass, but the specific institutional connection between the Inns and the theaters, especially the private ones, is a factor of some weight on its own level.

[61] See Webster's Induction to Marston's *The Malcontent,* lines 48 ff., in *Elizabethan Plays,* ed., C. R. Baskervill, V. B. Heltzel, and A. N. Nethercott (New York: Holt, Rinehart and Winston, 1934). The point about the increased size of the audience for stage satire is made by Maria Gottwald, *Satirical Elements in Ben Jonson's Comedy* (Wroclaw: Travaux de la Societé des Sciences et des Lettres de Wroclaw, Series A, no. 137, 1969), p. 24.

objects of satire became more specific, mocking the fop, the lover and the *nouveau riche* – all deviants from the urbane world view of the implied audience. The countryside ceased to be the locus of enduring values and was ridiculed as the home of the peasant and the boor.

The realist theatrical mode of satiric comedy was appropriated by writers celebrating urban life, reassuring its audience of the superiority of its values of style, leisure and elegant consumption.[62]

This became true as a fashionable world consolidated itself, a process Jonson observed, but observed critically – the theaters and Jonson himself mediated as well as transmitted the new urbane culture. It is time to say the obvious: Jonson's pronouncements on fashion and the fashionable are overwhelmingly negative. "Nothing is fashionable, till it be deformed," he wrote in *Timber*.[63] Fashion is the constant object of satire, extravagantly fashionable people are nearly always unmasked, fashion is perhaps the major embodiment of change, instability, superficiality – the negative pole of the opposition everyone now sees in Jonson between centrifugal energy and a "centered self."[64] This opposition is always loaded with ambivalence; in the case of fashion the ambivalence takes some special forms, not only moral or psychological but derived from the social situation of Jonson and his art. The pronouncements tell only half the story.

Plays denouncing fashionable gallants were attended most conspicuously by fashionable gallants, the topic being especially popular in the coterie theaters. One suspects that they did not especially mind being satirized: Impudence was their foremost characteristic, the hunger for attention positive or negative. Satire may have wounded individuals, but as a group they found that the theater responded to them satisfactorily. It represented them, providing a backhanded confirmation of their social power and initiative. Their own self-infatuation

[62] Kate McLuskie, " 'Tis but a Woman's Jar: Family and Kinship in Elizabethan Domestic Drama," *Literature and History* 9:2 (Autumn 1983), 230.

[63] Herford and Simpson, p. 581. Jonson's critics have not been slow to pick up on this point. See, for example, Jonas Barish, *Ben Jonson and the Language of Prose Comedy* (1960; rpt. New York: W. W. Norton, 1970), pp. 48–9, on the inherent badness of clothes. The use of cosmetics is associated with deception, according to Annette Drew-Bear, "Face-Painting Scenes in Ben Jonson's Plays," *Studies in Philology* 77 (1980), 388–401, and "Face Painting in Renaissance Tragedy," *Renaissance Drama* n.s. 12 (1981), 71–93. Alexander Leggatt regrets Jonson's emphasis on the issue of fashion, seeing an artistic problem in focusing on such "trivial vices": "Jonson has trouble dramatizing the idea that foppery is a real danger to the state," *Ben Jonson: His Vision and his Art* (New York: Methuen, 1981), p. 83. The comical satires are not all masterpieces and there is something disproportionate and awkward about Jonson's moralizing. But the issue needs to be set in the historical contexts of a society where the meaning of dress was not at all trivial, of a social dynamic in which the issue was pushed to the fore, and of Jonson's personal situation, which gave him a tortured relation to the question.

[64] The *locus classicus* is Thomas M. Greene, "Ben Jonson and the Centered Self," *SEL 10* (1970), 325–48.

and self-display are intimately related to the genesis of the art that portrayed them. The comical satires in particular are (again backhandedly) their own art form, sharing with them not only a scene, a social space, but also specific objects of attention and modes of perception.

Moreover the theatrical situation, particularly in the fashionable private theaters, imposed a certain paradox: One could write plays against fashion, but they had to be fashionable. Look, for instance, at the "character" Jonson gives of Fastidius Briske in the list of dramatis personae of *Every Man Out*:

> A neat, spruce, affecting Courtier, one that weares clothes well, and in fashion; practiseth by his glasse how to salute; speakes good remnants (notwithstanding the Base-violl and Tabacco:) sweares tersely, and with variety; cares not what Ladies fauour he belyes, or great Mans familiarity: a good property to perfume the boot of a coach.

Jonson is not only simultaneously preening and exposing his character but also making promises to the audience to show them the top of fashion and the cleverest tricks of the man about town. Fastidius Briske is morally a fake, but in the fashion world he is the real thing. Here and everywhere Jonson radiates perfect confidence in his judgment of what the fashion is. It is the confidence of an insider. Had the actors of the Master's of Courtship examination in *Cynthia's Revels* not been accurately taking off the latest fashions the scene would have been discredited before its point was made. Jonson could not afford not to be in the most perfect fashion.

Jonson's alter ego Crites hangs around the Fountain of Manners in plain clothes, like Jonson himself with his preferred poor scholar's garb, in glaring visual contrast to his surroundings. His judgment is disqualified by the fashionable – "you are no courtier" (V.4.542) – and he dismisses the whole business with sour contempt: "would any reasonable creature make these his serious studies, and perfections?" (V.4.174–5). Yet he has studied them. He acts as trainer for Mercury/Monsieur when he enters the lists against Asotus, and at the climax of the scene he shows he can play too: He discountenances Anaides by mimicking him. A playwright is professionally capable of meeting a courtier on this ground, of keeping up with fashion, since it is only a system of signs falling under his empirical eye.

This fashion competition takes place, with allegorical precision, in the context of social mobility. Cynthia's revels are a sort of open house, "In which time, it shall bee lawfull for all sorts of ingenuous persons, to visit her palace, to court her Nymphs, to exercise all varietie of generous and noble pastimes" (I.1.97–100). The barriers of rank are temporarily down; the price of admission is courtly clothes and manners, not courtly status, and into this clear field rush "these courtiers for high dayes" like Hedon, whom we are told does not have the means to be a courtier longer than the period of the revels (II.1.33).

The theme of climbing through acquiring courtly manners is centered on the citizen-son Asotus, and it is clear enough that the citizen-son Crites/Ben Jonson, making his bid for court favor, is in a sense his double and competitor. (And the instructor Amorphus' double also: At the beginning of the play we see Asotus pass from Crites' tutelage to Amorphus': at the end Crites again lays down the law. The Jonsonian poet is a higher form of the "instructor" figure, molding the soul as well as manners.) The Master need not compete on this level to have his noble nature recognized by Arete and Cynthia; but he finds it convenient to do so.

Jonson's career as a playwright continued to be closely bound up with fashion. If he began by following it, or rather stalking it with a savage gleam in his eye, he later made fashions, of some kinds at least, occupying a position of power at the center of things (expressed in *Epicoene* as clearly as in the court masques). Then he was left behind by fashion, a painful experience to which he reacts in a variety of ways in the introductory materials to *The Staple of News* (1626). The theme of the distraction of "showes" is introduced when the Prologue addresses Curiosity, Lady Censure, suggesting that her interest in the play she is about to see is merely as a fashion parade – "you come to see, who weares the new sute to day? whose clothes are best penn'd, what euer the part be? which Actor has the best legge and foote? what King playes without cuffes?" (39–42) – and is carried on in terms derived from the quarrel with Inigo Jones:

> For your owne sakes, not his, he bad me say,
> Would you were come to heare, not see a Play.
> Though we his *Actors* must prouide for those,
> Who are our guests, here, in the way of showes,
> The maker hath not so; he'ld haue you wise,
> Much rather by your eares, then by your eyes.
>   (The Prologue for the Stage, 1–6)

The Prologue expects the audience to be full of irrelevant chatter. People have come to pick up women and trade news about

> what is done, and where,
> How, and by whom, in all the towne; but here.
> Alas! what is it to his Scene, to know
> How many Coaches in *Hide-parke* did show
> Last spring, what fare to day at *Medleyes* was,
> If *Dunstan,* or the *Phoenix* best wine has?
> They are things – But yet, the Stage might stand as wel,
> If it did neither heare these things, nor tell.
>   (The Prologue for the Stage, 11–18)

The relation of the theater to news and fashion, to the life of fashionable society, is seen as accidental, and is bitterly resented. Jonson had for years been lecturing his audience on the manner and quality of its attention, but there is a new hardening of position here as the interest he harnessed in the comical satires slipped away from him. The poet wants to exercise his moral function

from a position high and aloof, neither springing from nor reacting to the
fashions of the day or the interests of an unworthy audience. In the wake of the
failure of *The New Inn* (1629) matters were still worse. In the Dedication to
the Reader he prefers any reader to the impertinent spectators who came
merely "To see, and to bee seene": "And doe trust my selfe, and my Booke,
rather to thy rusticke candor, than all the pompe of their pride, and solemne
ignorance, to boote." Candor had always been looked for, but "*rusticke* candor" is something Jonson's dramatic art gives us no examples of. In his poems
he could praise the life retired from the town (*The Forest* III. "To Sir Robert
Wroth"), but in his plays the only tenable alternative to extravagant fashionableness was sensible fashionableness.[65]

[65] *Underwoods* 42, "An Elegy," provides an interesting parallel, though here the context
of Jonson's relation to clothes is erotic and poetic rather than theatrical. Jonson
begins, in the manner of *Underwoods* 2 "A Celebration of Charis," or 9, "My Picture
Left in Scotland," by arguing that whatever his personal liabilities, he is, qua poet, a
lover, with privileges and interests that extend to ladies' dressings:

> Fathers and husbands, I do claim a right
> In all that is called lovely. . . .
> No face, no hand, proportion, line or air
> Of beauty; but the muse hath interest in:
> There is not worn that lace, purl, knot or pin
> But is the poet's matter.
>   (11–12, 14–17)

These things are *his business*. The poem will swing about in standard Jonsonian
fashion to dwell on the bad side of that business. The person the poem addresses, who
seems to be a wealthy citizen, is accused of promoting a general sexual passion for his
wife by squandering his "sordid bounty" on her wardrobe. His perverse pleasure
culminates in peeping through a hole at the servant in charge of his wife's wardrobe
as her clothes excite him to masturbation (51–60). (This poem also includes the sketch
of the tailor and his wife, picked up in *The New Inn*.) This leads to the point that there
are many "songsters" with a similarly fetishized and mindless admiration for clothes
and the poem closes with vituperation of those who would love "a goat in velvet."
    The point I want to make concerns the poem's turn, where Jonson establishes his
immunity to the citizen's game by pointing, autobiographically, to his connection
with the Court.

> But I who live, and have lived twenty year
> Where I may handle silk, as free, and near,
> As any mercer; or the whalebone man
> That quilts those bodies, I have leave to span:
> Have eaten with the beauties, and the wits,
> And braveries of court, and felt their fits
> Of love, and hate: and came so nigh to know
> Whether their faces were their own, or no.
>   (29–36)

The coincidence and implication of Jonson with the world of fashion follow the law Bourdieu outlines whereby the avant-garde artist and his avant-garde audience stay "miraculously" attuned to one another because of

> the structural and functional homology between a given writer's or artist's position in the field of production and the position of his audience in the field of the classes and class fractions. . . .
>
> Between pure disinterestedness and cynical servility, there is room for the relationships established, objectively, without any conscious intention, between a producer and an audience, by virtue of which the practices and artifacts produced in a specialized and relatively autonomous field of production are necessarily over-determined.[66]

Bourdieu talks of the "pre-established harmony" created between artist and audience by this homology – too strong a term for the contentious relations of Jonson and his audience, where the roles of both artist and audience were still unsettled, but the principle is the same, and allows us to look beyond the claims of pure disinterestedness and cynical servility that would fly with such abandon in the War of the Theaters. More on this shortly, but first I want to explore more concretely the relations in the theater of Jonson and the gallants. Dekker's *Gull's Horn Book* makes clear the basic socioeconomic reason why fashionable gallants loom so large in the drama:

> The theater is your poet's Royal Exchange. . . . Players are their factors. . . . Your gallant, your courtier and your captain had wont to be the soundest paymasters and I think are still the surest chapmen. And these by means that their heads are well stocked deal upon this comical freight by the gross when your groundling and gallery commoner buys his sport by the penny.[67]

It is not just that the gallants came regularly and paid more for their seats, though this was also true. (Those who sat in the "Lord's room" or on stage came through the players' entrance and paid six times the general admission price, additional money, moreover, that was profit for the players not shared with the landlord.)[68] The gallants were also closely involved in the social and professional life of the "poets" and players in the sort of coercive intimacy we see in *Poetaster*, as well as through the legitimate forms of friendship and patronage celebrated in Jonson's dedication of *Every Man Out* to the Inns of

There is self-irony in Jonson's sense of his status in the Court environment being not unlike that of the mercer and whalebone man, given leave to be intimate with his superiors, and there is satire on the fickleness and falsity of courtiers; but undoubtedly the force of the passage lies in Jonson's claim of superiority over the citizen on the grounds that he is closer to the center of things, an intimate of the most fashionable, and so unimpressible.

[66] Bourdieu, pp. 239–40.
[67] In E. D. Pendry, ed., *Thomas Dekker: Selected Prose Works, The Stratford-upon-Avon Library 4* (Cambridge: Harvard Univ. Press, 1968), p. 98.
[68] Bradbrook, p. 57.

Court. Most directly of all, the gallants dominated, or tried to dominate, the social situation in the theaters, to the point of conditioning or even interrupting the performances.

THE AUDIENCE ON STAGE

Jonson's new kind of play, devoted to the themes of social competition and display, and staging with a new immediacy the space, time, and social behavior of its London audience, developed an excrescence that dealt with the social issues concerning the theater most concretely by playing with the fact that the audience literally as well as figuratively shared the stage with the actors. At the margins of the stage the playing space and the seating space overlapped. Not only were the thrust stages surrounded on three sides by the audience, but gentlemen could rent stools on the stage itself at the private indoor playhouses, and at public houses like the Globe they could sit if not on the main stage – there is conflicting evidence on this point – at least in the "Lord's room," also used as an upper stage.[69] This situation figures in a number of inductions, played at the edge of the stage and at the edge of the dramatic illusion.

In part the issue is merely a physical one. Jonson's uncharacteristically polite request in the Prologue to *The Devil is an Ass* that the gentlemen allow the actors enough space to work in is merely a newer form of the cry of "make room!" which began medieval performances. But something more complex and interesting happens in the "critical"[70] inductions created by Jonson, with Marston and Webster and Beaumont right behind him; they are little playlets about the theatrical situation, with actors playing members of the audience and spectators sometimes forced into the fiction. At issue were the autonomy and social nature of the dramatic illusion, and finally the rival social claims of aristocratic audience and professional actors and playwrights to the space of the theater. This was a real struggle. We are told of one occasion, from a considerably later period, in which "a formidable riot broke out when an actor remonstrated with a nobleman for crossing the stage in front of the actors to speak to a friend, while a principal scene of *Macbeth* was playing, and was struck across the face for his pains."[71]

The inductions were a sort of carapace the plays threw up around themselves to protect the boundaries of the stage and deal with a recurrent set of problems. Their origins probably owe as much to the actors' improvised reactions to

---

[69] Dekker's *The Gull's Horn-Book* says "Whether, therefore, the gatherers of the public or private playhouse stand to receive the afternoon's rent, let our gallant, having paid it, presently advance himself up to the throne of the stage" (p. 98). Webster's Induction to the Globe production of Marston's *The Malcontent,* however, seems to make it clear that stage sitting was not permitted there.

[70] "The Critical Induction" is the title of chap. 4 in Thelma N. Greenfield, *The Induction in Elizabethan Drama* (Eugene: Univ. of Oregon Press, 1969), pp. 67–95.

[71] Irwin Smith, *Shakespeare's Blackfriars Playhouse* (London: Peter Owen, 1966), p. 223.

audience meddling as to classical models. The give and take between actors and spectators at the private theaters "may have developed into something like a wit combat between the stage and the spectators. To break the play or put the character 'beside his part' was a form of jest that spectators might find more attractive than an indifferent performance. . . . Such plays lacked the authority of art: they were a form of 'commoning.' "[72] As the problems remained much the same, the themes of the inductions fell into a formulaic pattern: the war with the gallants on stage (who, as Jonson complained in the Dedication to *The New Inn,* came "To see, and to bee seene. To make a generall muster of themselues in their clothes of credit: and possesse the Stage, against the Play. To dislike all, but marke nothing.") always had to be fought over again. Typically the worst sorts of disruptive behavior were described (as in *Every Man Out*) or mimicked and thereby discredited, in the hope that this would preempt such behavior.[73] In *Cynthia's Revels* a boy actor smokes tobacco, ostentatiously condemns the actors in word and gesture, and makes a series of demands on the playwright on behalf of the audience. This is also the method of the inductions to Marston's *What You Will* (1601) and *The Malcontent* (written by Webster for the King's Men [1600–01?] after they stole the play from the Blackfriars), Beaumont's *Knight of the Burning Pestle,* and, when Jonson returned later to this technique, *Bartholomew Fair, The Staple of News,* and *The Magnetic Lady.*[74]

The inductions were thus functional, as well as being brilliant *jeux d'esprit.* The "extra-dramatic" moments of Elizabethan drama, when an actor steps out of the dramatic illusion and suddenly occupies the same space as the audience in the theater, or (in the Inductions) emerges from the audience with the dramatic illusion coagulating around him, have exercised a certain fascination over modern theoreticians of the theater. Historians of the Elizabethan dramatic

[72] Bradbrook, p. 265.

[73] See John Sweeney III, "*Volpone* and the Theater of Self-Interest," *English Literary Renaissance 12* (1982), p. 230.

[74] By 1607 Beaumont could write "Gentlemen, Inductions are out of date" (Prologue to *The Woman Hater,* quoted in Herford and Simpson 9, p. 408); his own use of the technique in *The Knight of the Burning Pestle* is an extraordinary turn on the Jonsonian form. For an analysis, which also deals much more fully than I do here with the heritage of the early Tudor interlude, particularly Medwall's *Fulgens and Lucres,* see an earlier version of this section, "The Elizabethan Audience on Stage," *Themes in Drama 9,* ed., James Redmond (Cambridge: Cambridge Univ. Press, 1987), pp. 59–68. The problem with exhibitionistic gallants continued in the Restoration theater, when they were called fops and were seated in a corner of the pit near the stage called "Fop-corner." Playwrights continued to take potshots at them. See Robert B. Heilman, "Some Fops and Some Versions of Foppery," *ELH 49* (1982), p. 366 and n. 9. The Inductions in our period also have to do with backstage tensions among members of the theatrical company, among actors (*Cynthia's Revels*), or with the playwright (*Every Man Out, Cynthia's Revels,* Marston's *Jacke Drums Entertainment* [1600, pub. 1601], and *Bartholomew Fair*).

illusion (such as Muriel Bradbrook and Ann Righter[75]) see these moments quite differently: They do not see the dramatic illusion being broken down to produce a philosophical *frisson,* but a dramatic illusion still in the process of formation, not an anticipation of a modern technique, but a relic of the medieval theater. The revelation of theatricality does not usually come from the actors becoming conscious of themselves as creatures with a metaphysical or ontological problem, but it comes from outside, from the social demands of the audience.

Righter talks about the "tyranny" of the medieval audience over the play, how the inability to forget the audience limits the depth of the dramatic illusion, making it shallow and vulnerable, as if it were always about to be squashed flat against the screen in the back of the hall leaving the actors naked, exposed as poor servants in need of the toleration and cooperation of their masters whom they were seeking to entertain.[76] The inductions of the turn of the century, on the other hand, grow out of a sense of security and assertiveness on behalf of a three-dimensional dramatic world. The illusion is deep and resilient, able to withstand the blows of a hostile audience, even to mount offensive forays of its own, and to grow stronger through this sparring. This confidence had a social, even an economic, base. No longer a fleeting moment in the hall of a patron, at the disposal of his guests (Medwall's *Fulgens and Lucres* [c. 1497] has a pause between acts so the company can finish their dinner), the dramatic illusion is now at home, in a commercial theater, entertaining its own guests in a hall its own profits built. It has produced its own space. It still depends on its guests, but the relationship is now one of strong reciprocity.

This sense of security about the dramatic illusion led the players and playwrights to claim their space with a new confidence, but the gallants did not necessarily acquiesce. Their patronage was inflected with aristocratic arrogance, an attitude that they could take or leave the performance as they would a dessert. In *A Midsummer Night's Dream* Shakespeare remembers the old practices when he has the newly married aristocrats mock and interrupt the rude mechanicals offering their play.[77] Bradbrook tells us the actors did not mind this sort of thing, that disruption by the audience was a mark of acceptance.[78] Perhaps, but such was clearly not the attitude of Ben Jonson.

Jonson's strategy involved more than a headlong assault on the audience with his high claims for the dignity of art: The strategy in his inductions is to isolate those who claimed a social dominance over the play and hold them up

---

[75] Anne Righter, *Shakespeare and the Idea of the Play* (London: Chatto and Windus, 1962); M. C. Bradbrook, *The Rise of the Common Player.*

[76] "The Tyranny of the Audience" is the name of part of Righter's first chapter, pp. 31–40.

[77] It is consistent with Shakespeare's avoidance of the contentious situation of city comedy that his plays-within-plays look back to older theatrical conditions rather than out into the audience facing him; compare *The Taming of the Shrew.*

[78] Bradbrook, pp. 29, 123, 265.

to ridicule. The audience could be made to respond together as an audience, to agree that such people were interfering with its collective pleasure, that its interests were with the dramatic illusion rather than with the "commoning" of a social assemblage in the theater.[79]

Such a reorganization and splitting of the audience was possible because of the celebrated diversity of the Elizabethan audience, and the social tensions that accompanied it. The view from the stage was of a highly uneven social topography, not of a homogeneous audience, and when Jonson has the audience send forward its representatives, they always stand for some part of it, not for a homogeneous whole. Both points are illustrated in the Induction to *The Magnetic Lady,* where the Tribunes Probee and Damplay announce they are sent "from the people."

> Boy.   The people! which side of the people?
> Dam.   The Venison side, if you know it, *Boy. . . .*
> Pro.   . . . Not the *Faeces,* or grounds of your people, that sit in the oblique
>   caves and wedges of your house, your sinful sixe-penny Mechanicks—
> Dam.   But the better, and braver sort of your people! Plush and Velvet-
>   outsides! that stick your house round like so many eminences.
>
> (27–37)

This diversity was much restricted in the private theaters, but still the audience lacked the organizing principle obtaining at performances at Court or in the halls of aristocrats, where it would be clear who the patron was whose auspices organized the occasion. Those who used their social prerogative to sit on stage, and then abused it by interfering with the performance, were open to the charge of usurping a patronage that was not really theirs.

To sit on the stage was in any case to focus a great deal of social attention and therefore tension on one's self, in a situation inherently full of ostentation and status assertion. The differential in ticket prices produced a rough zoning of the space of the theater by social class, but this zoning was far from perfect or precise.[80] The tension between rank and ticket price grew stronger at the margins of the stage, focusing at the points of highest visibility, the "Lord's room" above the stage, and the stools on the stage. We hear a great deal about the conditions of occupying these privileged places. There were definite rules governing who could claim them – gentlemen in the height of fashion – rules not formulated or enforceable by the theater management. In the Induction to *The Staple of News* the Gossips Mirth, Tatle, Expectation, and Censure invade the stage looking for stools:

> Yes, o' the *Stage; wee are persons of* quality, *I assure you, and women of* fashion;
> *and come to see, and to be seene.*
>
> (8–10)

---

[79] See Bradbrook, pp. 98 ff., especially p. 118.
[80] Compare the Induction to *Bartholomew Fair,* where Jonson plays on the relationship between ticket price and wit. On this Induction see below, chap. 5.

But since women were not allowed on stage, the Prologue worries *"what will the* Noblemen *thinke, or the graue* Wits *here, to see you seated on the bench thus?"* In Beaumont's *The Knight of the Burning Pestle* the violation of decorum is compounded when the Citizen and his Wife force their way onto the stage. That they can pay to be there does not temper the affront; they are so oblivious to the social standards involved that they are not even using their position on stage for fashionable ostentation, but merely for a crass display of their wealth and power.

The dramatists always present sitting on the stage as an act of brazen social ostentation.

> Fitzdottrel.   To day, I goe to the *Black-fryers Playhouse,*
> Sit i' the view, salute all my acquaintance,
> Rise vp between the Acts, let fall my cloake,
> Publish a handsome man, and a rich suite
> (As that's a speciall end, why we goe thither,
> All that pretend, to stand for't o' the *Stage*)
> The Ladies aske who's that? (For, they doe come
> To see vs, *Loue,* as wee doe to see them)
> Now, I shall lose all this, for the false feare
> Of being laught at?
>   (*The Devil is an Ass,* I.6.31–40)

This desire to see and be seen is normally presented as something more suspicious than the nobleman's legitimate display of magnificence and social preeminence. Fitzdottrel's status is adequate, but he displays more wealth than he has: Wittipol has already explained that

> that's a hyr'd suite, hee now has on,
> To see the *Diuell is an Asse,* to day, in:
> (This *Ingine* [a broker] gets three or foure pound a weeke by him)
> He dares not misse a new *Play,* or a *Feast,*
> What rate soeuer clothes be at; and thinkes
> Himselfe still new, in other mens old.
>
>   (I.4.20–5)

Webster's induction to *The Malcontent* works with this sort of material, and Dekker's *Gull's Horn-Book* devotes a chapter (6) to "How a gallant should behave himself in a playhouse." He is to exploit the slippages between fashionableness and wealth and status by displaying himself on the stage.

> Sithence then the place is so free in entertainment, allowing a stool as well to the farmer's son as to your Templar . . . it is fit that he whom the most tailors' bills do make room for when he comes should not be basely, like a viol, cased up in a corner.
> Whether, therefore, the gatherers of the public or private playhouse stand to receive the afternoon's rent, let our gallant, having paid it, presently advance himself up to the throne of the stage . . . on the very rushes where the comedy

is to dance . . . must our feathered ostrich, like a piece of ordnance, be planted valiantly because impudently, beating down the mewes and hisses of the opposed rascality.[81]

Access to the edge of the commercial stage is, with a certain appropriateness, defined by tailors' bills rather than rank, and in this delegitimized and newly competitive space the gallant offers himself up to the fashion gaze, reveling in the social tensions he creates, or rather the ripples he makes in a current of tension already coursing through the theater.

The gallants, then, as Michael Shapiro has pointed out, were putting on a social performance of their own in competition with the dramatic performance;[82] the quarrel was over the relative importance and interest of these performances. The presence of the gentlemen on stage was a sign not only of the traditional aristocratic dominance over theatrical performances, but also of social climbing through fashionable behavior, in a context of general social mobility – the gallants were basking parasitically in the glamorous aura of the stage. That the stage was glamorous, or glamorous on this social level, was new. The commercial stage dates only from 1576, and it had only recently become an institution of fashion, in which social styles were set or confirmed, or at least Court fashions disseminated. (In *Histriomastix* a group of lawyers and merchants consider going to a play: "Why this going to a play is now all in the fashion" [p. 252], someone says, as if it were news that had just gotten to him.)

Jonson had uses for this new social power. From the first (that is, from *Every Man Out*) he sees the induction as an occasion not only to protect his play from the outrages of the audience – the sense of real danger facing the satiric playwright of which Asper's speech is so full had real justification, whatever the element of self-dramatization – but also to control the audience's responses, transforming their social habits, their habits of attention, which implied defining the purposes and status of his art.[83] The induction was his bully pulpit. The space he claims for his art is not only sovereign control of the boards, but the removal of a layer of socially mediated responses. Jonson wants direct access to the consciousness of the individual playgoer. (He will return to precisely this point in the Induction to *Bartholomew Fair* and I will have more to say about it later.) Asper instructs Mitis to stare down recalcitrant members of the audience, marking them out for future vengeance – this is an art object that can stare back at its viewer, in the mode of the fashion gaze, and with a mien of judgment rather than supplication.

> if in all this front,
> You can espy a galant of this marke,
> Who (to be thought one of the iudicious)

---

[81] Dekker, *The Gull's Horn-Book,* p. 98.
[82] Michael Shapiro, *Children of the Revels* (New York: Columbia Univ. Press, 1977), p. 70.
[83] John Gordon Sweeney III, *Jonson and the Psychology of Public Theater* (Princeton: Princeton Univ. Press, 1985), p. 8 and passim.

Sits with his armes thus wreath'd, his hat pull'd here,
Cryes meaw, and nods, then shakes his empty head,
Will shew more seuerall motions in his face,
Then the new *London, Rome,* or *Niniueh,*
And (now and then) breakes a drie bisquet iest,
Which that it may more easily be chew'd,
He steeps in his owne laughter. . . .
CORD. 'Tis true, but why should we obserue 'hem. ASPER?
ASP. O I would know 'hem, for in such assemblies,
Th'are more infectious then the pestilence:
And therefore I would giue them pills to purge,
And make 'hem fit for faire societies.
How monstrous, and detested is't, to see
A fellow, that has neither arte, nor braine,
Sit like an ARISTARCHVS, or starke-asse,
Taking mens lines, with a tabacco face,
In snuffe, still spitting, vsing his wryed lookes
(In nature of a vice) to wrest, and turne
The good aspect of those that shall sit neere him,
From what they doe behold! O, 'tis most vile.
MIT. Nay, ASPER.
ASP. Peace, MITIS, I doe know your thought.
You'le say, your guests here will except at this:
Pish, you are too timorous, and full of doubt.
Then he, a patient, shall reiect all physicke,
'Cause the physicion tels him, you are sicke.
                    ("After the second Sounding," 158–90)

Asper/Jonson thus returns to his manifesto about how the satirical artist is to be revered for his nearly sacred function. The audience should keep still, like a good patient, and endure all the purgatives, enemas, corrosives, and lashings the "physicion" decides will be good for him. This involves an extreme reversal of social expectations, of the relative status and therefore mode of address of the playwright and the upper reaches of his audience.

Marston responds to Jonson's induction in the one he wrote for *What You Will* a year or two later. The full stage direction shows just how naturally the induction could arise out of the theatrical situation:[84]

---

[84] Though exactly how completely the actors were disguised as audience members is still not clear. If the actors were adults, the disguise was potentially complete, but if they were boys it would have been obvious they were actors. Bradbrook points out that when Will Sly played a citizen sitting on stage in Webster's Induction to *The Malcontent* he would have been easily recognized as a leading actor. *John Webster: Citizen and Dramatist* (New York: Columbia Univ. Press, 1980), p. 114. The danger of *not* being recognized is illustrated by an anecdote from an Oxford University performance in 1607 where an actor, not recognized as such, started up out of the audience as Detraction to condemn the actors, and was "like to have been beaten for his sauciness." Bradbrook, *Rise of the Common Player*, pp. 278–9.

> Before the musicke sounds for the Acte, enter ATTICUS, DORICUS, and
> PHYLOMUSE; they sit a good while on the Stage before the candles are
> lighted, talking together, and on suddeine DORICUS speakes.[85]

He addresses an explosion of wit on trimming the lights to the tireman: This
is an indoor, private theater performance, probably by the Paul's Boys. Soon
they get onto the topic of what "Sir Sineor Snuffe, Mounsieur Mew and
Cavalero Blirt" may do to detract from the play's reception, and the author's
noble contempt for them. This is all very Jonsonian, though it is expressed in
unmistakably Marstonian images, the humors metaphor disgustingly elaborated: "Shall he be creast-falne, if some looser braine, / In flux of witte uncively
befilth / His slight composures?" The figure of "the poet" must be Marston,
but he is playing Jonson's role and it becomes apparent that he must also in
some sense *be* Jonson as his exaggerated contempt comes in for criticism.
Doricus finally has enough and tries to calm down the ranting friend of the
poet, Phylomuse:

> Now out up-pont, I wonder what tite braine,
> Wrung in this custome to mainetaine contempt
> Gainst common censure; to give stiffe counter buffes,
> To crack rude skorne even on the very face
> Of better audience.

The audience is an aristocratic one, which does not like to be threatened by the
likes of the poet and his friend, who are reminded that the "rules of art / Were
shapt to pleasure, not pleasure to your rules." The point, which is a preemptive
compliment to the audience, is that the battle Jonson is fighting has already
been won. The audience is good enough, its taste developed, and is a legitimate
source of authority in itself. The attack on it is cruder than it is, and the
obnoxious poet is threatened with social censure, with being dropped by a
society that does not really need him.

> Dor.   Ile here no more of him; nay, and your friend the author, the com-
> poser, the What You Will, seemes so faire in his owne glasse, so
> straight in his owne measure, that hee talkes once of squinting crit-
> ickes, drunken censure, splay-footed opinion: juicles huskes, I ha done
> with him; I ha done with him.
> Phy.   Pew, nay then—
> Dor.   As if any such unsanctified stuffe could finde a beeing monge these
> ingenuous breasts.

Doricus carries the argument, which is ended by tactful gestures. The audience's interest in artists' problems shouldn't be pushed beyond very moderate
limits, and sitting on the stage is rude to everyone, the audience as well as
the players:

[85] John Marston, *What You Will,* in *The Plays of John Marston,* vol. 2, ed. H. Harvey
Wood (Edinburgh and London: Oliver and Boyd, 1938), p. 231.

> Atti. Come, wee straine the spectators patience in delaying their expected delightes. Lets place our selves within the curtaines, for good faith the stage is so very little, we shall wrong the generall eye els very much.
>
> Phy.   If youle stay but a little, Ile accompany you; I have ingag'd my selfe to the author to give a kind of inductive speech to his commedy.
>
> Atti. Away! you neglect your selfe, a gentleman –

Again the "Prologus" Phylomuse reads is a Marstonian adaptation of Jonson, half defiance of the rude ("Sweet breath from tainted stomacks who can suck?") and half promising to do his best for the "gentle mindes" of the judicious. Marston's bow sweeps lower to the floor than Jonson's ever does (nor would Jonson ever refer to his works as "slight composures," which implies the trifles of a gentleman's leisure rather than the works of a professional),[86] a note of self-abasement mixing with the sense that Marston, as a gentleman himself, had an inside track with the gentlemen in the audience as Jonson never did. Atticus' horror at Phylomuse, a gentleman, agreeing to appear on a professional stage on behalf of a playwright sounds the note of condescension. Marston is doing Jonson a favor by arguing his case to his superiors. He does it because Jonson is the figure of the artist to be reckoned with, and Marston can see himself only in his image; but he thinks he can play the role better himself since he can outflank Jonson socially. This is a typical tactical move in the War of the Theaters.

THE WAR OF THE THEATERS

The rise and fall of this kind of induction is more or less coterminous with the War of the Theaters, whose serious thematic content – most obvious in Jonson's *Poetaster* and Dekker's *Satiromastix* – was the poet's relation to society. Even the less elevated aspects of the stage quarrel were connected to this problem. The clash of personalities was expressed through arguments, or at least posturing and lampoons, on the topic; the merely mercenary aspect (which Jonson notes in *Poetaster* [III.4.326] and more directly in the appended Apologetical Dialogue [lines 148–9] and Dekker cheerfully admits to in the epilogue to *Satiromastix*) shows at the least that there was a large public willing to pay money to see this issue, which one might suppose would interest only the artists themselves and their circle, degraded to the level of a bear baiting. That the theaters would quarrel publicly with one another suggests a new measure of self-confidence in the face of their common enemies.[87] The theater had attained stability as an arena within which social competition could take place. The baiting of the poets was another form of the vaunting contentiousness focused in the theaters – whether the bear won or the dogs, the management would get its take.[88]

---

[86] This distinction is a theme of Richard Helgerson, *Self-Crowned Laureates: Spenser, Jonson, Milton, and the Literary System* (Berkeley: Univ. of California Press, 1983).

[87] Bradbrook, *John Webster: Citizen and Dramatist*, p. 92.

[88] The noise of the War reached Cambridge, where the personal antagonism is commented on in *The Return from Parnassus*, Part 2 (IV.3.1769–73). The Parnassus plays

The epilogue to *Satiromastix* suggests this was all good clean fun; the bearish Jonson was clearly disgusted by the game, but could not resist playing it. The mood of the theaters had an oppressive and constraining aspect, too, as Bradbrook suggests: "Constant uneasy fear of detraction would not allow of the large freedom of the tragic mood; satire alone was possible."[89] The muse of the War of the Theaters is Envy, the emotion of social competition.

Envy appears everywhere in prologues and dedications to these plays, but most spectacularly in the prologue to *Poetaster*, "*Arising in the midst of the stage*" with her snakes. She is invested with powerful emotions, radiating a bad sexual energy. Her snakes have "soft, and amorous foulds" (7), and she has been intimately connected to the play since its inception: "these fifteene weekes / (So long as since the plot was but an *embrion*) / Haue I, with burning lights, mixt vigilant thoughts, / In expectation of this hated play" (14–17). She holds out her snakes to the players and "poet-apes" in the audience: "come, and eate, / And while the squeez'd juice flowes in your blacke jawes, / Helpe me to damne the Authour. . . . choose / Out of my longest vipers, to sticke downe / In your deep throats; and let the heads come forth / At your deep mouthes" (44–51). Jonson aggressively shoves the snakes down his enemies' throats, but the Envy, violence, and hideousness are supposed to be theirs, directed against the innocent playwright.[90]

Envy is foiled by the scene, set in Rome and hence supposedly immune to the sort of topical reading *Poetaster* in fact invites (and receives, both from its contemporary audience and from the looniest branch of Shakespeare criticism), and is foiled again by the calm of the audience; but before she can sink out of sight she is clobbered by

share the thematic issue of the place of the literary man in society, the question being what the market value of a university education was (see especially Part 1 of *The Return*, Act III). The social basis of the university production was quite different, however, and the situation of the London theaters is viewed from a distance, if not a comfortable distance (Part 2 of *The Return*, IV.3 and 4, are about the theater hiring – and humiliating – University wits). When the news of the War reaches "Elsinore" (*Hamlet* II.2) it is the rivalry of the *theaters* that the players talk about. In *Poetaster* Jonson also notes the economic difficulties of the men's companies, and cites the War as a way of winning back an audience. In this sense to talk of "the management" is misleading. The public may have enjoyed the prospect of its fickle favor making or breaking one company or another, but this very power would confirm it *as* a theater-going public, a player in the competition. For an interesting reading of *Hamlet* in the context of the War of the Theaters, see Joseph F. Loewenstein, "Plays Agonistic and Competitive: The Textual Approach to Elsinore," *Renaissance Drama* n.s. 19 (1988), 63–96.

[89] Bradbrook, *The Rise of the Common Player*, p. 275. She is speaking of the university drama as well as of the boys' theaters in London. In his "Apologetical Dialogue" Jonson turns away from the War and the buzzing theatrical situation it represents to announce that he is working on, precisely, a tragedy.

[90] Jonson's aggression toward his audience is a major theme of Sweeney's book, though he does not read Envy's prologue in particular depth.

an armed *Prologue;* know, 'tis a dangerous age:
Wherein, who writes, had need present his *Scenes*
Fortie-fold proofe against the coniuring meanes
Of base detractors, and illiterate apes,
That fill vp roomes in faire and formall shapes.
("The third sounding. PROLOGVE." 6–10)

The materials of Jonson's other inductions are here, but the lurid psychic coloring of the allegory heavily overlays the social setting and disrupts the economy of relations with the audience. The strategy of divide and conquer is replaced by simple defiance. It is difficult to move about gracefully in civil society in heavy armor, and armor-plating the scenes of a play tends to keep the audience out.

In any case the problem of the poet's relation to society and especially the theater had become so central that the induction could no longer contain it. The body of the play is given over to this theme, and Envy immediately reappears as the first word of the poem Ovid is composing at the play's opening (a translation of Ovid's Elegy I.15), which is a defence of poetry. In spite of its poor social reputation poetry brings eternal fame, though the poem recognizes that the contradiction can be costly and may well only be resolved posthumously. Recitation of the poem is interrupted by Envy's representatives, Ovid Senior, enraged that his son is at work on a play for the common players, the Tribune Lupus and the skeldering Captain Tucca (either of whom may have informed Ovid Senior of his son's activity).[91] Ovid Junior is thus beset by an alliance of forces opposed to theater.

The father objects because his son, a gentleman (though a younger son without an income), is being corrupted by association with socially inferior players who, he believes, are using him parasitically: "What? shall I haue my sonne a stager now? an enghle for players? a gull? a rooke? a shot-clogge? to make suppers, and be laught at?" (I.2.15–17). The situation is reminiscent of Knowell Sr. condemning his son's interest in poetry in *Every Man In,*[92] but the association with the common stage makes the prejudice and the tone much more vehement.

Lupus objects to the players on political grounds, as did the Aldermen of London, whom he clearly represents: "they will rob vs, vs, that are magistrates, of our respect, bring vs vpon their stages, and make vs ridiculous to the plebeians; they will play you, or me, the wisest men they can come by still; me: only to bring vs in contempt with the vulgar, and make vs cheape" (I.2.39–44). The theme of authority nervous about a subversive art will be amplified as

[91] Both the recitation of the poem on Envy and the interruption will be echoed in V.2 when Lupus breaks in on Virgil's reading of the allegorical description of Fame in the *Aeneid.*

[92] Herford and Simpson were so convinced that Jonson's own problems with his bricklaying stepfather were expressed in Ovid Sr.'s oppression of his son that they make the connection three times, 1, p. 6; 1, p. 429; and again in 9, p. 538.

Lupus persecutes Horace, and as Caesar – the other heavy father of the play – banishes Ovid for his parody banquet of the gods (in costumes borrowed from Histrio's theater company), and for his illicit courtship of the Emperor's daughter. Tucca picks up on both these points, though it is clear that he represents neither the social nor the political interests of the ruling class but its vices (in particular his own). "An honest decayed commander, cannot skelder, cheat, nor be seene in a bawdie house, but he shall be straight in one of their wormewood *comoedies*" (I.2.49–52).

Ovid denies involvement with the common players:

> I am not knowne vnto the open stage,
> Nor doe I traffique in their *theaters*.
> Indeed, I doe acknowledge, at request
> Of some neere friends, and honorable *Romanes,*
> I haue begunne a *poeme* of that nature.
> (I.2.63–7)

"Poem" was the word Jonson used, a bit ostentatiously, for his plays, and it is hard not to see here a fantasy of what Jonson would have liked his relation to the stage to have been – if not never actually to come on the boards, at least to have his art spring from the request of honorable friends rather than from the "traffique" of the theaters.

This denial ends the association of Ovid with the theater, if it does not stop the tirade about the penury and disgrace to which poetry brings its professors. Ovid still needs to find social support for his art, though the issue is not put starkly in exactly these terms. There is no hint of professionalism about him, as there is about Virgil and Horace, whom Mecoenas supports. Ovid has every reason to regard a society that denies the value of poetry with the baleful eye of the familiar Elizabethan malcontent, but he merely wishes plaintively for a world in which men's eyes are more dazzled by knowledge than by gold or titles. We will see him try the usual array of possibilities: studying law as his father wishes, visiting a citizen household in the exploitative gentlemanly manner, taking his chances at Court. This is very much a city comedy situation, but Ovid never turns into a scheming and predatory gallant in need of securing his status like a Middleton character, or for that matter like Quarlous and Winwife of *Bartholomew Fair*. Nor is he subjected to the picaresque adventures in unemployment of the heroes of the Parnassus plays. The instability of his social situation doubtless informs the erotic and imaginative disorders which lead to the catastrophic banquet – surely Caesar does not appreciate his daughter's affair with a penniless poet – but most of the critics of the play interpret his failings on the more elevated moral plane.

The cynics are Lupus and Tucca, who, as they second Ovid Senior's advice to study law, demonstrate their nouveau riche fantasies of what the law can bring: Legal success requires neither rank nor merit, only plodding and impudence (I.2.120–8). Ovid has fancy social connections (Caesar's daughter is in love with him, and his father points out that his companions Tibullus, Gallus, and Propertius are gentlemen of means) and his social life is a version of the ideal society based on a happy relation of rank and merit which will be more fully expressed in Caesar's patronage of Virgil. But there the relation is sealed by political power; here it is fugitive from Caesar's authority, and from Ovid Senior's, finding refuge in the fashionable end of civil society, where, however, it brushes up against, and employs for its amusement, the poetaster and fop Crispinus, the climbing citizen wife Chloe, and even Tucca. Ovid's friends Tibullus and Cornelius Gallus are ranked in his Elegy among the immortal poets, but we see them hanging out with him as gallants in the city comedy environment as if there were no more interesting place on earth to be. This is the society of Wellbred and Knowell, enlarged and glorified. The plot connections between the group of courtiers and the citizens are adventitious and never very important, leading some to think the city comedy materials irrelevant, but surely they map the ground on which poetry might be planted, an urban setting for urbane wit.[93]

Crispinus, the "poetaster" of the title, extends Ovid's social career downward. His path crosses Ovid's at the house of Chloe and Albius, where he instructs her in the manners of the aristocracy, and sings, apparently very pleasantly, for the assembled company. Here we see poetry and song as social arts, and the ambience is attractive enough, though here as everywhere there is competition. The famous singer Hermogenes coyly refuses to sing, so the company encourages Crispinus to provoke his rivalry – "O, this contention is excellent," says Gallus (II.2.154). Crispinus decides to pick up the trappings of a poet for their social cachet, to help him seduce Chloe. At the next gathering at her house he sings a lyric he has stolen from Horace, commencing the open hostilities between the poets and the poetasters (IV.3.52 ff.).

First, however (Act III.1), he torments Horace with his adulation, in a scene paralleling Act I: Again a poet is interrupted in the course of composing a poem. Here the problem is not a society that rejects poetry but one that degrades it, making it a mere commodity in the game of social ostentation (Crispinus is on his way to a broker's to rent a poet's gown) or a sleazy career opportunity. Crispinus recognizes Horace in the street as someone Mecoenas favors, and greets him, "How far'st thou sweete man? frolicke? rich? gallant? ha?" Horace replies, "Not greatly gallant, sir, like my fortunes; well" (III.1.14–16). As Jonson's projection, Horace (like Crites) remains middle class, albeit of a sublimed and noble cast. He is not a gallant himself, although as Crispinus insists on pointing out "thou art exceeding happy in thy friends and acquaintance; they are all most choice spirits, and of the first ranke of *Romanes:* I doe not know that *poet,* I protest, ha's vs'd his fortune more

---

[93] Herford and Simpson, Preface: "In addition Jonson has used once more certain stock situations and characters of his social satire, which had, so far as we can see, no personal, poetic, or historical relevance at all, but simply made for comic vivacity" (1, p. 421).

prosperously, then thou hast" (III.1.234–8). Horace finally blows up precisely when Crispinus suggests that Mecoenas' patronage can be gained by scheming, and that his circle is motivated by envy and competition – in other words, that it is like all other systems of patronage. Horace's anger is nobly provoked on his friend's behalf, but it is significant that this purity, of all others, is defended with violence.

The difference between poet and poetaster has so far been amply established without any reference to Crispinus' artistic abilities – it all has to do with the way the role of poet is played. Like Ovid, Horace is introduced to us entangled with his opposite; it is through the contrast that true values are revealed. Bourdieu explains this as inherent in the constitution of culture:

> The opposition between the "authentic" and the "imitation", "true" culture and "popularization", which maintains the game by maintaining belief in the absolute value of the stake, conceals a collusion that is no less indispensable to the production and reproduction of the *illusio,* the fundamental recognition of the cultural game and its stakes. Distinction and pretension, high culture and middle-brow culture – like, elsewhere, high fashion and fashion, haute coiffure and coiffure, and so on – only exist through each other, and it is the relation, or rather, the objective collaboration of their respective production apparatuses and clients which produces the value of culture and the need to possess it. It is in these struggles between objectively complicit opponents that the value of culture is generated, or, which amounts to the same thing, belief in the value of culture, interest in culture and the interest of culture – which are not self-evident, although one of the effects of the game is to induce belief in the innateness of the desire to play and the pleasure of playing. It is barbarism to ask what culture is for.[94]

If the whole structure of *Poetaster* demonstrates this point, Jonson is still very far from recognizing it – Bourdieu would say he "misrecognizes" it. It is this problem which he protests too much about, with constant strenuous declarations of independence and transcendence, ringing so false on an immediate emotional level that we are compelled to explore what is behind them.

At the moment the opposition of Horace and Crispinus is expressed rather calmly, without the violent symbolic antipathies of allegory, though Jonson will get to that, or with the violence of real life. (Jonson told Drummond "he had many quarrells with Marston beat him & took his Pistol from him, wrote his Poetaster on him" [*Conversations,* H&S I, line 284–5]). The opposition is a matter of comically exaggerated social discomfort, based on a horror of the banal that marks class distinctions. The contrast is precisely that between the petty bourgeoisie and the bourgeoisie in our day, and the bourgeoisie and the aristocracy in Jonson's: insecure ostentation and crude revelations of the material basis of things against "a sort of ostentatious discretion, sobriety and understatement, a refusal of everything which is 'showy', 'flashy' and pretentious, and which devalues itself by the very intention of distinction."[95]

---

[94] Bourdieu, p. 250.
[95] Ibid., p. 249.

We have to do here with classes defined by their relation to cultural rather than economic capital. As Bourdieu explains, cultural, social, and economic capital are defined differently and have a limited autonomy, though they are finally interdependent. Accumulating cultural capital, for instance, depends on a withdrawal from economic necessity, a withdrawal Jonson is always eager to emphasize.[96] The rates of conversion among these sorts of capital are always changing. Under the feudal system, for example, they were theoretically inconvertible. Jonson, as a humanist, militated for a high return on cultural capital. In his fable Horace and Virgil achieve a spectacular rate of conversion.

In spite of Crispinus' superior status – he is a gallant and Horace is not – Horace is in the superior position, with the connections and money Crispinus is actively seeking. But without any cultural capital to work with, Crispinus' trading in the literary marketplace is all based on his unimpressive stock of social capital, and is therefore fraudulent as well as pathetic. It is his lack of cultural capital that is emphasized. He parades his smatterings of everything, and serves as the intermediary to Chloe, who like Touchstone's Audrey has to be told what a poet is and how much he is worth on the market (compared, say, to a commander like Tucca, IV.3.50–1). The analogy of cultural to social and economic capital is close enough that all the forms of city comedy satire on social climbers can be brought into play.

Horace's economy thus maintains its air of austere mystery, while the mask of Crispinus' economy is torn off. Horace is freed from his torment when Crispinus is arrested for debt by the apothecary Minos. Such scenes, where the borrowed feathers of gallants are torn off, destroying their social pretensions, were popular in satiric comedy. Into this scene bursts Captain Tucca, the champion of false economies, who attempts to rescue Crispinus (whom he does not know, but he knows whose side he is on in this situation). Tucca's sword is taken away with risible ease, but he then displays his formidable talents as a fixer, patching things up between the gallant and the apothecary, extending credit and skeldering in all directions. Tucca is always working such deals. His *activity* is seldom remarked on because his talk is so astounding that it has monopolized critical attention; moreover his intriguing is so loosely related to the plot, or plots, that it does not call attention to itself. But Tucca is a very busy man – he is the only figure who runs through the whole play, turning up everywhere from Ovid's house to Chloe's and Caesar's. He is most at home, however, here in the street.

[96] Ovid makes the point at I.2.240–3: "would men learne but to distinguish spirits, / And set true difference twixt those jaded wits / That runne a broken passe for common hire, / And the high raptures of a happy *Muse,* / Borne on the wings of her immortall thought." Jonson's famous poverty, his necessities, do not contradict this principle – they make of him an early bohemian martyr for art ("He disuaded me from Poetrie, for that she beggered him, when he might have been a rich lawer, Physitian or Marchant," as he told Drummond: lines 615–16).

From Ovid to Crispinus marks one social descent; Crispinus falling into the hands of Tucca marks another, into the urban demimonde. It is precisely here that the theater reappears. Tucca hails the actor Histrio as he tries to sneak by, asserting his class superiority with insults that recall his speeches denouncing players in Act I: "no respect to men of worship, you slaue? What, you are proud, you rascal, are you proud? ha? you grow rich, doe you?" (III.4.123–5). He reminds him of the old days when Histrio was a fiddler eager for the Captain's business. It becomes clear that all this is a way of maintaining leverage within an ongoing relationship. Tucca's praise/abuse style always keeps class relations volatile; manipulating class prejudices is one of his principal methods of buoying himself up socially. Soon Tucca is making Histrio agree to give a supper for him. "There are some of you plaiers honest gent'man-like scoundrels, and suspected to ha' some wit, as well as your *poets;* both at drinking, and breaking of iests: and are companions for gallants. A man may skelder yee, now and then, of halfe a dozen shillings, or so" (III.4.152–6).

He introduces Crispinus to Histrio as a gentleman of good family who "pens high, loftie, in a new stalking straine," both of which facts are more than he knows, and tells Histrio to give him forty shillings as an advance on a play. (*Shillings* – this was the standard fee the London theaters paid; Tucca will shift back to sesterces as he gets Minos to invest more money in Crispinus on the strength of this prospective deal, "Suffer him not to droop, in prospect of a player, a rogue, a stager.") Tucca intends the sort of alliance of gentlemanly author and common players that had made the London theaters – "If he pen for thee once, thou shalt not need to trauell, with thy pumps full of grauell, any more, after a blinde iade and a hamper" (III.4.167–9).

Tucca's talk swings to other theatrical topics. He would like to bring his cocatrice to a bawdy play, but, in a clear reference to the Jonsonian comical satires playing at the private theaters, "they say, you ha' nothing but *humours, reuells,* and *satyres,* that girde, and fart at the time, you slaue." Histrio protests, "No, I assure you Captaine, not wee, They are on the other side of *Tyber*" (III.4.190–4). As in Act I, Tucca's concern with the genre of satire is personal: "I heare, you'll bring me o' the stage there"; and he threatens them if they do. He has his pages audition (thinking to rent them to Histrio as boy actors) in a sampler of overblown styles. And he inquires after the poor poet Demetrius, who has been standing silently by, promising to make a gathering for him so he can get some decent clothes if he is really as good as advertised.

By the end of the scene Tucca has offered Histrio his countenance if his company lacks a patron, for which service he expects two shares. He does not really have the status necessary for that role, but it is a sign of how multifaceted and intimate are his relations with the theater. Before he makes this offer he is told Demetrius has been hired to write a satire on Horace – not that anyone has anything against Horace, but "it will get vs a huge deale of money" (III.4.27). Tucca gets Crispinus in on this project and later takes over the direction of it himself ("I'le giue you instructions: I'le bee your intelligencer, we'll all ioyne, and hang vpon him like so many horse-leaches, the plaiers and all. We shall sup together, soone; and then wee'll conspire, i'faith" IV.3.125–9). Tucca thus becomes the impresario who joins the gentlemanly coterie playwright Crispinus (who is John Marston) with the "dresser of plaies about the town" from the popular theater across the Tiber, Demetrius (who is Thomas Dekker), to create a satire on Horace, who is Jonson. The play will be staged by the Chamberlain's Men as *Satiromastix,* and it was wind of this project that led Jonson to mount his preemptive strike, *Poetaster.*

So the generative, structuring opposition of the play is Horace versus the forces organized by Tucca, and one can argue that this is the principal thematic opposition as well. Jonson is setting himself up on the model of the great Roman satirist, a public moralist enshrined by the state and practicing a socially necessary and strictly principled art. Tucca is not only one of the guilty who is touchy about having his vices exposed, a dangerous object of satire, he is also the rival satirist, or rather the motive force behind a bad kind of satire, embedded in a nasty society, malicious, envious, libelous, mercenary, lewd, and snarling. In a subsequent scene (not in the Quarto edition) Horace makes the distinction to the lawyer Trebatius, and speaks favorably of the "iust decree" banning lewd and libelous satire, perhaps having in mind the decree under which Marston's satires had just been publicly burned (III.5.127–36). There is also a moral contrast of personalities. Against the perfect, coherent, and transcendent souls of Horace and Virgil (Horace says Virgil is "most seuere / In fashion, and collection of himselfe, / And then as cleare, and confident, as IOVE" V.1.105–07) is poised the double-faced Tucca, whose punishment in the final judgment scene will be to have a double-faced vizard put over his head – Tucca praises and abuses simultaneously, defends and subverts class lines, organizes the world of letters and slanders it, skelders and offers credit.

Socially *Poetaster* presents an unhappy polarization, with the middle ground of the ideal community of poets giving way, endangered from several directions. Horace shows up at Chloe's but seeing Crispinus there immediately leaves, driven out of his social space. Histrio plans to put Horace's gallant friends in his play, too, and they are caught in the ruin of Ovid's career when Caesar crushes his banquet at court, sending the citizens scurrying back to the City. Horace berates Histrio and Lupus for bringing down Caesar's wrath on the banquet: To curry favor they "prey vpon the life of innocent mirth, / And harmelesse pleasures, bred, of noble wit" (IV.7.41–2). He denounces informers as "the moths, and scarabes of a state; / The bane of empires; and the dregs of courts," but they are a threat to civil society too, like the Pooly and Parrot of whom Jonson had personal experience, who would affright the liberty of Jonson's company in "Inviting a Friend to Supper" (*Epigrams* CI, 36).

Horace looks on unhappily but can do nothing. Caesar pulls Gallus and Tibullus from the wreckage, because they are poets who can serve the state, and with Mecoenas they await Virgil, who is coming from the country, a model of virtue with no visible ties to the city. An austere company of poets is thus gathered around Caesar, amidst echoing stony rhetoric. He wants only poets who "can becalme / All sea of humour, with the marble *trident* / Of their strong spirits" (IV.6.75–7), so their poetry "can so mould *Rome,* and her monuments, / Within the liquid marble of her lines, / That they shall stand fresh, and miraculous, / Euen, when they mixe with innouating dust" (V.1.21–4). Horace meets Caesar's austerity with a severity of his own. When Caesar makes Crispinus' mistake and suggests that Horace as the poorest of the poets would be most likely to envy or detract from Virgil, Horace sharply rebukes him:

> CAESAR speakes after common men, in this,
> To make a difference of me, for my poorenesse:
> As if the filth of pouertie sunke as deepe
> Into a knowing spirit, as the bane
> Of riches doth, onto an ignorant soule. . . .
> But knowledge is the *nectar,* that kepes sweet
> A perfect soule, euen in this graue of sinne;
> And for my soule, it is as free, as CAESARS"
> (V.1.79–90)

Caesar accepts the rebuke: "for thy sake, wee'll put no difference more / Betweene the great, and good, for being poore." He accepts the equality of a poet's pure soul, setting Virgil's chair above his own. The violation of decorum is insisted upon, as Caesar tells Virgil

> "Vertue, without presumption, place may take
> "Aboue best Kings, whom onely she should make.
> VIRG. It will be thought a thing ridiculous
> To present eyes, and to all future times
> A grosse vntruth; that any *poet* (void
> Of birth, or wealth, or temporall dignity)
> Should, with *decorum,* transcend CAESARS chaire.
> "Poore vertue rais'd, high birth and wealth set vnder,
> "Crosseth heau'ns courses, and makes worldlings wonder.
> CAES. The course of heauen, and fate it selfe, in this
> Will CAESAR crosse; much more all worldly custome.
> (V.2.26–36)

The monarch's prerogative to alter the social order he presides over made him a very popular figure at the conclusion of comedies, but he rarely displaces himself to pay tribute to anyone's cultural capital. As a bid for royal favor this play is even less cannily politic than *Cynthia's Revels,* since it seems to accept patronage only on its own stringent terms. Jonson's severe classlessness intends no threat to the social order, only to open up a place for itself at the top, where it becomes an independent source of values – but this in itself was an extraordinary request.

This was the imaginative solution of a desperate man, fed up with the theater and looking elsewhere for patronage. Jonson found his Mecoenas (the next news we hear of him, from Manningham's diary for February 1602, is that "Ben Jonson the poet now lives upon one Townesend, and scornes the world" [H&S 1, 30]), and then his Caesar, as commissions to provide royal entertainments began to arrive. He was ready to rupture his social relations with the theater.

Poetaster provoked a storm of abuse: "citizens of standing, professional persons, lawyers and soldiers as well as players, indignantly protested against the outrage offered to their orders and to their persons" (H&S, I, p. 416). These were all offended special interest groups, but there was a more general offense in Jonson's attitude of turning his back on society as a whole, and this provided the natural basis for the counterattack.

The strategy of Dekker's Satiromastix, which recycles the figures of Horace, Tucca, Crispinus, and Demetrius, while shifting the setting to a vaguely archaic England, is to plunge Horace/Jonson back into society, showing his social relations; showing them in a highly unflattering light, certainly, but the central point is that Horace has a problem with admitting what they in fact were and conducting them in good faith. Everything mystified in Poetaster is demystified here, beginning with the discovery of Horace composing in his study (264). The situation parodies the scenes in Poetaster in which Ovid and Horace are similarly discovered, and is even closer to the "Apologetical Dialogue" Jonson appended to his play, which begins with visitors overhearing the author's sublime musings and ends when they are asked to leave because he is being swept away by inspiration. The lines Dekker's Horace is writing are about inspiration, but soon he has to hunt for a rhyme: "Immortal name, game, dame, tame, lame, lame, lame" (277). Writing poetry is work.

So is running a literary career. The entrance of Asinius Bubo, a gentleman gull under the spell of Horace's literary glamor who acts as his sidekick, agent, and intelligencer, is the occasion for exposing the mechanics of marketing the poetic product and the poet himself as a social commodity. Bubo is asked to praise the epithalamium Horace is writing on contract, and to applaud the points Horace scored in an ordinary when he recited his Odes and put down a gull who mewed at them. Later he will be sent off to distribute various papers, epigrams on Tucca and a letter to a gallant who was smitten by Horace's brilliance the night before. Horace has a stock of such letters to send to "any fresh suited gallant" the morning after such meetings, before he is out of bed, to amaze him with "the sodaine flash of my writing" (960–76).

Horace is always calculating his base of support, glorying in his reputation, figuring out how to throw his weight around. When Bubo reports that Tucca has been railing against him, Horace replies "I am too well ranckt Asinius to be stab'd with his dudgion wit," and threatens him with an epigram. When told of Crispinus and Demetrius' plan to bring him onto the stage as a bricklayer he relies on his organized power in the theater: "I can bring (& that they quake at) a prepar'd troope of gallants, who for my sake shal distaste euery vnsalted line, in the fly-blowne Comedies. Asi. Nay that's certaine, ile bring 100. gallants of my ranke" (408–13). At the end of the play, as Horace is made to take oaths of good behavior, he is accused of making the playwright's versions of the moves Jonson attacked in his inductions:

> you shall not sit in a Gallery, when your Comedies and Enterludes haue entred their Actions, and there make vile and bad faces at euerie lyne, to make Sentlemen haue an eye to you, and to make Players afraide to take your part. . . . Besides, you must forsweare to venter on the stage, when your Play is ended, and to exchange curtezies, and complements with Gallants in the lordes roomes, to make all the house rise vp in Armes, and to cry that's Horace, that's he, that's he, that's he, that pennes and purges Humours and diseases.
>
> (2607–16)

The audience would know how much truth there was in these charges. The audience's knowledge is kept in play: Tucca's claim that in the days when Jonson was an unsuccessful actor playing Hieronimo he borrowed a gown from a player and returned it lousy (631–6) is the sort of thing that would be talked over later – who knew the story?

The point that Jonson's literary talents could be rented is indisputable. In "To Fine Grand" (*Epigrams* LXXIII) Jonson revenges himself on a deadbeat by recounting the literary trinkets for which he has not been paid: a jest, tales, a song, a Greek poesy for a ring, a charm, a couple of anagrams, "an epitaph on my lord's cock." Tucca rubs the point in, forcing Horace to accept cast-off clothing from Crispinus and to sit up and beg for small change (610–72). This is not simple payment, either, though Tucca associates it with the payment for the epithalamium. The cast satin is taken in settlement of his dispute with Crispinus and Demetrius, and the "presse-money" is a sign of Tucca's patronage. Horace is free neither from the obligation to write for money nor from the social relations that go with it. When Horace is hired to rail against baldness at a party (as part of a rival suitors plot, c.1400 ff.) what is being bought is not alienable labor but the poet.

The exaggerated humiliations we see Horace endure are Jonson's punishment. What was held against him was not that he was a working professional – Dekker could hardly reproach him for that – but his resentment of the conditions of his work, which vents itself as back-stabbing of his patrons, an intellectual condescension to his social superiors masked by hypocrisy. It also vents itself as denial of real motivation, obsessively hidden in great clouds of high-minded rhetoric. One does not like to believe that Jonson was the liar Horace is, but Dekker certainly exposes the bad faith of the protestations of *Poetaster*.

There are three great scenes of humiliation as well as many lesser barbs. One is at the hands of Tucca, discussed above. The second is at a party. His slandering is exposed again, but the humiliation runs to a more general and personal judgment of Horace's social undesirability. He is made to overhear a lady harping on his bad face, his nasal voice, and the way he "talkes and randes" like a madman (1893 ff). When he is flushed out of hiding the assembled company decides to toss him in a blanket, a common shame punishment in early modern England. But first there is an informal trial, in which Horace, still trying to climb, claims that all the people he has attacked "enuy me / Because I hold more worthy company" (2015–17), and Crispinus and Demetrius make serious and high-minded reply to the effect that they do not envy Horace his success or his talent; but no one likes his obnoxiousness, and when Tucca asks for a verdict it is "Omnes. Blancket" (2053). This is reminiscent of Marston organizing a social consensus against Jonson in the prologue to *What You Will,* but without the element of class conspiracy – Horace's social liabilities would be liabilities in any setting.

In the event Horace is not tossed in a blanket but taken to Court for another trial scene, the final humiliation. (The official setting echoes *Poetaster,* though Dekker's King is no argument for absolutism – the satire on Horace coexists with a romantic plot that turns on the King's *droit de seigneur* over a courtier's bride and the successful resistance to it.) The conditions imposed on Horace have less to do with his art, which is always and genuinely respected, than with his manners in society. Horace/Jonson should rise, but he should not act like a social climber, using devious and hypocritical means. Again manipulation or resentment of his patrons is a central issue. His patrons are by definition his social superiors, but the emphasis is not on this social scandal but on Horace's own bad feelings and the bad manners in which they result. It is Horace who cannot stop thinking about class, not Dekker.

Satiromastix is an immeasurable help in understanding Jonson, dovetailing with his own work and completing the picture. It is hard not to believe that the accusations are truer than Jonson's denials, and this reader at least finds it easier to be affectionate toward the sane and genial *Satiromastix* than toward *Poetaster,* so stiff with ambitions and anxieties. Dekker was the first to admit that Jonson was the greater artist, and the psychological problems that left Jonson so open to satire reflect a serious historical problem: how the serious literary figure is to support himself. Jonson tried all the options, from the theater through the aristocratic patronage network to the Court. He had considerable success at all of them, all of them imposed indignities on him, and all of them failed him in the end. His career outside the drama is outside the purview of this study; it is now perhaps conventional wisdom to say the problem was soluble only by Dryden's time, when a better developed print market could support the dignity of the independent bourgeois artist.

The very unhappiness of *Poetaster* helped to define that dignity and independence, as – more successfully – Jonson manages to define the classless, free, and urbane values of high culture in "An Epistle answering to One that Asked to be Sealed of the Tribe of Ben" (*Underwoods* XLVII), even as it is clear that the subterranean emotional agenda of the poem is his struggle to deal with his bad emotions following Inigo Jones' victory at Court. The opening lines are "Men that are safe, and sure, in all they do / Care not what trials they are put to" – the familiar perfection of soul entailing invincibility. The ritual disconnection of values from contingent power relations is meant to purify Jonson's personality by sublimating his ego, and to elevate the Tribe of Ben (and defuse its critics) by removing it from a context of competition, making it into something more than a literary clique or personality cult.

Here as elsewhere Jonson's solutions do not appear bourgeois. The work of this poem is to replace a bad sealing of bad men "that never yet did friend, or friendship seek, / But for a sealing" (14–15), where the sealing is a legal contract which is all that holds an atomized society together, a minimal fixing of the ambient bad faith and lies, with the good sealing of the final line ("Now stand, and then, / Sir, you are sealed of the tribe of Ben"), which has a sacramental quality, like dubbing a knight. In *Poetaster* Jonson is clearly throwing his lot in with absolutism.

On the other hand one should not underestimate the tenacity with which Jonson stuck to a middle-class identity. That identity was a very personal thing and stuck to him – he probably could not have shed it if he tried. But there was an element of active resistance in his attachment to his poor scholar's garb; he invested in it as a public persona more than he needed to, with a pride that enlarged it, creating a dignified cultural identity not actively citizenly, but something other than aristocratic or that of a gentleman servingman imitating the style of the Court. Jonson did not rush to cash in his cultural capital for the established social goods. He acquired gentlemanly status in an appropriate way when the universities awarded him honorary Masters degrees. (He is described as a "gentleman" in the legal records from the Roe suit in 1610. H&S I, p. 228.) When James wanted to make him a knight in 1621 (an expensive honor James tried to impose on anyone he could) he declined (H&S I, p. 87), but he did become free of the city by officially joining his stepfather's guild, and was made City Chronologer as well as poet laureate.

I will have more to say shortly about the class character of Jonson's sensibility, but I do not want to reduce the War of the Theaters to individual psychological issues. I would rather emphasize that it is no coincidence that by the end of the War of the Theaters the contemporary London setting, the audience, and the figure of the playwright had all been newly defined and were newly visible to one another. These three elements had been provoking and developing each other in a three-way dialectic, finding their bearings by triangulation. The psychological and moral flaws of the satirist may have been brought into focus by the move onto the stage, as Kernan says,[97] but so were his social ones; beyond his flaws, once the satirist became visible he had to be located somewhere in the social field, as a combatant, the exponent of an immanent and likely partisan social power. The figure had to be politicized and disputed.

[97] Alvin Kernan, *The Cankered Muse: Satire of The English Renaissance,* Yale Studies in English, vol. 142 (New Haven: Yale Univ. Press, 1959).

This analysis of the social conditions of the theatrical situation brought with it a self-reflexive thickening of the dramatic medium, to the point of personal exasperation, the near stasis of plot, and inhibition of dramatic potential, whatever the extraordinary gains that were being made. By the time Jonson wrote *Volpone* he was more secure socially and emotionally. He had transcendentally died out of the visible role of satirist, and the audience was no longer directly confronted, a formal metamorphosis that is a central concern in recent books by John G. Sweeney, Peter Womack, and Alexander Leggatt. When he returned to the London scene his dramatic realism was more transparent. Approaching the scene with the same motives and most of the same topics, he developed a new depth of vision made possible when the skirmishing at the boundary of the stage quieted down.

EPICOENE

In *Epicoene* (1609 or early 1610), as Dryden famously noticed, Jonson "described the conversation of gentlemen in the persons of True-Wit, and his friends, with more gaiety, air, and freedom, than in the rest of his comedies."[98] He draws very close to the sensibility of the young gentlemen gallants, who play the normative role of Wellbred and Edward Knowell in *Every Man In,* a role that had been shouldered aside in the intervening plays by the heavy normative apparatus of *Every Man Out* and the Jonsonian alter egos Asper, Crites, and Horace. The element of moral equivocation is still in evidence, and the play opens on that note, as Truewit visits Clerimont in his lodgings, which have something of the epicurean hothouse atmosphere of Volpone's: "what, betweene his mistris abroad, and his engle at home, high fare, soft lodging, fine clothes, and his fiddle; hee thinkes the houres ha' no wings, or the day no post-horse" (I.1.24–7). Truewit makes speeches in the mode of Christian Stoicism, but they are dialogized even more thoroughly and intimately than Knowell Senior's: "Foh, thou hast read PLVTARCHS moralls, now, or some such tedious fellow," Clerimont tells him, "and it showes so vilely with thee: 'Fore God, 'twill spoile thy wit vtterly. Talke me of pinnes, and feathers, and ladies, and rushes, and such things: and leaue this *Stoicitie* alone, till thou mak'st sermons" (I.1.62–6).

We are not asked to take this exchange as a serious debate, much less as the speeches of a hardened sinner rejecting good counsel; Clerimont and Truewit are playing with attitudes. Truewit has already dropped his stoical mask once: to the question "Why, what should a man do?" he replies that he should lay bets, spend loudly, and visit the ladies. "These be the things, wherein your fashionable men exercise themselues, and I for companie" (I.1.39–41). Clerimont briefly rehearses the standard *carpe diem* argument that the time for moralizing is when age has lost youth's capacity, but again the tone is of

[98] "An Essay of Dramatic Poesy," in *Selected Works,* ed., William Frost, 2d ed. (New York: Holt, Rinehart and Winston, 1971), p. 469.

badinage, not profound conviction. The contradictory arguments make clear that these are men who have heard what can be said about how to conduct oneself, from the gravely moral to the strictly fashionable, and they do not particularly need more advice. The penumbra of moral argument merely emphasizes the fine-grained and confident secularism of the position they occupy, a secularism that does not deny other dimensions but conspires to get along without them, to paraphrase Raymond Williams. Dramatically the irony in Truewit's "and I for companie," and Clerimont's stylistic objection to Truewit's moralizing sound decisive; they both turn on the mood and style of one's manners. The real question – of the whole play as well as its opening – is indeed in what style and to what extent one wants to join in with the rest of society.

There is no neat answer to this question, just as there is no neat synthesis of epicurianism and Christian stoicism – or of the correlate tension in Jonson between a centered self and the noise of the world, or of the humanists' debate over whether one could serve the world or a prince without losing oneself.[99] The play symmetrically punishes Morose, whose self is so centered he has become an antisocial monster, and the fops Amorous La Foole and Jack Daw, who are mere reflexes of social chatter with no real selves at all. But the direction is always outward, into society. Clerimont is coaxed out of his den, and Dauphine falls in love with *all* the Collegiate ladies, who represent society, and are clearly understood by the three gallants to be as empty and worthless as Daw and La Foole:

> all their actions are gouerned by crude opinion, without reason or cause; they know not why they doe any thing: but as they are inform'd, beleeue, iudge, praise, condemne, loue, hate, and in aemulation one of another, doe all these things alike. Onely, they haue a naturall inclination swayes 'hem generally to the worst, when they are left to themselues. But, pursue it, now thou hast 'hem.
>
> (IV.6.64–71)

If this is less than glorious, there is not much evidence Jonson seriously condemns his gallants for having a go at the ladies.

The moral situation may be dialoguized, but the social one is more exclusive than in any of Jonson's other plays. The setting is restricted to the fashionable world of the Strand, a world that (as Stone says) was just achieving the apparent autonomy of a fashionable *monde*. L. C. Knights' medieval economic morality occasionally peeks out to interrogate the social basis of this autonomy, as when La Foole proclaims himself a rack-renter, or Truewit in his tirade against marriage talks conventionally of acres being sold to dress up a worthless woman. The restriction of social purview is one of the grounds for claiming this play as the beginning of the comedy of manners.

[99] See, *inter alia*, David Kay, "Jonson's Urbane Gallants: Humanistic Contexts for *Epicoene*," *Huntington Library Quarterly*, 39 (1975), 251–66.

There are still gradations and instabilities of rank, but they are much finer. Everyone is an aristocrat or his servant. Clerimont's elegant page has his own sexual career with the Collegiate ladies, and even the barber Cutbeard has enough Latin to pose as a Doctor of Canon Law. Only the Otters have the aura of Jonson's earlier social climbers. They are a great deal like the jeweler Albius and Chloe of *Poetaster*. She is "the rich *China*-woman, that the courtiers visited so often, that gaue the rare entertainment" (I.4.27–8), proud of her kinship with a gallant (Sir Amorous La Foole), and like Chloe taken up by her superiors, being a probationer of the College. Also like Chloe she is contemptuous of her socially inferior husband, with his rough popular festive culture, redolent of the bear-baiting pit ("Neuer a time, that the courtiers, or collegiates come to the house, but you make it a *shrovetuesday!* I would haue you get your *whitsontide*-velvet-cap, and your staffe i' your hand, to intertaine 'hem," III.1.5–9); but he understands, correctly, that all he has to sell is his "humour," and that the gallants will want to see his famous collection of drinking cups.

The fops are real knights, and the gallants and even Morose have connections with the Court. The ladies' College is "an order betweene courtiers, and country-madames, that live from their husbands" (I.1.75–6), socially intermediate between the Court and the rural gentry. Their *"hermaphroditicall* authoritie" may reflect the new independence of women in the new social formation of the urbanized gentry – women had used to be left at home when the men came up to London in term time, but now their presence was beginning to be important in defining polite society.

Thus this society, like that of Restoration comedy but unlike that in Jonson's other plays, appears to be relatively uniform in its class character, autonomous, and stable. In the absence of the scramble for social status and wealth a number of the features I have been describing in Jonson's other plays recede in importance or, like fashion, are transformed. Clothes are talked about much less, despite – or rather because of – the fact that we can assume everyone is fashionably dressed. The real gentlemen talk about clothes more than Daw and his like but their conversations consist neither in display nor complaining about newfangledness, but in serious discussions of the arts of social appearance. No one needs the services of a professional instructor, though the College serves to regulate manners, and when Dauphine decides he wants to conquer the ladies he recognizes that there is an art to it which he can learn from Truewit: "How cam'st thou to study these creatures so exactly? I would thou would'st make me a proficient" (IV.1.53–4). Truewit's advice owes more to the Ovidian art of love than to the courtesy manuals. Money is hardly ever mentioned, because no one needs to cadge it or exchange it for social status (or vice versa). Dauphine's inheritance is at stake and Morose indulges himself in imagining the shifts Dauphine will be put to when he is cut off (II.5.100 ff.), but we never see any such thing and the relation of this central plot to the themes and materials of the play are remarkably abstract. The *Epicoene* world is luxurious, with fancy meals and coaches, but there is nothing fantastic about its luxury as there is in *Volpone* or *The Alchemist,* and neither money nor luxury is connected with the disruptive energies of capitalism as they are in *The Alchemist* and *The Devil is an Ass.*

At issue is the definition and consolidation of polite social space, and, most of all, a competition for sway within it. There is a politics of factions: the Collegiates, however faithless they are to one another, still gain strength by collectively crying "downe, or vp, what they like, or dislike in a braine, or a fashion" (I.1.78–9) and entertain the Wits and Braveries, who are fashionable cliques of gallants. Their arrogation of a "most masculine, or rather *hermaphroditicall* authoritie" sets the ground for the war of the sexes that will be fought out in Restoration drama. Though there is little social climbing in the sense of crossing status barriers, there is a great deal of personal ostentation, of which the clearest examples are the fops Daw and especially La Foole, who shouts his invitations from an upstairs window so the whole street will know with whom he is dining.[100]

The stake in this game is the social commodity, reputation. The ladies cry reputations down or up, and the gallants plot to destroy them (those of Morose, Epicoene, Daw, La Foole) or to create them (Truewit is always staking his reputation on pulling off something, for example, building Dauphine's reputation with the ladies within a matter of hours). Maintaining a reputation is more complicated than learning the gestures a Sogliardo had to learn to get himself past the door of a fashionable ordinary. Reputations exist in a tightly knit social world, held together by gossip, and Jonson delivers such a world in *Epicoene,* as he never had before, and most brilliantly in Act I, where the expository work of introducing the main characters and themes is accomplished in that gentlemanly "air" Dryden liked so much: The air thickens into a new atmosphere, where the manner of what is said, the hints and assumptions, the character of a shared social life, are the real objects of representation. Jonson gets the conversation of gentlemen best in this play – and I think it must have been the first act Dryden was thinking of – because he gives them their own environment in which to be free and gay. The fictive world has a new density, because analysis is swallowed up in imitation of gentlemanly conversation;

---

[100] The fops of the exclusively aristocratic world of the Restoration stage are trying to climb into fashion and a personal reputation, but this struggle has been so completely detached from climbing in social status that they are no longer a threat. Robert B. Heilman can argue that

> Aside from being [morally] inferior, the fop is usually good-natured and even-tempered; so he is a pleasant fellow to have around in a society of tense competitors. . . .
> The vanity regularly attributed to the fop is his conviction that he has made it; he is beyond competition. He is a relaxed man, a pleasant relief in a Hobbesian world. *ELH 49* (1982), 391–2.

There is no such relaxation in Jonson's handling of the fops.

humors will still be displayed using the old techniques, but in the case of the gallants we share their company without disruptive objectification. The satiric objects, the fops and Collegiate ladies, occur naturally as features of the gentlemen's social network. There is none of the sense of foraging about the streets of London for entertaining specimens that we get in *Every Man In,* and *Every Man Out* looks socially unfocused in comparison, with its accidental collisions of dramatis personae on the road to London, and *Cynthia's Revels* (the other play restricted to the fashionable world) seems artificially constructed with its opposed sets of courtiers.

The setting for this initial free gentlemanly conversation is Clerimont's dressing room. *"He comes out making himselfe ready,"* followed by his boy. Many a Restoration comedy will follow Jonson's lead by beginning in a gallant's dressing room; it is the natural place for expository gossip, for the plotting of a social or erotic career, or for honest talk about social values. It is where one makes one's self ready to go out into society by constructing a public character, and as such is made to order for a dramatist's business.

The dressing room scene assumes people have a private side as well as a public social one, and that the relationship between them is comfortable. Jonson previously had taken us behind the scenes for satiric purposes only. The scene in Livia's dressing room in *Sejanus* (1603), where the murder of her husband is discussed along with her makeup, is full of deadly irony. When Jonson's maurauding dramatic eye tracks Bobadill to his lair in *Every Man In* (I.3) the intent is invasive; we intrude with Matthew at an unfashionable hour to find Bobadill asleep on a bench with the basin of last night's vomit beside him, and we watch him struggle with the incongruity of his gentlemanly pretensions and his poor lodgings at Cob the water-carrier's. The forms of gentlemanly life that have drifted down (or been snatched) from above bump uneasily against the brute facts of poverty and social stigma. By the end of the scene Bobadill has cadged a breakfast off Matthew and is launched again.

Clerimont can be seen in his dressing room because he has nothing to be ashamed of and is inwardly sound, to adopt the terms of his lovely lyric, which is appropriately placed in this scene:

> *Still to be neat, still to be drest,*
> *As, you were going to a feast;*
> *Still to be pou'dred, still perfum'd:*
> *Lady, it is to be presum'd,*
> *Though arts hid causes are not found,*
> *All is not sweet, all is not sound.*

Truewit responds that ladies should "paint and professe it. CLERIMONT. How, publiquely? TRV. The doing of it, not the manner: that must bee priuate. Many things, that seeme foule, i' the doing, doe please, done" (I.1.110–15). Those who profess to be fashionable similarly make it clear that the time and money have gone into their appearance, but keep the actual process mysterious. They make it clear that their company is exclusive, but mystify the principles of exclusion and do not like to show the act crudely.

Jonson's satire had been playing around these principles, exposing through his fools the side of the process that should be occluded. The surest sign of a fool in Jonson is generally that he does not know how to hide the preparations for social appearance. We must all look in the glass, but should not do so in public. Truewit argues for fashion, and for decorum; he thinks women should have dressing rooms, but we should not know when they are at work in them: "nor, when the dores are shut, should men bee inquiring, all is sacred within, then. Is it for vs to see their perrukes put on, their false teeth, their complexion, their eye-browes, their nails?" (I.1.116–19). But as he speaks a satiric note creeps into his voice – the list begins to resemble Otter's description of his wife being assembled from manufactures all over the city, and taking herself apart at night like a great German clock (IV.2.92 ff.). Truewit launches into a satiric anecdote:

> And a wise lady will keepe a guard alwaies vpon the place, that shee may doe things securely. I once followed a rude fellow into a chamber, where the poore madame, for haste, and troubled, snatch'd at her perruke, to couer her baldnesse: and put it on, the wrong way.
> CLE. Oh prodigie!
> TRV. And the vn-conscionable knaue held her in complement an houre, with that reuerst face, when I still look'd when shee should talke from the t'other side.
> CLE. Why, thou should'st ha' releeu'd her.
> TRV. No faith, I let her alone as wee'l let this argument.
>
> (I.1.128–39)

Clearly Truewit, and Jonson, are complicit with the "rude fellow." Two sensibilities are struggling in Jonson, one weaving a fabric of elegant social life and the other eager to tear it.

To some extent these motives succeed one another, the gaiety, air, and freedom of the first act giving way to a noisy satiric hammering once the gallants get out into society. Dryden admired the perfect form of the plotting but its untempered and savage tone is unlike the cultivated libertine cynicism of Restoration comedy. The sadism of displaying and playing on humors is nowhere clearer: Dauphine has to be restrained from maiming Daw as part of the jest (IV.5.134–6), and Otter is beaten by his wife before an assembled audience, to the sound of drums and trumpets (IV.2.103) – sublime comedy, but sublimed from the oldest and crudest farce. The party is now more than simply an object and framework for satiric analysis; it is organized as a succession of cruel games at someone's expense, a "comedy of affliction."

What drives the savage satire is not an objection to polite society as such, but Jonson's irritation at those who fill up social space with their undeserved reputations. For him reputation still ought to be connected (if not reducible) to honor, that is, masculine valor and female chastity. The basis of his concern is not connected to the cultural context of cavalier or heroic drama, where honor is an endless theme, but to instincts rooted in an older and less exclusively aristocratic formation. It comes down to a staunch sense of personal integrity, which has a bodily dimension: Those who do not have integrity can be shown to be an assemblage of artificial parts (like the ladies), or can be made to offer the sacrifice of parts of their body to avoid risking a duel (like Jack Daw).

In a highly interesting article Susan Staves has suggested that the fops, with their horror of violence, their delicate overrefinement, their interest in clothes and singing and so forth – all regarded as effeminate – were in the avant-garde of the refinement of manners and of sex-role changes. By the eighteenth century table manners were thought to be a good idea and masculine brutality a bad one, and the fops began to be viewed more charitably.[101]

I have been arguing that Jonson was himself an agent in this process of refinement, and the gentlemanly conversation is not the only evidence that could be adduced from *Epicoene*. Truewit and Clerimont mock women who bray when they laugh and take huge strides like ostriches, and they like modulation in ladies' behavior ("I loue measure i' the feet, and number i' the voice: they are gentlenesses, that oft-times draw no lesse than the face," IV.1.51–2). But we can also see the limits of Jonson's refinement. In this play, so full of sexual ambiguities, he judges the fops to be effeminate and punishes them for it. We remember that the author of the scene in which they refuse to duel had killed two men in single combat, though Jonson also wrote against dueling with the conviction of one who had thought the matter over deeply (*Underwoods* 26, "An Ode [High-spirited friend]"). He stands for a rugged middle way between crudeness and overrefinement. As the ladies shift their interest from Daw and La Foole to Dauphine, following the fops' humiliation, they praise Dauphine's appearance but like it that he is not

> so superlatiuely neat as some, madame, that haue their faces set in a brake!
> HAUGHTY.   Ay, and haue euery haire in forme!
> MAVIS.   That weare purer linnen than our selues, and professe more neatnesse, then the *french hermaphrodite!*
>
> (IV.6.23–7)[102]

Jonson wields their physicality as a weapon against the refined, an opportunity for revenge – Lady Haughty's lips are oily, Clerimont suspects the hidden

---

[101] "A Few Kind Words for the Fop," *SEL* 22 (1982), 413–28; see particularly pp. 420–1.

[102] Compare *Every Man Out*, where Fallace, the citizen's wife and daughter of the boorish Sordido, is smitten by what Jonson pretty clearly sees as the over-fastidiousness of Fastidius Briske, though it looks like ordinary decency to a modern reader: "how cleanely he wipes his spoone, at euery spoon-full of any whit-meat he eates, and what a neat case of pick-tooths he carries about him, still! O, sweet FASTIDIVS! o fine courtier!" (IV.1.38–41).

motives of her art, and the fops are intercepted on their way out to the garden to urinate. A grosser sensibility enters the play through Otter, he of the bear-baiting pit, who thinks "Wiues are nasty sluttish *animalls*" (IV.2.56); his wife objects to his grossness, which is a sign of his social inferiority, but the spirit of the bear-baiting pit percolates up through the play, so that the din of "polite" society torments Morose like the rough music of a charivari: "The spitting, the coughing, the laughter, the neesing, the farting, dauncing, noise of the musique, and her masculine, and lowd commanding" (IV.1.7–10).

So it is tempting to see Jonson as a sort of Silenus Alcibiades, his mountain belly and rocky face containing the elegant gallant Clerimont within – the poet laureate who was his own antimasque, the courtier who could also present himself as the sweating and drunken poet glimpsed backstage in the Induction to *The Staple of News*. But the opposition is not always so neat. The opposition between popular festive and refined aristocratic cultures was still forming and should not be exaggerated; it would become better defined even as the strong tension over manners slackened. Much later Squire Western would drink himself into a stupor to the delicate sounds of Sophia's harpsichord, without the contrast implying an unsettled cultural conflict. But in *Epicoene,* where we are halfway between the comedy of manners and the bear-baiting pit, the opposition is tense and productive of attention without being altogether sharp. The gentlemen are the agents of the play's gay aggression.

On the subjective level both bear-baiting and the comedy of manners express interpenetrating facets of Jonson's sensibility, and it seems clear that he was not tailoring that sensibility to fit a genteel audience. Even as Jonson carefully recreates the fashionable society immediately adjacent to the fashionable Whitefriars theater for which he wrote *Epicoene,* he declines to exploit the fancy social ambience in his marketing of the play. The dedication is to Sir Francis Stuart, a sea captain and drinking companion to whom Jonson appeals as a judge rather than an "Vndertaker." This must be the truth, not flattery, since Stuart would not have been in a position to give Jonson much of a boost. From a practical point of view he was wasting the dedication. And the uncharacteristically democratic Prologue for once goes out of its way *not* to define an elite among the audience who alone are worth pleasing:

> Truth sayes, of old, the art of making plaies
> Was to content the people; & their praise
> Was to the *Poet* money, wine, and bayes.
> But in this age, a sect of writers are,
> That, onely, for particular likings care,
> And will taste nothing that is populare.
> With such we mingle neither braines, nor brests.
>
> (1–7)

Jonson promises there will be something here for waiting wenches as well as lords and knights (22–3).

Having thus laid the foundations for Restoration drama, Jonson promptly abandoned them. For him this was only an unstable moment, a moment of discovery not consolidation. He did not want the restricted coterie conditions of Caroline or Restoration drama, nor the restricted social purview, and would not let them claim him.

4

Representing the Underworld: The Alchemist

REPRESENTING THE UNDERWORLD

Like the middle class which seemed (until this decade) always to be rising, criminals seem always to become more professional. Jonson, who reveled in the spirit and arcana of professions, created in *The Alchemist* a criminal operation whose imaginative extravagance and moral logic tend to distract one from its practical plausibility, which is to say from its social logic. But Jonson thought carefully about how these criminals organized themselves, and how they were attached to society. In fact he managed, so I argue, to formulate a new conception of criminality. This conception has little to do with the Foucauldian creation of a criminal subject by a new penal apparatus – that apparatus had not yet been constructed. It has to do rather with a new structure of economic and social opportunities. It is striking about Jonson's thought, and against the grain of most contemporary thinking, that he professionalizes criminality without hypostasizing it; he is finally less interested in criminality per se than in the society that produces it. Subtle and Face and Doll represent new social possibilities, are figures of and for new spaces, fissures, and energies in London society; their operation may go up in fumes at the end of the play, but the vast, restless, generative metropolis does not dissolve:

> Our *Scene* is *London,* 'cause we would make knowne,
> No countries mirth is better then our owne.
> No clime breeds better matter, for your whore,
> Bawd, squire, impostor, many persons more.
> (Prologue, 5–11)

A number of social historians have argued that the Early Modern Period was the first to define crime as a problem, to identify crime not as unacceptable behavior on the part of a member of the community, but as the practice of reprobates beyond the pale. Both Calvinist theology, with its sharp and absolute division between the elect and the damned, and economic dislocations that increasingly divided society into a prosperous and respectable elite and an impoverished and "rough" underclass enter into this new ideological formulation.[1] Criminals began to be seen as members of an antisociety.[2]

This transformation is visible in the rich stage tradition of roguery. Mak and Gill are clearly part of the community of *The Second Shepherd's Play*. The shepherds know them and know how to deal with them, without rejecting them, appealing to outside authorities, or passing judgment on their souls. But as the morality tradition progressed its structure changed, as David Bevington has shown, "from a struggle for the soul of a universal man to a series of contrasts between those who are unquestionably saved and those who are irreparably damned."[3] So Tom Tosspot and Ralph Roister, Cuthbert Cutpurse and Pierce Pickpurse (from Fulwell's *Like Will to Like Quoth the Devil to the Collier*) progress straight toward their bad ends. As I have noted, in such plays the scene of the crimes – or sins, since the signs of depravity are drinking, swearing, roistering, whoring, and brawling, at least as much as criminal activities per se – is the familiar alehouse or tavern. The morality stage presented a world that was sharply divided into cultures of good and evil, but neither was foreign.

[1] T. C. Curtis and F. M. Hale, "English Thinking about Crime, 1530–1620," in Louis A. Knafla, ed., *Crime and Criminal Justice in Europe and Canada* (Waterloo: Wilfred Laurier Univ. Press, 1981), pp. 111–26; Michael R. Weisser, *Crime and Punishment in Early Modern Europe* (Hassocks, Sussex: Harvester, 1979), p. 1; V. A. C. Gastrell, Bruce Lenman, and Geoffrey Parker, ed., *Crime and the Law: the social history of crime in Western Europe since 1500* (London: Europa, 1980), p. 8; Jean-Christophe Agnew, *Worlds Apart: The Market and the Theater in Anglo-American Thought, 1550–1750* (Cambridge: Cambridge Univ. Press, 1986), pp. 61–73; John L. McMullan, *The Canting Crew: London's Criminal Underworld 1550–1700* (New Brunswick: Rutgers Univ. Press, 1984), especially pp. 3, 15 (and on a new harsher attitude toward the poor, coordinate with the new attitudes toward crime, pp. 39–45); Christopher Hill, *Reformation to Industrial Revolution* (London: Weidenfeld and Nicolson, 1967), pp. 40–1. Cynthia B. Herrup, "Law and Morality in 17th Century England," *Past and Present* 106 (Feb. 1985), 102–23, stresses the religious and moral elements in the distinction, and argues that these elements kept the distinction from being altogether sharp; see also her "Crime, Law and Society: A Review Article," *Comparative Studies in Society and History* 27, no. 1 (January 1985), 159–170. J. A. Sharpe, "The History of crime in late medieval and early modern England: a review of the field," *Social History* 7 (May, 1982), 187–203, is not so sure much changed. A seminal article in this field is Douglas Hay, "Property, Authority and the Criminal Law," in *Albion's Fatal Tree: Crime and Society in 18th Century England,* ed., Douglas Hay, Peter Linebaugh, John G. Rule, E. P. Thompson, and Cal Winslow (London: Allen Lane, 1975), pp. 17–63.

[2] A. L. Beier thinks this element first appears in England in Barclay's translation of Sebastian Brandt's *Ship of Fools* (1508), *Masterless Men: The Vagrancy Problem in England 1560–1640* (London: Methuen, 1985), p. 7.

[3] David M. Bevington, *From "Mankind" to Marlowe, Growth of Structure in the Popular Drama of Tudor England* (Cambridge, Mass.: Harvard Univ. Press, 1962), p. 152.

The roguery and cony-catching pamphlets detailed a specifically criminal milieu, and introduced an element of cultural estrangement. They are a species of ethnological literature, describing an alien and exotic population. This is perhaps clearest in the case of the literature about rural vagabonds, stemming from John Awdeley's *The Fraternity of Vagabonds* (1561) and Thomas Harman's *Caveat for Common Cursitors* (1566), which purports to give the inside story about the visible army of the destitute tramping the English countryside in greater numbers in the mid-sixteenth century than in any other period of history.[4] Having fallen out of village society, this population was imagined to have evolved its own elaborate social structure and customs, blending in the imagination with gypsy lore (as Jonson blended them in *The Gipsies Metamorphosed*).

Harman was a Justice of the Peace with practical motivations and some sociological purposes, but the literary tradition seized on these materials for their exoticism, and constructed out of them a pastoral realm of freedom and ease even as the Poor Laws were forcing real vagabonds into workhouses.[5] Awdeley and Harman's information was simply rehashed for the next eighty years, without being updated. *Martin Markall, Beadle of Bridewell* (1610) by S[amuel] R[id?], for instance, points out that Dekker's pamphlets are plagiarized from Harman, and that he is passing off as current terms used forty years before he was born.[6]

In any case, around the turn of the century the stage inherited from the pamphlets a new color and detail with which to spice its long tradition of Vices, bad alehouse companions, rogues, beggars, braggart soldiers, and tricky servants. Even while the tavern world expanded into the representation of

---

[4] The classic collection of cony-catching pamphlets, including Awdeley and Harman, is A. V. Judges, *The Elizabethan Underworld* (London: Routledge & Kegan Paul, 1930). The classic studies of this literature are F. W. Chandler, *The Literature of Roguery*, vol. 1 (New York: Houghton Mifflin, 1907), and Frank Aydelotte, *Elizabethan Rogues and Vagabonds* (1913; New York: Barnes and Noble, 1967). The most sophisticated and suggestive accounts I have seen of the cony-catching literature, with a number of thematic parallels to my own work, are Lawrence Manley's "Ghosts: Project(ions) of Greene and Nashe," and "Cony-Catching: Anatomy of Anatomies," unpublished mss.

On the number of destitute vagabonds, see P. A. Slack, "Vagrants and vagrancy in England 1598–1664," *Economic History Review*, 2d series, 27 (1974), 360–79; A. L. Beier, "Vagrants and the social order in Elizabethan England," *Past and Present 64* (1974), 3–29; and Beier's *Masterless Men*, pp. 14–16, on the difficulty of arriving at accurate statistics on the number of vagrants.

[5] See Aydelotte, p. 74. Both the romanticizing of the freedom of the beggar's life, and an early warning that new social policies were brewing that would curtail it, are to be found in Erasmus' "Beggar Talk" (1524). *The Colloquies of Erasmus*, trans. Craig R. Thompson (Chicago: Univ. of Chicago Press, 1965), pp. 248–54.

[6] In Judges, pp. 406–09. Aydelotte treats the plagiarism issue at length.

fashionable society as a whole, blurring the boundaries that made it a distinct setting, the roguery scene was being developed with a new specificity and extensiveness; a world (not necessarily the real one) was growing around it. There is a marked dissociation between the fascination with the figure of the rogue in the theater and the genuine alarm the Tudor government felt in the face of a politically dangerous multitude of sturdy poor; the very status of vagabond was made a crime[7] and vagabonds were branded and whipped from parish to parish, the judicial form of the unanimous social ostracism Harman invoked:

> The honorable will abhor them, the worshipped will reject them, the yeomen will sharply taunt them, the husbandmen utterly defy them, the labouring men bluntly chide them, the women with a loud exclamation wonder at them, and all children with clapping hands cry out at them.[8]

But the rogue found himself quite welcome in the theater. There the audience could indulge, in safety from his vermin and pilfering, the curiosity and fascinated ambiguity always accompanying the figure of the rogue. The audience could also think through, via the status crime of vagabondage, the themes of social identity and political organization that had become unavoidable in England's postfeudal society, and that now preoccupied the drama.[9]

By the time we arrive at plays like Fletcher and Massinger's *Beggar's Bush* (1622) all interest in real beggars has frankly disappeared; the beggar lore simply provides costumes and scenery for a drama about another class entirely, and has coagulated into speeches like the following, where the canting terms that provided much of the interest of the pamphlets turn into titles of an alternative commonwealth:

> Come Princes of the ragged regiment,
> You o' the blood, Prig my most upright lord,
> And these (what name or title, e're they beare)
> Jarkman, or Patrico, Cranke, or Clapperduggeon,
> Frater, or Abram-man: I speake to all
> That stand in faire Election for the title
> Of king of Beggars, with the command adjoyning,
> Higgen, your Orator, in this Inter-regnum,
> That whilom was your Dommerer.[10]

Brome's *The Jovial Crew* (1641) uses elaborate techniques to pose its exotic subjects. They are heard singing their anthems before they enter the stage, with dances and "postures" and masquelike speeches. The plot and mood are dominated by slumming young gentry being taken on a safe guided tour of the

[7] Beier, *Masterless Men*, p. xxii.
[8] Quoted in McMullan, p. 41.
[9] On this preoccupation, see Agnew, passim.
[10] *Beggar's Bush*, ed., John H. Dorenkamp (The Hague: Mouton, 1967), II.1.1–9.

vagabond life, and the play contains a whole society gone underground: "Hedge lady-birds, hedge-cavaliers, hedge-soldier, hedge-lawyer, hedge-fiddlers, hedge-poet, hedge-players, and a hedge-priest among 'em." [11] Everyone will be raised from beggardom at the denouement.

The disguise motif (associated with beggars since ancient times) is indispensable in these plays, because of the shallowness of interest in real beggars. (Even in *King Lear,* which is truly concerned about the plight of the poor, the beggar is a disguised aristocrat.) The setting is used to costume extraneous fantasies and ideological topics: in *Beggar's Bush,* a reconciliation of aristocracy and bourgeoisie; in *The Jovial Crew,* a debate over political happiness, and anxieties current just before the Revolution. The vagabonds are valued imaginatively because they are outside the social order; this structural otherness is the only important fact about them. The ideological and fantastic character of the investment of the figure of the beggar can be gauged by the fact that both plays distinguish sharply between real peasants, who are treated with contempt, and the spiritual nobility of the vagabonds – a reversal of the class interests and propaganda of propertied Englishmen. The genre is, in short, a branch of pastoral. [12]

Though there is no sharp distinction between rural and urban roguery – the rogues went back and forth, and the same authors tended to write about both environments – the figure of the urban cony-catcher has a different career. [13] The urban underworld was based in another huge population of the chronically or seasonally unemployed, ranging from twenty to fifty percent of London's total, according to John McMullan; [14] but in the pamphlet literature the

[11] Richard Broome, *A Jovial Crew,* ed., Ann Haaker (Lincoln: Univ. of Nebraska Press, 1968), V.1.76–8. This is a relatively good play because it is at least interested in the experiences of its young people on their summer vacation, if it doesn't care about the beggars; some truths about the social situation of beggars do get revealed reflexively. Other plays of this genre include Chettle and Day's *The Blind Beggar of Bednal Green* (1600), Middleton's *More Dissemblers Besides Women* (before 1623?), and Middleton and Rowley's *The Spanish Gipsy* (1623). Compare the false beggar in Massinger's *A New Way to Pay Old Debts* (1621). On the representation and falsification of the life of the rural poor in Tudor and Stuart drama, see Kate McLuskie, " 'Tis but a Woman's Jar: Family and Kinship in Elizabethan Domestic Drama," *Literature and History* 9:2 (Autumn 1983), 228–30; and Anat Feinberg, "The Representation of the Poor in Elizabethan and Stuart Drama," *Literature and History* 12:2 (Autumn 1986), 152–63.

[12] The vogue for plays about rural beggars coincides with improvements in the transportation system that made pleasure excursions into the countryside around London popular. Compare McLuskie: "In later drama . . . rural life . . . was idealized as the playground of aristocrat and courtier, inhabited by picturesque gypsy folklore and jolly beggars" (p. 230). Jonson's *The New Inne* (1629) has this character.

[13] On the difference between rural vagabonds and urban roguery, see Aydelotte, pp. 21–2, 76.

[14] McMullan, p. 10

cony-catcher does not usually appear as one of the destitute. *A Manifest Detection of Dice Play* (1552) by Gilbert Walker(?), from which the urban branch of the cony-catching literature springs, claims that cheaters at dice had risen in the last twenty years from a very few whose estate was "the next door to a beggar" to half an army, looking "for a good hour to creep into a gentleman's room of the Privy Chamber."[15] The urban con man must look respectable, may appear to be a gentleman, may even, as in Walker's dialogue, appear to be a courtier with a luxurious house and a bejeweled wife with which to awe his middling gentry victim. The urban underworld is thus an invisible empire. Not much account is given of the social origins of the cony-catcher, except when he is recruited from the ranks of the prodigals undone by other cony-catchers.[16] It is through moral choice that men and women opt into the life of crime. They prefer deception to truth and "idleness" to work. ("Idleness" is a term that would be applied even to the frantically busy professionals of *The Alchemist:* the "Argument" says of the servant Face, "Ease him corrupted".) Walker defines cony-catchers in moral and philosophical, not sociological, terms:

> For the first and original ground of cheating is a counterfeit countenance in all things . . . the foundation of all those sorts of people is nothing else but mere simulation and bearing in hand. And like as they spring all from one root, so tend they all to one end: idly to live by rape and ravin, devouring the fruit of other men's labours. All the odds between them be in the mean actions, that lead towards the end and fixed purpose.[17]

Appearances are totally deceptive, but the distinction between criminal and society is absolute, principled, and vehement.

The urban underworld was thought to be as highly organized as the rural vagabonds' hierarchy of upright men, rufflers, patricoes, autem morts, counterfeit cranks, and the rest. The "laws" of this countersociety were its illegal scams: "prigging law" is horse stealing, "sacking law" is prostitution, and so on. By a similar reversal, these idlers were thought to be organized into crafts. The guild structure is projected onto the underworld. An example is Walker's account of the "corporation" that organized the scam called "barnard's law," in which the dupe is encouraged to think he is cheating the cony-catchers, rather as Mammon thinks he is taking advantage of the unworldly Doctor. (Like the

---

[15] In Judges, p. 34. An allusion dates the writing of the pamphlet to 1544.

[16] On gentleman cony-catchers and their social origins, see Gamini Salgado, *The Elizabethan Underworld* (London: Dent, 1977), p. 31. Many of the rank and file were recruited among ex-soldiers or sailors, or cast-off serving men. In *The Merry Wives of Windsor* (1600), as Falstaff liquidates his band of disreputable feudal retainers to pursue wealth through trading on his social status in civil society, Pistol turns to cheating at dice: "Let vultures gripe thy guts! for gourd and fullam [types of false dice] holds, / And high and low beguiles the rich and poor!" (I.3.85–6). Falstaff recommends to him "a short knife [for purse-cutting] and a throng!" (II.2.17). This is very accurate sociology.

[17] In Judges, p. 36.

scams in *The Alchemist,* barnard's law requires a number of actors playing extended dramatic roles.) Walker attributes to this corporation all the essential features of a craft guild: a long apprenticeship under the tutelage of masters, wardens who allocate shares of the market, a specialized vocabulary, a standard of quality of workmanship, and a common treasury supported by a regular rating for the relief of members in trouble.[18] The canting vocabulary is mysterious because it is the language of a "mystery": "But always ye must consider that a carpenter hath many terms, familiar enough to his 'prentices, that other folk understand not at all; and so have the cheaters."[19] Each scam has its own vocabulary, so that the one who draws in the cony is called a "verser" in versing law, a "taker" in barnard's law, a "setter" in cony-catching law, and so forth.[20]

Whether these terms and forms of organization had any basis in reality has been sharply debated by historians; they certainly express the Elizabethan taste for profuse classification. The more serious recent studies of crime in Early Modern England have abandoned the attractive anecdotes of the pamphlets for statistical studies of court records.[21] But the interesting question which remains

[18] "Their craft, of all others, requireth most sleight, and hath marvellous plenty of terms and strange language; and therefore no man can attain to be a workman thereat, till he have had a good time of schooling, and by that means do not only know each other well, but they be subject to an order such as the elders shall prescribe. No man so sturdy to practise his feat but in the place appointed, nor for any cause once to put his foot in another's walk! . . . Some of them are certainly 'pointed, as it were, by their wardens to keep the haunt, with commission but a short while, and to interchange their places as order shall be made, to avoid suspicion. By occasion whereof, whensoever any stroke is workmanly stricken, though it were at Newcastle, the rest of the fig-boys that keeps resident in London, can forthwith prognosticate by whom the worthy feat was wrought. . . .

"Another help they have, that of every purse that is cleanly conveyed, a rateable portion is duly delivered into the treasurer's hands, to the use, that whensoever by some misadventure any of them happen to be taken and laid in prison, this common stock may serve to satisfy the party grieved, and to make friends to save them from hanging." In Judges, pp. 48–9. This language of guild organization is sometimes mingled with or replaced by pedagogical terminology: schools, novices, scholars, colleges, and so forth. For examples, see Judges, p. 42. *Martin Markall Beadle of Bridewell: His Defence and Answers to the Bellman of London* by S. R[id?] (1610) takes the analogy with guild organization so far as to claim that rogues born into the mystery do not have to pay the entrance fines required of others "as being made free by his father's copy" (in Judges, p. 415), and speaks of an "old manuscript, remaining on record in Maunders' [beggars'] Hall" (p. 420).

[19] Walker, in Judges, p. 36. This passage is plagiarized by Greene in *A Notable Discovery of Cozenage* (1591).

[20] For a table of such terms, see Robert Greene's *A Notable Discovery,* in Judges, p. 135.

[21] "Generally the present study finds that legal records present a different picture from the literary one," says Beier, *Masterless Men,* p. 7. See especially chap. 8: "The Underworld Uncovered." See also Beier, "Vagrants and the Social Order in Elizabethan England," pp. 3–29, and the response by J. F. Pound in ibid. 71 (May 1976),

about the cony-catching literature, as T. C. Curtis and F. M. Hale argue, is why this tightly focused selection from contemporary illegality should have aroused so much interest. The answer is that it served to make the underworld, and threatening social change, comprehensible. As Jean-Christophe Agnew writes,

> In the face of the accumulating pressures of enclosures, disestablishment, and demobilization, new forms of social, political, and imaginative order were improvised to keep people and things in their place. Like the estates literature that preceded it, rogue literature served as a figurative act of settlement: exposing, dissecting, and classifying all that threatened to confuse the social relations of Elizabethan England, tying the loose ends of commerce and crime back to the frayed fabric of society. . . . The effect of these fictions was to assimilate an otherwise erratic pattern of itinerancy and trespass into a more familiar notion of deliberate, if dubious, guild activity: a freemasonry of crime whose arts and mysteries the pamphlets purported to lay bare.[22]

Curtis and Hale would add that the effect of Greene's pamphlets, that fleshed out the underworld in fuller fictional form, was double: they both reduced the underworld to familiar categories and solidified its otherness.

> [I]n making crime comprehensible, the idea of the underworld gives crime an identity. The reverse is also importantly true: what the ordinary citizen does, even if wrong, even if illegal, is not a crime, for that is done by professionals, criminals who inhabit the underworld. Crime becomes a special form of, and something slightly apart from, the illegal; there is a distance and distinction between the two; the way is thus clear for the idea of crime to be moulded as a container to receive the undesirable in whatever may be the appropriate form, and with whatever may be the appropriate explanations for their character and actions, while simultaneously, by their absence from the underworld,

(note 21 cont.) 126–9. Salgado believes in the literature (see, for example, p. 44). McMullan takes a moderate position (see p. 2), but claims: "Like other city corporate bodies the cutpurses, thieves, prostitutes, and cony-catchers possessed their own versions of seigneuries collectives which lent a shape and stable structure to urban crime. Criminal areas were mirror reflections of trade and guild quarters, and . . . they borrowed from legitimate trades some of their characteristics: division of labor, collective styles, particular codes of behavior, and work discipline" (p. 20). For other examples of the new history of crime based on statistics from court records, see John Beattie, "The Pattern of Crime in England, 1600–1800," *Past and Present* 62 (1964); J. S. Cockburn, ed., *Crime in England 1500–1800* (Princeton: Princeton Univ. Press, 1977); John Brewer and John Styles, eds., *An Ungovernable People: The English and Their Law in the Seventeenth and Eighteenth Centuries* (New Brunswick: Rutgers Univ. Press, 1980); V. A. C. Gastrell et al., *Crime and the Law;* Michel Weisser, *Crime and Punishment in Early Modern Europe* (Hassocks: Harvester, 1979). This shift from the anecdotal to the statistical is commented on by J. A. Sharpe. The best example of the old anecdotal form of writing on the underworld, based on literary sources, is still Aydelotte; Salgado is a recent example.
[22] Agnew, p. 65.

the ordinary citizen's activities are somehow condoned. Greene's world is therefore at once therapeutic and justificatory.[23]

The appearance of the criminal underworld as an issue, like the appearance of the population of the dispossessed and destitute, was a sign of the breakdown of the feudal order, but neither the rogue population nor the idea of an underworld were inherently capitalist. The cony-catching literature is a post-feudal phenomenon, part of what Michael Walzer calls the "steady stream of mournful criticism, sometimes brilliant invective, sometimes naive analysis, most often, perhaps, only a kind of conventional chatter"[24] accompanying deep social change that could not be understood. The final words of Aydelotte's book on the pamphleteers are, "They expressed the unrest of their time: they could not direct its aspiration."

Hence the conservative character of most of the cony-catching literature, which often links professional cony-catching and other immemorial kinds of sharp dealing. The model of estates satire sometimes leads the pamphleteers to assert the universality of deception. *The Defense of Cony-catching* (1592) by "Cuthbert Cony-Catcher" – who may be Robert Greene[25] – attacks Greene for exposing the small-time criminal when society is full of wickedness. (*Martin Markall* paraphrases this argument while carrying out a similar attack on Dekker.)[26] There follows a parade of the enemies of the old economic morality – usurers, brokers, millers with heavy thumbs, and so on – who are shown at their tricks, but then (each anecdote following the same pattern) are foiled and publicly humiliated. Far from suggesting that a new and dangerous form of criminality has appeared, then, the pamphlet celebrates society's ability to cope with its traditional enemies. The cony-catching aspects of plays like *The Merry Wives of Windsor* carry the same meaning.

Curtis and Hale make the point that the cony-catching plays developed the argument, left undeveloped in the pamphlets, that all of society is based on

---

[23] Curtis and Hale, 123–4.

[24] Michael Walzer, *The Revolution of the Saints* (1965; rpt. New York: Atheneum, 1976), p. 205.

[25] "Cuthbert Cony-Catcher," *The Defense of Cony-Catching,* in *Cony-Catchers and Bawdy Baskets: An Anthology of Elizabethan Low Life,* ed., Gamini Salgado (Harmondsworth: Penguin, 1972), pp. 339–77.

[26] "If then it be all one in city as in country, among rich as amongst us poor, and generally in all trades and occupations deceit and abuses (sith it is so that he that cannot dissemble cannot live), why then should you be so spiteful, Goodman Sansbell, to inveigh against us poor souls above the rest, who, of all others, in shifting are the most simplest souls in this overwise world. . . . had you such a mote in your eye that you could not see those fox-furred gentlemen, that harbour more decit under their damask cassocks, than is in all the poor rogues in a country, brokers I mean, and usurers, that like vultures prey upon the simple, those that are moths in a commonwealth." In Judges, pp. 391–2. See James A. S. McPeek, *The Black Book of Knaves and Unthrifts* (n.p.: Univ. of Connecticut Press, 1969), chap. 6, "The 'Theefe in Societie' and the Knave of Fashion."

deceit. As a cheater explains to a prodigal he is recruiting in Walker's *Manifest Detection,*

> "Though your experience in the world be not so great as mine, yet am I sure ye see that no man is able to live an honest man unless he have some privy way to help himself withal, more that the world is witness of. Think you the noblemen could do as they do, if in this hard world they should maintain so great a port only upon their rent? Think you the lawyers could be such purchasers if their pleas were short, and all their judgments, justice and conscience? Suppose ye that offices would be so dearly bought, and the buyers so soon enriched, if they counted not pillage an honest point of purchase? Could merchants, without lies, false making their wares, and selling them by a crooked light, to deceive the chapman in the thread or colour, grow so soon rich and to a baron's possessions, and make all their posterity gentlemen? What will ye more? Whoso hath not some awkward way to help himself, but followeth his nose, as they say, always straight forward, may well hold up the head for a year or two, but the [third] he must needs sink and gather the wind into beggars' haven."[27]

This passes without comment in the dialogue of Walker, whose worldliness and relativism are very close to those of More and Erasmus. For Greene, who plagiarized this passage in *A Notable Discovery of Cozenage*,[28] it only proves that the cony-catchers are "given up into a reprobate sense and are in religion mere atheists, as they are in trade flat dissemblers." But, as Curtis and Hale say, "[w]hat Middleton and Jonson did was to posit a world wherein this really was the case – wherein deception, gulling, was the respectable norm, and the one motivating force in human action was greed for gold."[29]

Curtis and Hale do not seem to notice the contradiction between these two ideological functions of the underworld, as Other and as model for the rest of society. Both, certainly, are responses to the dislocations of early capitalism, which was creating an army of the unemployed and encouraging economic activities that were illegitimate in the traditional order.

The inversion by which the underworld is made the model for society is, in an obvious respect, a way of morally denouncing society. In Jonson at least there is a sardonic character to this reversal, and it can be read in several ways: he is ironically trying to awaken the audience to the vices it treats as respectable; he is on a badly needed moral holiday; or his moralism has given way to a bleak pessimism.

This is not the same sort of mirroring that projects the guild structure onto the underworld, a projection of social form, not moral content. It is Jonson's social, as opposed to moral, understanding that interests me here. Crime is parasitic, and hence derives its form from the economy; the gulls create the

[27] In Judges, p. 38.
[28] In Judges, pp. 133–4.
[29] Curtis and Hale, p. 120.

rogues, not only in the moral sense that poetic justice gives them what they deserve, but in the economic sense of creating a structure of opportunity for crime. The cony-catching pamphlets had usually, though not exclusively, located the disturbing problem where new money was floating around, on which a "fast set" battened. The literature is full of the traditional laments about "these times," always said to be worse than any in memory, but the extent of plagiarism demonstrates that the pamphleteers were willing to be a generation or two behind in their sociological analysis.

In spite of the manifold continuities between the cony-catching literature and *The Alchemist,* Jonson's work is a new departure because his play's sociology is fuller, much more acute, and up to date. His expanded dramatic realism specifies social situations and relations to a greater extent; he simply gives us more, and better integrated, information. Further, and more important, what is happening to his society can be seen to have a systematic character, beyond moral formulas. Jonson sees not only how the old order is breaking up, but the form and pressure of a new economy. We are not dealing with a full analysis of the transition from feudalism to capitalism, but Jonson's specific and decisive step was to imagine an underworld no longer structured on the guild model, but on a capitalist one. The fundamental problem is not the appearance of a new criminal profession, nor the perversion of the estates, but a new economy, working through both society and the underworld.

THE ALCHEMIST

Subtle and Doll and Face are clearly underworld figures, professional criminals, setting them off from Jonson's sharp gallants and from the inspired amateur Volpone, who glorifies more in the cunning purchase of his wealth than in the glad possession. They have evolved directly out of the cony-catching pamphlet literature. In the course of the argument that opens the play Face shows how easily they could slip back into it, threatening to "haue / A booke, but barely reckoning thy impostures, / Shall proue a true *philosophers stone* to printers" (I.1.101–03). Surly speaks like an author of such a pamphlet, exposing the tricks of the cony-catchers; their techniques are drawn freely from the scams described in the pamphlets. They define themselves as organized against the rest of society: When Doll asks how their camp fares, Face replies "As, with the few, that had entrench'd themselues / Safe, by their discipline, against a world" (III.3.34–5). To reinforce their solidarity Doll provides strong images of the punishments hanging over them if they get caught (I.1.163–74). We never hear of Subtle having done anything besides cony-catching; a prostitute like Doll could not easily reenter straight society; Surly recognizes Face as a well-known underworld figure, supervising a large prostitution ring (II.3.300 ff.).

The play presents us immediately with strong images of something we do not otherwise see, Subtle and Face in poverty, images slung around as part of the violent opening argument. Poverty is in itself an insult, as Jonson mocked Dekker's tattered clothes in *Poetaster,* and Dekker replied by remembering

Jonson trudging after a players' cart with his pumps full of gravel in *Satiromastix*. These images cannot be denied, and show the abyss out of which the cony-catchers emerged. Face met Subtle

> at *pie-corner,*
> Taking your meale of steeme in, from cookes stalls,
> Where, like the father of hunger, you did walke
> Piteously costiue . . .
>
> .   .   .   .
>
> When you went pinn'd vp, in the seuerall rags,
> Yo' had rak'd and pick'd from dung-hills, before day,
> Your feet in mouldie slippers, for your kibes,
> A felt of rugg, and a thin thredden cloake,
> That scarce would couer your no-buttocks . . .
> When all your *alchemy,* and your *algebra,*
> Your *minneralls, vegetalls,* and *animalls,*
> Your coniuring, cosning, and your dosen of trades,
> Could not relieue your corps, with so much linnen
> Would make you tinder, but to see a fire.
>
> (I.1.25–8, 33–42)

Subtle is the very specter of poverty in its urban form, a *lumpen* utterly outside society and nearly expelled from life itself. In return Subtle can reproach Face with having been a servant, stuck with the smallest of the *menu peuple,* living "vnder ground, in cellars, / Or an ale-house, darker than deafe *John's;* beene lost / To all mankind, but laundresses, and tapsters" (I.1.84–6).

> Make it not strange. I know, yo'were one, could keepe
> The buttry-hatch still lock'd, and saue the chippings,
> Sell the dole-beere to *aqua-vitae*-men,
> The which, together with your *christ-masse* vailes,
> At *post and paire,* your letting out of counters,
> Made you a pretty stock, some twentie markes,
> And gaue you credit, to conuerse with cob-webs,
> Here, since your mistris death hath broke vp house.
>
> .   .   .   .
>
> Thou vermine, haue I tane thee, out of dung,
> So poore, so wretched, when no liuing thing
> Would keepe thee companie, but a spider, or worse?
> Rais'd thee from broomes, and dust, and watring pots?
>
> (I.1.51–8, 64–7)

Doll, we learn later, is an Irish fruitseller's daughter. These origins are quickly forgotten. They are not the real durable truth about these people, in contrast to Jonson's social climbers whose nature often shows through their pretensions. All traces of origin are effaced by their constant and impeccable role-playing. The transformation they have undergone is almost as dramatic as that by which they entice their victims. Beggary had always been strongly associated with deception; now deception is distilled out as a quintessential energy brewed in a repressed nether world. Their role-playing allows them to have their run, makes them presentable in a theater with little interest in starving cheaters, minor servants, and fruitseller's daughters. As Walker would have us believe, they are essentially deceivers, but now this is understood socially as well as morally. It is hard to imagine them falling back on their "real" social identities.[30]

Acting is their essential professional skill, underlying and universalizing the particular scams. Subtle and Doll, the "Argument" tells us, are "A cheater [that is, a gambler with false dice], and his punque; who, now brought low, / Leauing their narrow practise, were become / Cos'ners at large" (4–6). Subtle is the alchemist, but he is also a conjurer, astrologer, professor of the science of quarrelling, pickpocket, and so on. Face may have a regular position as "superintendent" of prostitutes, as Surly claims, but we never see him do anything so routine. Their acting is not the specialized and routinized deception of the cony-catching pamphlets, but free improvisation.[31] Perhaps this explains the remarkable fact that though the play is fascinated with professional vocabularies, it steers clear of cony-catching cant, though Jonson employs the cant with gusto in *The Gipsies Metamorphosed,* and Surly recognizes its parallel with alchemical jargon ("What a braue language here is? next to canting?" II.3.42). This may be partly because the audience needs to understand Subtle and Face and Doll when they talk to each other, but it is also true that their scamming moves so quickly that the vocabulary, overly specialized on the model of the guilds, cannot keep up with them.

There are only residual traces of guild structure and vocabulary in the play (it would be "a mastery" to gull Surly); there is a decisive shift toward imagining the underworld as connected to, and reflecting in its mobile and flexible organization, the new protocapitalist economy of London. It is well understood that the guilds were losing their relevance to economic activity in this

[30] For an opposing view see Alvin Kernan, who thinks that "Subtle may appear most reverent, grave, wise, and stuffed with erudition and arcane knowledge, but he remains no more than the poor creature described by Face" in the passage I have quoted; and Face "is still no more than Jeremy the butler" as described by Subtle. *The Cankered Muse: Satire of the English Renaissance,* Yale Studies in English, vol. 142 (New Haven: Yale Univ. Press, 1959), p. 183. This argument rests on conservative assumptions about social identity. Its sharp dichotomy between real social essence and mere appearances leaves little room for people to remake themselves into another identity, or to create new identities (for example, a fashionable modern con-man) that are not grounded in the traditional social order. Such assumptions make it very difficult to recognize the sorts of slippages that were a central problem in city comedy and in Jacobean society.

[31] Charles Read Baskerville noticed that other rogues, like Jonson's, change quickly from one occupation to the other. On the same page is one of his typically extreme assertions that Jonson owed everything to books, in this case literary treatments of roguery, and little or nothing to observation of real life. *English Elements in Jonson's Early Comedy* (Austin: Univ. of Texas Press, 1911), p. 14.

period.[32] The model of a long apprenticeship in a narrow specialization was being undermined by a new pattern of employment. As Joan Thirsk has shown, the new business enterprises mushrooming up and then often collapsing required little in the way of capital investment in machinery, and created an employment pattern in which it was quite common to hold many different jobs during a career as a worker.[33] If one remembers that seasonal and casual employment was about all many of the London poor could hope to find,[34] and that the fallen gentlemen who made up another sector of the cony-catching population were educated not in a particular skill but with the capacity to serve the state, amateurishly, in a variety of employments, one sees a work force in which mobility, adaptability, and imagination were important qualities.

The "Argument" makes the "tripartite indenture" sound like shares in an acting company: "they here contract, / Each for a share, and all begin to act" (7–8). R. L. Smallwood points out that their enterprise "masquerades as a fully constituted trading 'house', with 'credit' to be maintained, as a 'venture tripartite' based upon an 'indenture' uniting its members."[35] It looks like a joint stock company, the newest form of capitalist organization. The tripartite indenture invites speculative investment in a potential monopoly (both Mammon and Tribulation point to the difference between *making* the stone and *owning* it[36]), and brokers the base metals with which Lovewit's house fills up.

[32] On the guilds, see T. H. Marshall, "Capitalism and the Decline of the English Guilds," *Cambridge Historical Journal*, 3 (1929), 23–33; J. R. Kellet, "The Breakdown of Guild and Corporation Control over the Handicraft and Retail Trade in London," *Economic History Review*, 2d. ser., 10 (1958), 381–94.

[33] Joan Thirsk, *Economic Policy and Projects: The Development of a Consumer Society in Early Modern England* (Oxford: Clarendon Press, 1978), pp. 171–2: "Men and women might in the end continue in the same occupation for 40 years . . . but they did not plan on this basis. Rather their careers suggest a more flexible, even casual, attitude to the choice of an occupation. This explains why new ventures could be launched quickly and spread without much preparation. . . . Jobs came and went unceremoniously and did not call for deep-laid plans." Compare Agnew, p. 64: "only the faintest of lines separated the multiple by-employments of the rural outworker from the multiple impostures of the professional rogue." Beier describes a "Wiltshire musician seized in 1605, who was "sometimes a weaver, sometimes a surgeon, sometimes a minstrel, sometimes a dyer, and now a bullard," and who was accused of having 'no trade to live by'!" *Masterless Men*, p. 88.

[34] McMullan, pp. 26–9.

[35] R. L. Smallwood, " 'Here in the Friars': Immediacy and Theatricality in *The Alchemist,*" *Review of English Studies* n.s. 32, no. 126 (1980), 145. On the business imagery see also Edward B. Partridge, *The Broken Compass* (New York: Columbia Univ. Press, 1958), pp. 139–44; Alan C. Dessen, "*The Alchemist:* Jonson's 'Estates' Play," *Renaissance Drama* 7 (1964), 38–41.

[36] On this point see Cyrus Hoy, "The Pretended Piety of Jonson's *Alchemist,*" *Renaissance Papers, 1956*, pp. 15–19, and Alan C. Dessen, *Jonson's Moral Comedy* (Chicago: Northwestern Univ. Press, 1971), p. 119.

Another capitalist institution appears as Face tells Kastril the Doctor has a sort of magical equivalent of the Royal Exchange;

> Hee'll shew a perspectiue, where on one side
> You shall behold the faces, and the persons
> Of all sufficient yong heires, in towne,
> Whose bonds are currant for commoditie;
> On th'other side, the marchants formes, and others,
> That, without help of any second broker,
> (Who would expect a share) will trust such parcels:
> In the third square, the verie street, and signe
> Where the commoditie dwels, and do's but wait
> To be deliuer'd, be it pepper, sope,
> Hops, or tabacco, oat-meale, woad, or cheeses.
> All which you may so handle, to enioy,
> To your own vse, and neuer stand oblig'd.
>
> (III.4.87–99)

Forcing someone who was borrowing money to take up worthless commodities was a well-known form of sharp dealing, so Face's business sense has a touch of the underworld about it, but it nevertheless extends to a centralized market in credit and commodities. The tripartite indenture looks beyond the profits to be made picking pockets or cheating country gulls at cards, though it by no means disdains such practices. The sense for what wealth was stirring is deeper and wider.

Most decisive is the transformation of a certain form of knowledge of society into a kind of capital. The pamphlets introduce some figures of a universal erudition, like the "taker-up" in "barnard's law":

> The taker-up seemeth a skilful man in all things, who hath by long travail learned without book a thousand policies to insinuate himself into a man's acquaintance. Talk of matters in law, he hath plenty of cases at his fingers' ends, and he hath seen, and tried, and ruled in the King's courts. Speak of grazing and husbandry, no man knoweth more shires than he, nor better which way to raise a gainful commodity, and how the abuses and overture of prices might be redressed. Finally, enter into what discourse they list, were it into a broom-man's faculty, he knoweth what gains they have for old boots and shoes.[37]

So Face can talk with easy authority about the tobacco business with Drugger and has a devastatingly accurate knowledge of Dapper's milieu. Everyone is spoken to in his own language. This prodigious learning is used in "barnard's law" merely to entice a cony to be cheated at cards; Face and Subtle and Doll use it as the basis of an open-ended improvisation. The power of this social knowledge exceeds the purpose for which it was originally collected in barnard's law – it is now the most universal, centralized, detailed, disposable,

[37] Greene, *Notable Discovery*, in Judges, p. 121; plagiarized from Walker, p. 47.

effective social knowledge there is. It permits manipulation of the whole range of society. Stephen Greenblatt has shown how the literature about the underworld sought power over it by revealing its secrets.[38] Here the knowledge that gives power is held by the cony-catchers, is their stock in trade.

This sort of social knowledge, also being purveyed as a commodity in courtesy books, and displayed in satiric comedy, had become valuable because the pressure of social mobility was rendering social appearances problematic as a sign of status.[39] Just as the cony-catchers have evolved from guildlike specialization to free improvisation in the widest markets available, so their victims are caught in the updraft that is loosening social categories. The satirical conception of the play is rooted in estates and professional satire, and the range of characters suggests a morality play about how greed and folly afflict all the estates.[40] But the victims' relations with the cony-catchers are all based on unsettled ambitions within the social order and/or on dreams that would explode it, a situation "greed" only begins to describe, and estates satire (a dying genre) could not represent. Even Abel Drugger, who is completely and irremediably petty bourgeois, is starting a fashionable business – or so Face implies, perhaps seducing him into fashionableness (I.3). Subtle would seduce him out of his citizenry altogether, saying he will be called to the Lord Mayorship next spring, "But hee'll be wise, preserue his youth, and fine for't: / His fortune lookes for him, another way" (I.3.40–1), encouraging this small consciousness to look beyond the hierarchy of the guild system. The lawyer's clerk Dapper's desires are easily inflated until he wants to leave the law (I.2.91). The Puritans have already withdrawn into their own society, and now want dominion. Mammon's dreams of wealth and power cannot be entertained within the monarchy of England (IV.1.147 ff.).

Alchemy is the grand symbol for this volatile state of affairs. The object of limitless desires, it promises infinite wealth and transformative power through operations scarcely more mysterious than the workings of capital, whose fantastic logic had not yet been dulled by familiarity.[41] Alchemy makes a neat metaphor for nascent capitalism, and *The Alchemist* fits neatly in the development of Jonson's economic thought between *Volpone,* in which a real pile of

[38] Stephen J. Greenblatt, "Invisible bullets: Renaissance authority and its subversion, *Henry IV* and *Henry V,* " in *Political Shakespeare,* ed., Jonathan Dollimore and Alan Sinfield (Ithaca: Cornell Univ. Press, 1985), pp. 36–40.

[39] Agnew connects the cony-catching pamphlets with the courtesy books, and speaks of a "crisis of representation," p. 73.

[40] Dessen, *"The Alchemist."*

[41] Walter Cohen has made this connection, citing the language Marx uses in describing interest bearing capital and the commodity form – "appears," "occult," "metaphysical," "theological," "mystical," "mystery," "magic," "necromancy," and so forth. *Drama of a Nation: Public Theater in Renaissance England and Spain* (Ithaca: Cornell Univ. Press, 1985), pp. 296–300.

gold draws "interest" in the old center of mercantilism, and the direct satiric exploration of capitalist "projection" in *The Devil is an Ass*.[42]

Less metaphorically, *The Alchemist* suggests that this social volatility will circulate through the fashionable demimonde of profligate gallants, ordinaries ("There's gaming there, and tricks," says Kastril apprehensively, III.4.49), brothels, and Paul's Walk, all places where respectable society and the underworld meet, and where social identity is mobile, uncertain, and frequently fraudulent. This terrain is the true scene of this, as of nearly all Jonson's plays, though that may not be immediately apparent, as our cony-catchers have enclosed themselves in Lovewit's house and are usually intent on projecting an image of reclusive and learned purity. But it is constantly alluded to, and is the necessary complement of the wide-ranging satire: a realistic portrayal of a criminal operation, which must have a specific terrain to work on, a criminal culture defined sociologically by its points of contact with society. These are the turbid waters in which Face fishes for gulls; Drugger is encouraged to cater to bespurred gallants, drawing them into his shop with a lodestone buried under the threshold; Dapper is encouraged to think he will ruin all the gamesters in town. Mammon frequents these scenes, and they are among the first to be transformed by his exalted vision. He will bring cures for the pox to the ordinaries, and no more shall thirst for rich fabrics

> To be displaced at *Madame Avgvsta*'s, make
> The sonnes of *sword*, and *hazzard* fall before
> The golden calfe, and on their knees, whole nights,
> Commit idolatrie with wine, and trumpets:
> Or goe a feasting, after drum and ensigne.
>   (II.1.17–21)

It is in this milieu that he knows the gamester Surly, who is the only real threat to Subtle, Face, and Doll, because he is another professional at their game. He, too, is a cony-catcher of sorts. Mammon suggests that he "deal[s] with the hollow die," is a whoremaster, and extorts money from young heirs with violence (II.1.9–14). He does not normally pretend, however, to be anything but what he is. His friendship with Mammon is "legitimate," an association not in crime but in a social network centered in whorehouses and ordinaries.

This milieu produces not only the real threat to the cony-catching operation, but also its real opportunity, in the form of Kastril and his sister Dame Pliant.

[42] In *The Devil is an Ass* gold has been superseded altogether by the technical/financial wizardry with which Meerecraft can turn anything into money, as he boasts in his famous speech (II.1). Meerecraft, who is the heir or rather reincarnation of the morose and brilliant Subtle, has moved up the social scale, and now inhabits the fringes of the Court. His only visible connection with the underworld is his brutal cousin Everill, whom he would be glad to be rid of, but even Everill receives dinner invitations from the likes of Lady Tailbush.

Kastril is "Of some three thousand a yeere, and is come vp / To learne to quarrell, and to liue by his wits, / And will goe downe againe, and dye i' the countrey" (II.6.60–2). The ethos of the gambling life is a commodity that can be sold to him, in the form of a set of lessons; he is lured with the glamor of being a prodigal ruined gallant living by his wits, a style of life, Face suggest, that is worth the necessary price of losing his estate (III.4.83–4).

Dame Pliant has also "come vp here, of purpose / To learne the fashion" (II.6.37–8), more respectable fashions in her case. Kastril's real motive in bringing her up is to sell her off on the marriage market to a "dubbed boy." As Raymond Williams has explained, the London marriage market was also adjacent to the underworld, which preyed off it, part of the same spectacle of luxury and fraud.

> For just because the city ordinarily concentrates the real social and economic processes of the whole society, so a point can be reached where its order and magnificence but also its fraud and its luxury seem almost, as in Rome, to feed on themselves; to belong in the city, and to breed there, as if on their own. Thus parasites collect around the real services, as in the legal and social underworlds of seventeenth-century London.
>
> There is another service which the city increasingly provided, as a result of changes in the laws of inheritance. It became a necessary marriage-market (what was later called "the season") for the relatively scattered country landowners. Around this, again, collected the pimps and procurers as well as the professional escorts, the keepers of salons, the intermediary rakes and whores.[43]

Face is instantly ready to deal in this market. He tells Kastril the Doctor is

> then for making matches, for rich widdowes,
> Yong gentlewomen, heyres, the fortunat'st man!
> Hee's sent too, farre, and neere, all ouer *England,*
> To haue his counsell, and to know their fortunes.
>   (III.4.101–04)

Much turns on this intersection between the cony-catchers and the marriage market. The tripartite indenture is not really in the business of turning its social knowledge into salable commodities (like lessons in quarreling), but of fraudulent trading on that knowledge. Dame Pliant thus replaces the Philosopher's Stone as the object of general pursuit, capable of transforming Face, Subtle, or Surly into honest (that is, respectable) men. She is fatal to the tripartite indenture. As soon as she appears Face and Subtle begin to conspire against Doll, and then against one another. She brings with her also the marriage-plot formulas of new comedy, which will have her married respectably to Lovewit, thereby permitting the rehabilitation and triumph of Face, who has performed a genuine service in the market for marriages. The play toys with the idea that

---

[43] Raymond Williams, *The Country and the City* (New York: Oxford Univ. Press, 1973), p. 51.

something can come of nothing, but substance is finally the issue; we move from the tripartite indenture to a marriage between the substantial property holders Lovewit and Dame Pliant.

The rehabilitation of Face is of great interest, because for Face the barrier between the underworld and straight society proves to be permeable. The famously "difficult" denouement helps to clarify the relations between criminal fraudulence and a society that defined itself in opposition to the underworld, but was not unwilling to receive stolen goods. Face deserves to win, because he can shark best, as he proves decisively when he rescues everything from Surly's triumphant Fourth Act reversal. The logic of his acceptance as the comedy ends is doubtless connected to the pleasure his wit has provided the audience.[44] But there is also another, social logic at work here, partly through the comic tradition and partly related to contemporary thinking about the nature of criminality. Face wins because he is legitimately attached to the house; he can fall back on the role of Jeremy the butler, and the ancient role of a tricky servant helping his master to a good marriage. Doll challenged Face, when he threatened to expose Subtle to the law:

> Who shall take your word?
> A whore-sonne, vpstart, *apocryphall* captayne,
> Whom not a puritane, in black-*friers,* will trust
> So much, as for a feather!
>
> (I.1.126–9)

But Lovewit's neighbors think "*Ieremie* / Is a very honest fellow" (V.2.37–8), and believe him rather than their senses. He has some credit to fall back on after all.

Face's real strength is his ability to participate in a comic settlement that reins in but does not reject the practices of a new social economy, accommodating it to the strength and durability of the status quo. The play opened with a crisis in the triple indenture, with Subtle claiming he had countenanced Face (pun intended) by sharing his knowledge, and Face claiming to have countenanced Subtle by providing the house, the material means of production. Having mastered Subtle's skills Face is in possession of their entire capital, so to speak, and is in a position to push his partners out. Face's possession is only momentary, however; as he was to Subtle, Lovewit is to him. Lovewit's possession of the house is absolute, and allows him to subsume the wit that provided such a handsome return on his investment. England's ruling class thus managed to negotiate the transformation in the form of their property from feudal to capitalist.

Subtle goes up in fumes, but the alchemical episode accelerates Face's promotion and sublimes him from household drudge to an unspecified but undoubtedly more advantageous position. A servant again, Face must humble

---

[44] For an example of this conventional interpretation, see Alexander Leggatt, *Citizen Comedy in the Age of Shakespeare* (Toronto: Univ. of Toronto Press, 1973), p. 76.

himself to fit into the denouement; as he tells the audience, "My part a little fell in this last *Scene,* / Yet 'twas *decorum*" (V.5.158–9). But Lovewit has promised to "be rul'd by thee in any thing, *Ieremie*" (V.5.143), and to help his fortune (V.5.151). Face will surely not hang up his words and fashion and go back to the cellar where Subtle found him. His relationship to society and the economy has been transformed.[45]

None of this should be taken to mean that Jonson approved of this settlement. L. C. Knights established Jonson's credentials as a critic of nascent capitalism. Walter Cohen argues for an extreme divergence in Jonson between the social action of the plot and the moral judgment on that action; this seems right, but what perhaps deserves emphasis is the great sensitivity with which the action of the plot registers historical change in the form of new social possibilities.[46]

Jonson's formulation of criminality is, then, subversive of the new therapeutic bourgeois category of criminal Otherness which informed the cony-catching pamphlets. His dramatic practice investigates and reveals, rather than marginalizing crime and then investing this marginal terrain with extraneous concerns. This latter is the pastoral mode of *The Gipsies Metamorphosed;* but in his city comedy Jonson thinks corrosively about the transformation of central social forms. *The Alchemist* is specific about the terrain of criminal activity without containing and demonizing it within a subculture: The points of contact, and the negotiations of the border with straight society, are of the greatest interest. The underworld is not the antithesis of society, but its continuation, its shadow; the concept of the underworld is based not on a containing form that gives criminality a shape and an identity, but on an energy playing through, and – within limits – breaking open all social forms, creating fissures and releasing jets of steam, and the myriad little explosions that give *The Alchemist* its effervescence.

[45] I disagree with Judd Arnold, who thinks that "If [Face] takes his exposure with better grace than Subtle, he takes it with no greater profit"; Arnold therefore has to claim that Lovewit's promises are made sarcastically. "Lovewit's Triumph and Jonsonian Morality," *Criticism* 11 (1969), 162.

[46] Cohen, p. 291. Compare Lawrence Venuti's intelligent Althusserian reading of the end of *The Alchemist* in "Transformations of City Comedy: A Symptomatic Reading," *Assays III* (1985), 107.

5

Festivity and the Dramatic Economy of Bartholomew Fair

In medieval and Early Modern Europe festivity was, in the first place, a mode of social expression and organization – a point Bakhtin insists on in his great book on Rabelais, although the point is regularly lost as Bakhtin's notion of the festive is imported into Anglo–American criticism, where festivity tends to become a purely symbolic or moral structure.[1] Because it was fundamentally a social phenomenon the sort of festivity Bakhtin describes disintegrated as its social basis disintegrated, and was reformulated in conformity with the new social conditions. The reformulation involved limiting its radical social aspects and emphasizing a more inward and detachable symbolic and moral meaning. Such a process is very complex and does not happen overnight, but it seems clear that in 1614 Jonson felt he was writing at a moment of disintegration and reformulation, and intervened with his characteristic energy. At times he is quite polemical about it.

I want to call attention to this historical aspect of the play, its role as witness of, and agent in, the transformation of festivity – an aspect that focuses with peculiar sharpness and delicacy the fundamental economic, social, cultural, and moral transformation of the Early Modern period. We will investigate three sectors of the "dramatic economy" of the play: the commercial economy of Bartholomew Fair as Jonson represents it; the economy of dramatic relations

---

[1] Mikhail Bakhtin, *Rabelais and his World,* trans. Helene Iswolsky (Cambridge, Mass: M.I.T. Press, 1968). Some other studies very much in sympathy with this one – and in the case of the Bristol and Stallybrass and White books, drawing upon it and extending it – were written around the time it first appeared as an article in *ELH* 51 (1984): Michael D. Bristol's "Carnival and the Institutions of Theatre in Elizabethan England," *ELH* 50 (1983), 637–55, and *Carnival and Theater: Plebeian Culture and the Structure of Authority in Renaissance England* (New York and London: Methuen, 1985); Peter Stallybrass and Allon White, *The Politics and Poetics of Transgression* (Ithaca: Cornell Univ. Press, 1986); Peter Womack, *Ben Jonson* (Oxford: Basil Blackwell, 1986), especially pp. 131–5; and Leah S. Marcus, *The Politics of Mirth: Jonson, Herrick, Milton, Marvell, and the Defense of Old Holiday Pastimes* (Chicago: Univ. of Chicago Press, 1986).

within the play; and the theatrical economy of relations with the audience. More than a pun holds the larger dramatic economy together: its parts are interrelated and interdependent, changing together as part of the same broad historical process.

In Bakhtin's "festive marketplace" there is a "temporary suspension, both ideal and real, of hierarchical rank," preserving utopian memories of a primitive communism. All exchanges are between equals, and are frank and free, as is language, often to the point of obscenity and abuse. The physical body is reviled and celebrated; the air is full of a universal laughter.

> The marketplace of the Middle Ages and the Renaissance was a world in itself, a world which was one: all "performances" in this area, from loud cursing to the organized show, had something in common and were imbued with the same atmosphere of freedom, frankness, and familiarity. . . . The marketplace was the center of all that was unofficial; it enjoyed a certain extraterritoriality in a world of official order and official ideology, it always remained "with the people."[2]

The utopian features of the festive marketplace cannot be understood apart from a good deal of squalor and violence and trickery; and detailed historical study of carnival behavior tends to qualify the absoluteness of Bakhtin's utopian claims.[3] Still the main lines of Bakhtin's account of carnivalesque social behavior seem sound. This ancient pattern was still flourishing in Rabelais' France, but as Susan Wells has pointed out, it was breaking down in Jonson's London:

> just as the literal marketplace was, during the Jacobean period, becoming marginal, slowly being replaced by the private shop . . . so also the metaphorical arena of the marketplace, the arena of openness and play, outside the scrutiny of the church and the direct concern of the crown, was becoming compromised. . . . first, by becoming simply the location of exchange and profit rather than a gathering place, a common space; second, by being circumscribed more tightly by the "official order", by losing its "extraterritorial status" and becoming integrated with the central apparatus of the government. . . .
>   Thus, while Bakhtin's *Rabelais* can present the marketplace as the place where the rights of the "lower bodily stratum" are legitimized, and where the

---

[2] Bakhtin, p. 155.

[3] Recent studies of the politics of carnival, for instance, have shown that it was often manipulated by powerful political factions, and carnival was also a time for organized violence against groups such as women and Jews. See Natalie Zemon Davis, *Culture and Society in Early Modern France* (Stanford: Stanford Univ. Press, 1975), Emmanuel Le Roy Ladurie, *Carnival in Romans,* trans. Mary Feeney (New York: George Braziller, 1979), and Martin Ingram, "Ridings, Rough Music and the 'Reform of Popular Culture' in Early Modern England," *Past and Present* 105 (1984) 79–113. Leah Marcus' sophisticated study is directed specifically at Jonson and his cultural context.

popular subversive tradition of laughter, parody, skepticism, and utopian hope could be preserved, so straightforward a relationship to the marketplace was impossible for Marston, Middleton, and Jonson. Their marketplace, their city, and their space of celebration, were different.[4]

City comedy, Wells goes on to say, explores the contradiction between the old communal marketplace, with its corporate ideology, and the new economy that rendered it obsolete. It is city comedy

> in which the popular festive traditions were most tellingly brought to bear on the problem of forming a new self-understanding for the commercial city. And indeed, the city comedy is rooted in forms that were connected, either organically or by analogy, with those traditions, and was performed before audiences who would have been both aware of the traditional forms of celebration, and unable to accept those forms uncritically.[5]

Wells provides a very apt description of the problematic of *Bartholomew Fair*. The play is built directly on the representation of the festive marketplace, and nowhere does Renaissance literature bring us closer to the sights and sounds and smells of a popular celebration. All the central motifs of Bakhtin's festivity are here: The material bodily principle is magnificently embodied in the enormous flesh of the pig woman Ursula and in her booth, which caters to all the body's needs (eating, drinking, defecating, fornicating); the fair people speak a pungent billingsgate; a mood of holiday license is evoked amid the noise and confusion and crowds. The plots follow the uncrowning, mocking, and humiliation of the bourgeois characters' pretensions to honor (Win Littlewit and Mistress Overdo), righteousness (Rabbi Busy), and authority (Justice Overdo and Humphrey Wasp). The play ends with a symbolic leveling, in which Justice Overdo is forcibly reminded that he is also Adam, merely flesh and blood, and is made to invite everyone home for dinner.

But there is at the same time a current setting the other way. It is finally decisive, drawing us away from participation in the festive marketplace and toward a criticism of it. We will look at how this works in the plot and in the relationship Jonson sets up with the theater audience, but the character of the Fair itself needs to be discussed first.

This most durable of fairs was changing – changing its face (Stow had noticed that the fairgrounds in Smithfield, just northwest of the walls, were being surrounded and encroached upon by the expansion of the city; and in the year of the play the fairground was paved for the first time and improved in various other ways) and changing its function, or rather the relations among its functions. Very broadly, the Fair's history relates the specialization and fragmentation of the religious, commercial, and recreational aspects of what was

[4] Susan Wells, "Jacobean City Comedy and the Ideology of the City," *ELH* 48 (1981), 38–9.
[5] Ibid., p. 45.

originally one indivisible event. Its religious associations had been destroyed at the Reformation, when the monastery of St. Bartholomew was dissolved (except that heretics continued to be burned there, but that ceased also after 1611). Commercially, according to the Fair's historian, Henry Morley,[6] Bartholomew Fair was for centuries the most important cloth fair in England, and was important for trade in horses, cattle, and leather goods as well. During the Middle Ages all the shops in London were forced to close during fair time, and set up booths in the Fair if they wanted to continue to do business. (Such legislation was a standard accompaniment of the legal privilege of holding a fair.) But by 1614 the Fair no longer swallowed up the whole city, no longer *was* the city in a holiday mode[7]; it now seemed an appendage of its commercial life, and its national and international role as a hub of trade had perhaps begun to decline, though this decay did not become serious until the Restoration. The commercial fair maintained its festive character, and as late as the Commonwealth could invent new customs that perfectly express the festive mode.[8]

Jonson's attention is devoted more or less exclusively to the pleasure fair that had grown up beside the commercial one. Northern, the clothier "who does change cloth for ale at the Fair here," is the sole representative of the cloth fair, and he is plainly off work when we see him. Jordan Knockem is a horse-courser, and may have some connection – apparently not an active one – with the livestock market, but he is also called a "Ranger of Turnbull" in the dramatis personae, and it is in the capacity of whoremaster and gamester (as well as acting proprietor of Ursula's booth) that we see him. The pleasure fair is where the fun and the money were, and that is where the future of the Fair was too. From 1661 to the middle of the eighteenth century, in spite of frequent attempts to prune it back, the Fair ran for a fortnight or even longer, rather than the statutory three days at the end of August. Critics complained that

[6] Henry Morley, *Memoirs of Bartholomew Fair* (1880; rpt. Detroit: Singing Tree Press, 1968). The description of the Fair that follows is based on Morley. I have also consulted Cornelius Walford, *Fairs Past and Present: A Chapter in the History of Commerce* (1883; rpt. New York: Augustus M. Kelley, 1968). The section of this disappointing book concerned with Bartholomew Fair (pp. 164–244) is derived almost entirely from Morley. On markets and fairs generally, see Fernand Braudel, *The Wheels of Commerce: Civilization and Capitalism, 15th–18th Century, Vol. 2.* Jean-Christophe Agnew's *Worlds Apart: The Market and the Theater in Anglo-American Thought, 1550–1750* is a brilliant handling of its subject.

[7] Compare Braudel: "True fairs were those for which a whole town opened its gates. In these cases, either the fair took everything over and became the town, or rather something more than the conquered town; or else the town was strong enough to keep the fair at arm's length – it was a question of respective weight" (p. 83).

[8] "Lady Holland's Mob" consisted of a company of tailors who met in a tavern – the same one that housed the Court of Pie-Powders – the night before the Fair opened. They elected a chairman, and at the stroke of midnight streamed into the street, brandishing their shears, the chairman announcing the opening of the Fair and thereby preempting the Lord Mayor's ceremony which took place twelve hours later. The crowd then ran riot through the streets of Smithfield (Morley, pp. 181–5).

three days were enough for business, and that everyone knew the prolonged Fair "to be a mere Carnival, a season of the utmost Disorder and Debauchery, by reason of the Booths for Drinking, Music, Dancing, Stage-plays, Drolls, Lotteries, Gaming, Raffling, and what not."[9] The ever increasing crush of people from the burgeoning metropolis finally made it impossible to conduct business. "The element of sober trade was choked by its excessive development as a great pleasure fair . . . the cloth trade in Bartholomew Fair died naturally; but the other trades that perished from it, died by suffocation."[10]

The consequence of this separation of business and pleasure was that pleasure became a business. In Jonson's play the marketplace is sharply divided into buyers and sellers, two distinct classes. This economy of the pleasure fair is special because real money is traded for more or less worthless goods and services: hobbyhorses and gingerbread men, pig sold at inflated prices for the privilege of eating it in the Fair, and all the staples of the vices of mind and body. Jonson wrote other plays about greed; the theme of this one is folly. The buyers and sellers are also hucksters and fools, and since the conditions of the Fair encourage the free play of the natural law that decrees that fools and their possessions should be separated by fair means or foul, the hucksters become sharpers and criminals, and the fools their gulls.

Appropriately Ursula's booth, where the pigs roast and the ale flows and the tobacco smokes in festive plenty, is also the front for the main criminal activities: It receives the purses that Ezekiel Edgworth and Nightingale steal, it houses Whit's prostitution ring, and hosts the fights Knockem arranges so cloaks can be stolen in the confusion. And the pig is overpriced, the ale and beer sold in false measures, the tobacco adulterated.

Nor are Urs and company the only criminals in the Fair, though they are the biggest operators. All the fair people are ready to commit crimes when the occasion arises. The theme of adulteration – the first "enormity" Justice Overdo encounters, and a timely one[11] – opens with Lantern Leatherhead's threat to reveal that Joan Trash's gingerbread progeny are made of stale bread, rotten eggs, musty ginger, and dead honey (II.2.8–9). Lantern Leatherhead and Joan Trash will strike their booths and steal away without delivering the goods Cokes has paid for. The costermonger will dump his basket of pears in front of Cokes, by arrangement with Edgworth, so Cokes can be robbed as he scrambles for the fruit. This is a minor moment, but typical, and nicely symbolic of what has happened to the festive: The heap of fruit which should accompany a communal feast is wasted as a ploy in a criminal operation. The world of the carnival is being restructured into the world of the cony-catching pamphlets.

---

[9] Quoted in Morley, p. 295.
[10] Ibid., p. 272.
[11] The Proclamation of the Lord Mayor opening the Fair in 1604 required that wine, beer, and ale be sold in ensealed measures, "And that no person sell any bread, but if it keep the assize, and that it be good and wholesome for man's body" (Morley, p. 110).

The fairground has become a place where the representatives of the folly of a huge city fall into the clutches of an underworld. Within this underworld some of the communal solidarity of the festive marketplace is preserved. In spite of the abusive language the fair people use among themselves (in itself a mark of the festive marketplace) they pull together: When Ursula is scalded everyone leaps to her aid; Joan Trash and Lantern Leatherhead call one another "brother" and "sister" when they are not quarreling; all the crimes are committed by a *team*. Ezekiel Edgworth, the Fair's golden boy, stands at the center of the economy of the underworld as virtuoso cutpurse, jovial principal customer of Ursula's whorehouse, and patron of a tarnished golden world of liberality and festive plenty. He always has money in his purse, we are told again and again, and always pays for everything (II.3.62–3, II.4.25–6, 70). He offers to give Knockem half of what he has, though Knockem does not seem to be in on his game.

The underworld preserves memories of a primitive communism and the freedom of exchange among equals, but being contained within an underworld changes their nature. The liberty of the fair people is limited, evasion rather than a true (even if temporary) release. The law may in many ways be made over in the image of the Fair (the watch is corrupt, in league with the informer/bawd Whit, more interested in extorting five-shilling fines than in keeping the peace; Justice Overdo is a fool, and his court of Pie Powders is a unique and perhaps faintly ridiculous legal institution adapted to the Fair), but it hangs heavy over them. Their talk is full of references to the cart, the whip, and the gallows. The disguised Overdo overhears Lantern Leatherhead and Joan Trash threatening each other with his name, and is satisfied: "I am glad, to heare, my name is their terror, yet, this is doing of Iustice" (II.2.27–8). The authority of his bench will continue to structure relations in the Fair, if only in a negative way; he is looked for on the bench even while he himself is in the stocks.

More important than the criminalization of the Fair is the creation of class barriers within it. Bakhtin insists on the "temporary suspension, both ideal and real, of hierarchical rank . . . during carnival time" – it is of the essence of carnival that *everyone* participates, and on equal terms. The underworld has an obvious vested interest in preserving the distinction between itself and its victims. (Punk Alice complains when Mistress Overdo begins to compete in her market: "The poore common whores can ha' no traffique, for the priuy rich ones," and beats her, IV.5.69–70.) The class lines are asserted from above as well.

The main plot (or plots – our descriptive vocabulary breaks down in the face of the profusion of this play) involves the disintegration of the two parties of bourgeois[12] fairgoers we meet in Act I. Each individual is separated from his

[12] Cokes is landed gentry, but I group him with the bourgeois characters for the sake of convenience. Mistress Overdo, his sister, comes from the same background but is married to a very lowly justice. Though Overdo is now wealthy enough to buy the wardship of Grace Wellborn, Wasp remembers when he was a humble scrivener (IV.4.162–5).

party, and stripped of the emblem of his social position. Cokes loses his money and most of his clothes, as well as his fiancée, Busy his hypocritical superiority, and so on. By Act V the leveling is complete, and the fair people and fairgoers go off to feast together.

This pattern is saturnalian, yet I would agree that the bourgeois characters and their destinies are conceived in the terms of satiric comedy. Jonson's play mixes the two kinds of comic structures, and mixes the two kinds of social concerns C. L. Barber associates with them:

> Satirical comedy tends to deal with relations between social classes and aberrations in movements between them. Saturnalian comedy is satiric only incidentally; its clarification comes with movement between poles of restraint and release in everybody's experience.[13]

The bourgeois characters are all immediately recognizable types from other city comedies: Cokes the gullible heir, unable to hold onto his property; Wasp the irascible but impotent guardian; Mistress Overdo, whose trivial social pretensions do not disguise the heart of a whore; John Littlewit, infatuated with his own negligible wit and his connections in the subliterary world of petty taverns and puppet theaters; his pretty and mindless wife, fair game for everyone since her husband is too foolish to hold onto her; her canting mother and her mother's hypocritical Puritan suitor. They are all ready for a fall: The conventions of city comedy demand their humiliation.

Jonson despised the particular milieus from which they sprang, and as individuals they represent the disjunction between social and moral status that provides much of the tension in city comedy. They are propelled out of their class positions and into the Fair by their own folly and vice, and poetic justice is there done to them. (When Cokes is robbed Wasp asks him, "Are you not iustly seru'd i' your conscience now?" II.6.110–1). Quarlous, Winwife, Edgworth, and Nightingale are all concerned, in what is presented as a principled and quite disinterested way, that people get what they deserve. When all the strands of plot are taken together it may appear that everyone is losing his class character in one universal rhythm and experience; but it is also possible to see the plot as a collection of destinies being met by (and *as*) individuals, expressed through conventions with an exact and limited social meaning. Jonson had as much scorn for those who, like Littlewit and Cokes, could not recognize class distinctions, could not recognize when they were degrading and making fools of themselves, as he had for inept and unworthy social climbers like Mistress Overdo, and as much contempt for those who couldn't hold on to their own as he did for those motivated by raw acquisitiveness. This study of social and moral status and the sorts of social mobility attendant on it is inherently quite different from the suspension of rank during a period of festivity.

[13] C. L. Barber, *Shakespeare's Festive Comedy* (Princeton: Princeton Univ. Press, 1959), p. 8.

There are three characters who are neither fools nor knaves: Quarlous, Winwife, and Grace Wellborn. Grace represents female virtue in a rather schematic way, and is a victim of the corruption of the social order: Specifically, she has been sold to Justice Overdo in the notorious Court of Wards. Quarlous and Winwife are also characters we recognize from city comedy, young gentlemen with wit and education (Quarlous says he has been to Oxford and the Inns of Court) but no money, on the make in the more fluid sectors of Jacobean society, usually to be found, as here, preying on the fortunes and women of foolish citizens. All three are from the gentry, but their class membership is threatened by legal or pecuniary problems. More or less from the moment we meet them we assume that the business of the comedy will be to confirm and secure them in their social position. This solidification of the hierarchy of rank runs counter to the festive in more than an abstract thematic way.

Grace and Winwife's marriage and Quarlous' fortune are made possible by the Fair, yet they never really participate in it. This point is made over and over very distinctly. Almost the first thing we hear Grace say is "Truely, I haue no such fancy to the *Fayre;* nor ambition to see it; there's none goes thither of any quality or fashion" (I.5.130–2). She is carried along anyway, but her icy reserve is never broken. Winwife and Quarlous follow, but they make it clear that they are trailing Wasp and Cokes, rather than visiting the Fair itself. They always enter their scenes looking for Wasp and Cokes, and speaking of them as a show: "Wee had wonderful ill lucke, to misse this prologue o' the purse, but the best is we shall haue fiue *Acts* of him ere night: hee'le be spectacle enough!" (III.2.1–3). The fair is an affront and a nuisance for Winwife, and for Quarlous at best a way to pass the time until Cokes reappears.

> *Winwife:*   That these people should be so ignorant to thinke vs chapmen for 'hem! doe wee looke as if wee would buy Ginger-bread? or Hobby-horses?
>
> *Quarlous:*   Why, they know no better ware then they haue, nor better customers then come. And our very being here makes vs fit to be demanded, as well as others. Would *Cokes* would come!
>
> (II.5.13–19)

When Jordan Knockem recognizes them and extends the hospitality of the Fair, Winwife wants to refuse, and Quarlous accepts only in order to quarrel. Both insist on the distinctions Knockem assumes the Fair has suspended.

> *Knockem:*   . . . will you take any froth, and smoake with vs?
>
> *Quarlous:*   Yes, Sir, but you'l pardon vs, if we knew not so much familiarity betweene vs afore.
>
> . . .
>
> *Knockem:*   Master *Win-wife,* you are proud (methinks) you doe not talke, nor drinke, are you proud?
>
> *Winwife:*   Not of the company I am in, Sir, nor the place, I assure you.
>
> (II.5.34–6, 50–3)

Later when Edgworth has stolen the marriage license for Quarlous, he offers to share his whores with his customary liberality – "I can spare any Gentleman a moity" – but Quarlous rebukes him violently:

> Keepe it for your companions in beastlinesse, I am none of 'hem, Sir. If I had not already forgiuen you a greater trespasse, or thought you yet worth my beating, I would instruct your manners, to whom you make your offers. . . . I am sorry I employ'd this fellow; for he thinks me such: *Facinus quos inquinat, aequat.*   (IV.6.22–6. 28–30)

As the bourgeois parties of fools and coxcombs disintegrate Winwife, Quarlous, and Grace find each other and establish their own little society in the midst of the Fair, based on the contrary values of self-possession and manners that reflect a gentlemanly bearing:

> *Winwife:*   . . . will you please to withdraw with vs, a little, and make them
> thinke, they haue lost you? I hope our manners ha' beene such
> hitherto, and our language, as will giue you no cause, to doubt
> your selfe, in our company.
> *Grace:*   Sir, I will give my selfe, no cause; I am so secure of mine owne
> manners, as I suspect not yours.
>
> (III.5.293–9)

When Quarlous and Winwife turn on one another in their competition for Grace, she chooses her husband by lottery, as valentines were chosen – a carnivalesque motif, but again her attitude is antithetical to everything the Fair stands for.

> Sure you thinke me a woman of an extreme leuity, Gentlemen, or
> a strange fancy, that (meeting you by chance in such a place, as this
> . . .) I should so forsake my modesty . . . as to say This is he, and
> name him.
> *Quarlous:*   Why, wherefore should you not? What should hinder you?
> *Grace:*   If you would not giue it to my modesty, allow it yet to my wit;
> giue me so much of woman, and cunning, as not to betray my selfe
> impertinently.
>
> (IV.3.21–31)

(Compare the speech of Rosalind's C.L. Barber quotes as an example of the mood of revelry in courtship: "Come, woo me, woo me! for now I am in a holiday humour, and like enough to consent" *As You Like It* IV.1.68–9.)[14] Her strategem of the lottery is designed to keep Quarlous and Winwife both in expectation and working for her until she is safely out of the Fair. Quarlous circumvents this strategy, but it is a clever one.

Grace is an altogether unlikely heroine for the play, given that the dynamic of festivity forces everyone to join in its spirit and derides and punishes those who do not – but she is the heroine of the play, not of the Fair, and these are

[14] *Ibid.*, p. 6.

two distinctly different things. The "super-plot"[15] that centers on Grace is as formal as her character: a pure comic plot of a girl dispossessed by a ridiculous but powerful blocking figure, representing an unjust and foolish society, who escapes from his authority with the help of the young man she will marry. This plot floats on top of the plots involving the bourgeois characters, which in turn are perched on top of the Fair itself. It is there to represent a potential society of sense, which Justice Overdo will not be able to provide even after his chastening. We would like to believe in Grace, and in Winwife for her sake, but as with Celia and Bonario in *Volpone* their virtue is too cut off from the central energies of the play.

The plot reflects this problem by having its natural economy disrupted by Quarlous, a character with the more ambivalent virtues of the city comedy gallants. Winwife may have gotten Grace, but Quarlous has managed to acquire a legal document transferring Grace's wardship from Justice Overdo to himself – and he will make her compound for the privilege of marrying Winwife just as Justice Overdo would have done. This twist by which boy gets girl but his friend gets her money is highly unusual, if not unique. Quarlous has also contracted a marriage for himself with Dame Purecraft, who has £6,000 and a roaring business defrauding her Puritan brethren. To make this match he sacrifices our sentimental interest and his own sexual gratification – it was Quarlous who in Act I lectured Winwife on the foulness and unnaturalness of chasing this particular widow – but it is a nicely symbolic union, uniting the two sharpest operators in the play.

How are we to understand this deflection of the most fundamental comic plot type, in which none of the gentle characters recoup their positions entirely, Winwife and Grace because they are left without her fortune, and Quarlous because he is saddled with an unpresentable wife? It is not hard to see why Quarlous ends up holding all the cards. We have seen that he is as hostile to the Fair as Winwife or Grace, but he is much more willing to plunge in than the squeamish Winwife. He is querulous and it gives him opportunities to quarrel. More important, he plunges into the marketplace because he needs money and there is a lot of property lying around loose for those aggressive enough to seize it from its imbecilic owners. He understands the marketplace as a place for accumulation, not festivity. His disguise as a madman shows he understands how to manipulate the symbol system of the Fair without believing in it himself.[16] Like the cutpurses of the cony-catching pamphlets and the under-world figures of this play, he understands the uses of disruption. They turn every fight, every spilled basket, every commotion caused by another crime, into an opportunity for the man with a quick wit and a quick hand. The Fair

---

[15] I borrow this term from Umphrey Lee, "Jonson's *Bartholomew Fair* and the Popular Dramatic Tradition," *Louisburg College Journal of Arts and Sciences* I (June 1967), 10.

[16] This is an example of the sort of understanding Stephen Greenblatt discusses as central to the powerful new cultural awareness of the Renaissance. *Renaissance Self-Fashioning* (Chicago: Univ. of Chicago Press, 1980).

for them is such a disruption on a giant scale, its festive trappings bait for their traps. Quarlous is playing a larger game; for someone in a socially marginal position a general disruption will create openings. Grace and Winwife stand to profit from the same situation, but Quarlous has the virtues – alertness, aggressiveness, the ability to improvise, a detached but practical intelligence, and a willingness to get his hands dirty – that make one master in this world. It is not especially reassuring to leave things in Quarlous' hands, but it makes sense.

The social function of festivity, we are told by everyone who has thought about it, is revitalization of the social order, but what constitutes revitalization depends on specific historical circumstances. The festive moment is essentially conservative in a strong and stable society, potentially revolutionary in an unstable or sclerotic one. Jonson's play provides a complex diagnosis of his society. The bourgeois victims of the saturnalian pattern stand to profit (somewhat paradoxically) from the spirit of festivity in orthodox ways – a moral regeneration consequent on their humiliation, a truer relation to society to compensate for the loss of the dominance (social or economic) they should never have had. Before the social order is restored (and the bourgeois characters are restored to their positions as well as limited to them by the universal forgiveness of the denouement) the satirist wreaks his will on them. Jonson's particular social concerns and his individual moral focus cut across the older social patterns of festivity, but they displace rather than erase them.

Quarlous and Grace and Winwife are never touched by anything like the spirit of festivity. The benefits they derive from the Fair are all practical. For the disenchanted lovers the Fair has only this in common with the world of romance, that it is full of accidents and happy chances through which they gain their freedom. The temporary unraveling of the social fabric allows them to reestablish who they rightfully *are,* by nature and birth. This is the sort of plot that makes people say comedy is a conservative form. The plot draws the lovers through the Fair, but their relationship with it is always accidental. Quarlous, on the other hand, does his own plotting in the Fair: He establishes not what he *is,* but what he can *do.* His attitude is also postfestive, but he sees how to get ahead in the rough scramble the Fair permits. The suspension of normal social relations leads not to a primitive equality, or to a pristine and ideal social order, but to an acceleration of the processes of social Darwinism. In the long run the realism of the English upper classes toward the changes in the economy, their participation in and mastery of those changes, insured the stability of their rule and the relatively smooth and rapid development of English capitalism. Here, as in *The Alchemist,* it is not too much to see in Jonson's distortion of the normal comic economy a registering of this historical perception.

In a sense, then, Jonson's implied historical analysis of the disintegration of the festive marketplace requires and guarantees Quarlous' role. Socially Quarlous, Winwife, and Grace are, I believe, like Wellborn and Knowell, Jr., of *Every Man In,* the necessary objects of identification for the audience, or at least that part of the audience Jonson was most concerned to reach, the part Wells says could no longer accept uncritically the traditional forms of festivity. This function is implied by their formal roles in the plot, and if it is not earned by the depth or warmth of their characters, it is made inevitable by the lack of any possible alternative. Like the gentlemen of Jonson's audience, we certainly do not want to see ourselves in the Overdos, or in Busy, in any but the most universal and metaphorical way. We may be attracted to the underworld figures, to Edgworth and Nightingale in particular, but our admiration must be romantic and voyeuristic. We know that in real life we would be their victims, not their friends. Similarly the cony-catching pamphlets may betray a fascination with the glamor and freedom and wit of the criminals, but the pamphlets are always addressed specifically to the very gentlemen, lawyers, country yeomen, and so on, liable to be robbed; and they were sold, in the first place, as instructions in how not to be taken, what to watch for. The way the Fair is presented is calculated to put us on our guard, to suggest that if we cannot, like Quarlous, master its noise and confusion, its tricks and deceptions, we had better stay aloof, like Winwife and Grace. Their detachment and condescension and even scorn are models for our own reactions, or at least for a crucial part of them – the part that has most to do with our own social identity, the cool judgment only fools fail to consult before they give themselves over to the confusion of the Fair, the part that warns us not to let go, that sets us apart.

Jonson wrote an Induction to explore the issue of the audience's relation to the play, and the play's relation to the Fair, which is of the greatest interest for our examination of the social meaning of festivity. The central fact is clear enough: The Fair, still very much alive in Smithfield, is being represented in a commercial theater, before a paying audience, at a different time of the year. It is thus torn out of its social context and made an object of art, and Jonson wants to be sure his audience sees the difference, that they reconstitute themselves as the proper sort of audience, not as a crowd in the festive mode.

The Induction begins with the appearance of the Stage-keeper, an exponent of the popular tradition, who complains about Jonson's appropriation of the Fair. He begins by accusing Jonson of failure accurately to represent, or we might say reproduce, the Fair itself.

> When't comes to the *Fayre*, once: you were e'en as good goe to *Virginia*, for anything there is of *Smith-field*. Hee has not hit the humors, he do's not know 'hem; hee has not conuers'd with the *Bartholmew*-birds, as they say; hee has ne're a Sword, and Buckler man in his *Fayre*, nor a little *Dauy*, to take toll o' the Bawds there, as in my time, nor a *Kind-heart*, if any bodies teeth should chance to ake in his *Play*. . . . But these Master-*Poets*, they will ha' their owne absurd courses; they will be inform'd of nothing! . . . would not a fine Pumpe vpon the Stage ha' done well, for a property now? And a *Punque* set vnder vpon her head, with her Sterne vpward, and ha' beene sous'd by my witty

> young masters o' the *Innes o' Court?* . . . hee will not hear o' this! I am an Asse!
> I! And yet I kept the *Stage* in Master *Tarletons* time, I thanke my starres. Ho!
> an' that man had liued to haue play'd in *Bartholmew Fayre,* you should ha' seene
> him ha' come in, and ha' beene coozened i' the Cloath-quarter, so finely! . . .
> And then a substantiall watch to ha' stolne in vpon 'hem, and taken 'hem
> away, with mistaking words, as the fashion is, in the *Stage*-practise.
>
> (10–45)

The Stage-keeper's demands modulate from having actual characters transferred from the Fair to the stage, to the reenactment of social rituals characteristic of fair time (ducking whores), to fidelity to the popular tradition in the
theater. The naturalness of the transitions may remind us of the very strong
popular dramatic tradition always associated with the Fair, and of Bakhtin's
comment that the marketplace was "a world which was one: all 'performances'
in this area, from loud cursing to the organized show, had something in
common and were imbued with the same atmosphere."

But our playwright meets this attempt by the popular tradition to reclaim its
own directly: "Hee has (*sirreuerence*) kick'd me three, or foure times about the
Tyring-house, I thanke him, for but offering to putt in, with my experience!"
(28–30). The Book-holder is sent out to drive the Stage-keeper off the stage,
and to establish the proper relation with the audience, even while recognizing
the stake of the Stage-keeper and the popular audience in the play:

> the *Author* hath writ it iust to his *Meridian,* and the *Scale* of the grounded
> Iudgments here, his Play-fellowes in wit. Gentlemen . . . I am sent out to you
> here, with a *Scriuener,* and certaine Articles drawne out in hast betweene our
> *Author,* and you.
>
> (55–60)

The opposition between the popular and coterie theaters is here perfectly
expressed: groundlings versus gentlemen; the Stage-keeper with his memories
of an improvisational popular theater versus the Book-holder and Scrivener,
men of the master-poet's written text; the communal possession of, and participation in, a tradition that was always extra-official, "with the people," versus
legal relations expressed in the formal articles the Scrivener reads out:
"ARTICLES of Agreement, indented, between the *Spectators* or *Heareres,* at the
Hope on the Bankeside, in the County of *Surrey,* on the one party; And the
Author of Bartholmew Fayre in the said place, and County on the other party."

The Articles, to which the audience must agree before the play will begin, are
half in jest, but they also impose serious conditions that could hardly be more
exactly calculated to oppose festivity as a social form. The first (and most
fundamental) requires the audience to remain in the places their money or friends
have put them in for two and a half hours, while the other party presents them
with a play. The audience is legally separated from the stage, made physically (if
not mentally) passive, turned into consumers of a commodity rather than participants in a ritual. This is what Bakhtin says carnival cannot allow:

> In fact, carnival does not know footlights, in the sense that it does not acknowledge any distinction between actors and spectators. Footlights would destroy a carnival, as the absence of footlights would destroy a theatrical performance. Carnival is not a spectacle seen by the people; they live in it, and everyone participates because its very idea embraces all the people. While carnival lasts, there is no other life outside it.[17]

The second Article grants that "euery person here, haue his or their free-will of censure, to like or dislike at their owne charge, the *Author* hauing now departed with his right: It shall bee lawful for any man to iudge his six pen'orth, his twelve pen'orth, so to his eighteene pence, 2. shillings, halfe a crowne, to the value of his place: Prouided alwaies his place get not aboue his wit" (85–91). The play can be sold as a commodity, but judgment cannot (though it is being conceived of as private property). Differentiating his audience into more or less fit and unfit, after bringing them all under contract, is a project Jonson pursued through his whole theatrical career. It is always possible that a man's place will get above his wit, but the organization of society into classes provides the metaphor for the hierarchy of wit, and the correlation between the two is assumed to be roughly accurate. (Jonson's own search for patronage at higher and higher social levels is based on this assumption.) Jonson does not value the opinions of his audience equally. He does not address them as a community of equals, but as a society differentiated by classes, and the experience of the play and their reactions to it will validate and reinforce that differentiation, not break it down.

The third Article deepens the isolation of the spectator, as it continues Jonson's old war with the self-appointed opinion makers in the theaters, stipulating that "euery man heere, exercise his owne Iudgment, and not censure by *Contagion*, or vpon *trust*, from anothers voice, or face, that sits by him, be he neuer so first, in the *Commission of Wit*: As also, That hee bee fixd and settled in his censure, that what hee approues, or not approues to day, hee will doe the same to morrow" (97–103). The audience is not to respond together, as a crowd, in one rhythm; they are to restrict their experience to what is provided from the stage, not what their fellows contribute. Judgment is an affair of the isolated individual, free of time and space. The effect Jonson was aiming at would later be achieved by lowering the house lights. Eugene Waith has shown that Jonson returned to medieval techniques in staging *Bartholomew Fair*,[18] but the conditions he tries to establish anticipate those of a later theater. Again, we may contrast these conditions with what Bakhtin has to say about festive laughter:

> [I]t is not an individual reaction to some isolated "comic" event. Carnival laughter is the laughter of all the people. Second, it is universal in scope; it is directed at all and everyone, including the carnival's participants.[19]

[17] Bakhtin, p. 7.
[18] Eugene M. Waith, ed., *Bartholomew Fair* (New Haven: Yale Univ. Press, 1963), "Appendix 2," p. 212.
[19] Bakhtin, p. 11.

The fourth Article stipulates that "no person here, is to expect more than hee knowes, or better ware then a *Fayre* will affoord: neyther to looke backe to the sword and buckler-age of *Smithfield,* but content himselfe with the present" (114–17). This is a direct reply to the Stage-keeper, limiting his rights of expectation, but, confident now of having established the conditions of his theater, Jonson can accommodate the popular tradition. He meets the Stage-keeper's demands, one by one: "Instead of a little Davy to take toll 'o the bawds, the author doth promise a strutting horse-courser. . . . And then for Kindheart, the tooth-drawer, a fine oily pig-woman with her tapster to bid you welcome." (The list can be extended further: Quarlous, a witty young master of the Inns of Court, asks after a ducking stool for Ursula, an ex-punk, now bawd; Cokes plays something like the part Tarleton once did; there is a watch with mistaking words.) Although Jonson will not go so far as Shakespeare in his *Tales* and *Tempests* to please a popular audience, "yet if the *Puppets* will please any body, they shall be entreated to come in." Jonson reels off his menu with his own relish and energy of language. He transforms the popular materials, giving them back animated with his own magnificent art, displaying the fruit of his imagination with what we might be tempted to call festive abandon.

It is festive, however, in a sense quite different from that of the popular tradition.[20] Michael McCanles has described Jonson's notion of festivity quite accurately as a much more refined comic spirit, expressed not in a social convulsion but in an individual moral posture. Ideally the festive does not oppose quotidian values; both are contained and reconciled within a single awareness, laughing but sane. The model for this typically humanist moral stance is Jonson's imitation of Martial, "Inviting a Friend to Supper." McCanles enumerates elements that *Bartholomew Fair* shares with Bakhtin's festive, but finds that the play does not really fit Bakhtin's definition.[21] Neil Rhodes takes the same position in an argument about Jonson's style – his comic prose has its roots in the Rabelaisian tradition Bakhtin describes, but "his moral earnestness pulls him in an opposite direction," toward the eighteenth century desire for " 'correctness', for purity and firmness of language."[22] The point I am concerned to make here is that the disjunction in the meaning of festivity is thematized and insisted on by Jonson, and can be historicized much more fully than is generally done. It is not enough to locate it in the literary history of prose style, or to account for it as a function of a purely personal moral sensibility, or a purely moral distinction between a "true" and a "perverted" festivity.

---

[20] I am not arguing that Jonson tried to eliminate festivity from the theater, only that he changed its character. Theatergoing is still a social and festive event, and can be described in terms of ritual behavior, but we have to recognize a displacement in these terms (which have been displaced several times in the history of the theater). The displacements are at least as interesting as the continuities.

[21] Michael McCanles, "Festival in Jonson's Comedy," *Renaissance Drama* n.s. 8 (1977), 215–16.

[22] Neil Rhodes, *Elizabethan Grotesque* (London: Routledge & Kegan Paul, 1980), p. 140.

The transvaluation of festivity depends ultimately on the transformation of the social base that had supported it. As surely as enclosures and rack-renting undermined the festive life of the countryside, the changing functions of Bartholomew Fair changed the nature of the festive marketplace. In both country and city the more visible ideological and legal attacks on the traditional extraterritoriality of the festive were led by the Puritans and the legal apparatus of the government. In that battle Jonson was a conservative: The Fair defends itself gloriously against the Puritan and the Justice of the Peace in his play; the aristocratic values of poems like "To Penshurst" are well known; his "sons" would get sentimental about hock-carts and May-days.

Still humanism had transformations of its own to wreak on the patterns of the disintegrating traditional society.[23] If Jonson's conflicts with the popular tradition are concealed by the content Bartholomew Fair shares with it, they are revealed by the pointedness and violence of his appropriation of that content. On every level he is willing to absorb the popular tradition, but unwilling to be absorbed by it.

This is clearest when the popular tradition in the theater gets in the way of the career Jonson was inventing for himself, and the Master-Poet kicks the Stage-keeper. In spite of the affection Jonson obviously felt for certain aspects of the popular tradition in the theater, he was also very alive to everything in it that was moldy, stale, crude, and outmoded. No one believed more vehemently that as a method of producing plays it was worn out. He built his career more clearly than anyone ever had on the assumption that the future lay with a new kind of artist, a figure he himself was busy constituting. This figure was articulated (and propagandized for) in the language of humanism. Perhaps its central feature was the personal autonomy the traditional society could not support, but the emerging capitalist society did. The Jonsonian man of letters had a high profile as an individual, was a citizen of austere independence of judgment; his productions were thoroughly his own because they were thoroughly coherent and original, the product of an individual genius (this was true even when he was imitating someone else); he expressed proprietorship of his own productions by editing his own Works;[24] and when he wrote for the

[23] For another approach to the historical meaning of Jonson's "Induction," see Don E. Wayne, "Drama and Society in the Age of Jonson: An Alternative View," in Renaissance Drama n.s. 13 (1982): "In Bartholomew Fair the Articles of Agreement point ironically to the increasing reliance on arbitrary regulation (contract law), in the absence of the more spontaneously recognized mechanisms of social control provided by a coherent and viable system of belief. . . . But despite the fact that the Articles of Agreement are satiric in intent, the author reveals himself to be implicated in his own satire and in the new contractual basis of social obligation." Compare also Leo Salingar, "Crowd and Public in Bartholomew Fair," Renaissance Drama n.s. 10 (1979), 141–59.

[24] On Jonson's editing of his own works, see especially Joseph F. Loewenstein, "The Text in the Marketplace," Representations 12 (1985), 101–15; Jonas Barish, "Jonson

theater he expected – against all odds – that complex institution to bend entirely to his will, embodied in a written text, at least for the duration of the performance. Jonson's self-definition as an artist depended on his making it clear to his audience that they were spectators of his art rather than participants in what was going on on stage, either as Fairgoers or as coproprietors of the popular theater. He always stresses that he has created an object for contemplation, pointing to its aesthetic and moral coherence. Jonson's art envelops the fair, but the Fair must not envelop his art.

The corollary of this definition of the author is an audience as defined in the Induction to this most Brechtian of Renaissance plays, a watchful, wakeful audience, with enough personal autonomy to make independent judgments, and enough aesthetic experience and training to make the right ones. Such an audience is also an historical product, and Jonson could not, and did not, assume that it already existed in adequate form. The prefaces, epistles, inductions and epilogues to all his plays are largely taken up with cajoling or coercing it into being. The members of Jonson's ideal audience were antithetical to the crowd of fairgoers in their psychosocial organization, and in the functions art played in their lives. The experience of festivity in its original social form had less and less to offer them, and it contradicted more and more clearly the polished manners and inward depth that characterized the seventeenth century gentleman. There was a social need to redefine festivity, toward the sensibility McCanles finds embodied in "Inviting a Friend to Supper," and away from the grossness of fat Ursula. This new perspective is a consequence and a cause of the disintegration of the older pattern, and it guarantees the roles of Grace and Winwife and Quarlous in this incarnation of the Fair.

The more polished classes did not stop going to the Fair – if Grace was right in saying that no one of quality or fashion went in 1614, things had certainly changed by 1667 when Pepys, on one of his many excursions (usually at the head of a pleasure party), saw the King's mistress Lady Castlemaine emerging from a puppet booth. Pepys went to see *Bartholomew Fair,* too, which was often revived just before or after fairtime. (During the Fair itself the theaters would sometimes close, and their companies move into booths at the Fair for extremely lucrative runs.)[25] It is odd but appropriate that the dynamics of the commercial theater drew *Bartholomew Fair* back toward Bartholomew Fair.

and the Loathed Stage," in *A Celebration of Ben Jonson,* ed., William Blisset, Julian Patrick, and R. W. van Fossen (Toronto: Univ. of Toronto Press, 1973), pp. 27–54; Timothy Murray, "From Foul Sheets to Legitimate Model: Anti-Theater, Text, Ben Jonson," *New Literary History,* 14 (1983), 641–64; A. Richard Dutton, *Ben Jonson: To the First Folio* (Cambridge: Cambridge Univ. Press, 1983); Richard C. Newton, "Jonson and the (Re-)Invention of the Book," in *Classic and Cavalier: Essays on Jonson and the Sons of Ben,* ed., Claude J. Summers and Ted-Larry Pebworth (Pittsburgh: University of Pittsburgh Press, 1982), pp. 31–58.
[25] Morley, p. 284.

The companies could capitalize on the play's realistic aspects, offering it as a fore- or after-taste of the real thing. But the nature of fairgoing had changed again – there is nothing in *Bartholomew Fair* like Pepys' slumming – and there is at least one piece of documentary evidence to show that Jonson's play was attached to the Fair by the culture of the Restoration because the theatrical relation developed in it did in fact serve as an exemplary model for fairgoers, a model of the proper structure of perception, moral relation to experience, and social relation to community, called for by the Fair in particular but relevant to life in general. This document is a letter written by one Sir Robert Southwell to his son, who was in London with his tutor at fairtime in 1685.

> Dear Neddy,
> I think it not now so proper to quote you verses out of Persius, or to talk of Caesar and Euclide, as to consider the great theater of Bartholomew Fair, where, I doubt not, but you often resort, and 'twere not amiss if you cou'd convert that tumult into a profitable book. You wou'd certainly see the garboil there to more advantage if Mr. Webster and you wou'd read, or cou'd see acted, the play of Ben Jonson, call'd Bartholomew Fair: for then afterwards going to the spot you wou'd note, if things and humours were the same to-day, as they were fifty years ago, and take pattern of the observations which a man of sense may raise out of matters that seem even ridiculous. Take then with you the impressions of that play, and in addition thereunto, I should think it not amiss if you then got up into some high window, in order to survey the whole pit at once. I fancy then you will say – *Totus mundus agit histrionem,* and you wou'd note into how many various shapes humane nature throws itself, in order to buy cheap, and sell dear, for all is but traffick and commerce, some to give, some to take, and all is by exchange, to make the entertainment compleat.
>
> The main importance of this fair is not so much for merchandize, and supplying what people really want; but as a sort of Bacchanalia, to gratify the multitude in their wandering and irregular thoughts.[26]

It is the whole broad humanist moral tradition that turns the Fair into a theater or a book, but it is Jonson's play that gives point to the metaphor. Neddy is to see the Fair through Jonson's play, and his experiences in the Fair should simply double the experience in the theater: "Take then with you the impressions of that play, and in addition thereunto, I should think it not amiss if you then got up into some high window, in order to survey the whole pit at once." The high window serves as a box in the theater, a half-crown seat. It removes Neddy from harm's way, and provides the necessary distance for reflection. Without this distance – the aesthetic distance of book or theater – the Fair means nothing at all, is simply a "tumult" or "garboil." (Book and theater are now effectively synonymous, and stand together against the Fair.) There is no question of a social relationship with the Fair, or even of direct experience or involvement of any kind. The "man of sense" observes everything, but is never touched.

[26] Quoted in Morley, p. 224.

No one in Jonson's play is allowed to take notes with this much detachment, and we may well regret the loss of Jonson's ferocious engagement. The spirit of festivity has really passed away. Still Southwell realizes the tendencies in Jonson I have been discussing. He is the ideal audience Jonson stipulates in his Induction. He also shares with Jonson a sense of the Fair as a great revelation of the social and moral fabric, and particularly of the false economies supported by human folly. (He develops this theme at some length.) He has faith that moral reflection can encompass the Fair, in all its uniqueness and particularity, and as his letter continues it becomes clear that the attempt to do so was intensely stimulating.

As London grew the Fair grew, until the Jonsonian humanist moral tradition associated with it was crushed to death, as the commercial fair had been, by the huge press of fairgoers. The literary tradition of the Fair ends with Book 7 of Wordsworth's *Prelude*,[27] where it epitomizes everything unnatural and inhuman about London. It comes up in Wordsworth's discussion of the relations that the structures the mind builds for itself have with outward things. Bartholomew Fair is his example of

> A work completed to our hands, that lays,
> If any spectacle on earth can do,
> The whole creative powers of man asleep!–
> For once, the Muses' help we will implore,
> And she shall lodge us, wafted on her wings,
> Above the press and danger of the crowd,
> Upon some showman's platform.
>
> (679–85)

The movement out of the crowd – tenser now – onto the showman's platform continues the structure of detached observation, and the point will be, as it is in Jonson and Southwell, the Fair as testing-ground for a special kind of seeing and comprehension, again an elite accomplishment, though now the "man of sense" has been replaced by the man with the Spirit of Nature upon him. But the structural similarities are less impressive than the changed scene. It is hard to think of Wordsworth as an audience: The isolation of the spectator has deepened past the point where we can place him in any social relationship. Having escaped from the press and danger of the crowd, he becomes a seer, a lonely prophet.

What he sees is not a play but a phantasmagoria:

> What a shock
> For eyes and ears! what anarchy and din,
> Barbarian and infernal – a phantasma,
> Monstrous in colour, motion, shape, sight, sound!
>
> (685–8)

[27] Wordsworth's visit to the Fair must have occurred in 1795. The Fair's popularity declined rapidly thereafter. By the time the 1850 *Prelude* was published it was virtually dead, and five years later it was legally so. I quote from the 1850 text, ed., J. C. Maxwell (Harmondsworth: Penguin, 1972).

There are Prodigies of all kinds to gaze at, and the masses who have come to gaze. The ones are too unreal and the others too anonymous to fashion drama out of. No faces or character types emerge; the theme of a moral economy is obviated by the epistemological problem and an industrial image:

> Tents and Booths
> Meanwhile, as if the whole were one vast mill,
> Are vomiting, receiving, on all sides,
> Men, Women, Three-year's Children, Babes in arms.
>   (718–21)

Jonson may have participated in the breakdown of the cohesion of his society, and of the popular theater audience in particular, but that cohesion is still very much with him. He was playing to an audience of the widest possible social range, from the groundlings at the Hope theater, a place "as durty as *Smithfield,* and as stinking euery whit," as Jonson ungraciously says at the end of the Induction, to the King, before whom the second performance of the play was given; and in the world he represents a surprising number of people already know each other when the play begins. Connectedness was a fact in the social fabric, not just a possibility for the individual mind, as in Wordsworth.

That connectedness is denied and violated in several ways, as we have seen, but it is also reasserted at the end of the play, symbolically and ideologically, by the dinner at Justice Overdo's house to which everyone is invited. The communal feast is a central festive symbol and event. The New Comedy convention that ends the play with an off-stage feast is highly convenient for Jonson, because it follows naturally from his comic plot, and because it postpones the feast until after the play is over. The feast would be the genuine festive experience, but it is hard to imagine it in the light of the still unresolved (and perhaps unresolvable) divisions the play has opened up. Can Grace really sit down with Ursula? How will Winwife get along with Quarlous, who has just defrauded his fiancée of her inheritance? The postponement confirms what the whole play has indicated, that real social festivity has become a utopian idea – not the utopian reality remembered and temporarily realized in Bakhtin's festive marketplace, but a purely symbolic event.

Index